To Lori Nelsen and Suzanne Innes-Stubb

**Books are to be returned on or before
the last date below.**

**7-DAY
LOAN**

**Books are to be returned on or before
the last date below.**

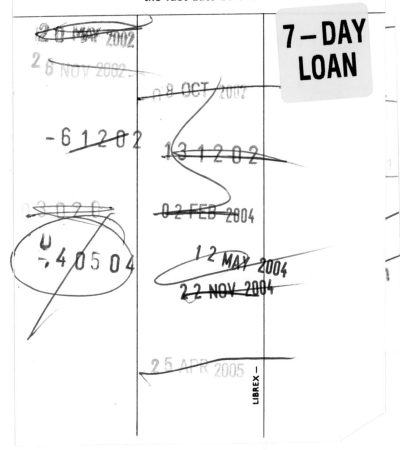

**7—DAY
LOAN**

2 0 MAY 2002

2 6 NOV 2002

0 8 OCT 2002

- 6 1 2 0 2

1 3 1 2 0 2

0 2 FEB 2004

- 4 0 5 0 4

1 2 MAY 2004

2 2 NOV 2004

2 5 APR 2005

LIBREX —

SECOND EDITION

THE

EUROPEAN

UNION

Readings on the Theory and Practice of European Integration

edited by

Brent F. Nelsen
Alexander C-G. Stubb

Published and distributed in Europe exclusively
and outside the Americas, Japan,
and Australasia nonexclusively by
MACMILLAN PRESS LTD
Houndmills, Basingstoke, Hampshire RG21 6XS
and London
Companies and representatives
throughout the world

ISBN 0-333-73241-3

A catalogue record for this book is available
from the British Library.

This book is printed on paper suitable for recycling and
made from fully managed and sustained forest sources.

10   9   8   7   6   5   4   3   2   1
07 06 05 04 03 02 01 00 99 98

Printed and bound in the United States of America

Contents

Preface

Second chances are rare, but welcome.

We put together the first edition of this book to meet our own need for a supplementary classroom text that explored in greater depth the ideas introduced in the standard descriptions of the history, institutions, and policies of the European Union (EU). We suspected that other instructors had a similar need, but we were rather surprised at the positive reception our book enjoyed on both sides of the Atlantic. Even more surprising—and gratifying—were the reports we received from people who were using the book outside the classroom as an introduction to the major themes in the study of European integration. But as satisfied as we were with the way the book was meeting student needs, we were also well aware (or were gently made aware by our friends and colleagues) of its imperfections. Time, too, took its toll as several of the chapters became dated and new work became available. So here we are, with a welcome second chance to improve on previous work.

This second edition, more than the first, is focused on the ideas informing the theory and practice of European integration rather than on EU policymaking, which is exhaustively covered in Helen Wallace and William Wallace (eds.), *Policy-Making in the European Union* (Oxford University Press, 1996). To a remarkable degree, both politicians and scholars have feasted on the same intellectual stew when thinking about the process of uniting Europe. In this stew are chunks of federalism, scraps of functionalism and neofunctionalism, bits of intergovernmentalism, and a few assorted economic lumps. The flavors have always been blended, but whether we look at the rhetoric of politicians or the writings of academics, no matter what the postwar decade, we can still discern these major ingredients. Thus, we designed the book to reflect the stew. We added some material to the historical sections (Parts 1 and 2) to better represent the development of the major approaches to integration. Care was also taken to achieve a diversity of national perspectives. We did the same to Part 3 (where most of the material is new) after making several agonizing decisions. Our goal in this final part was to include work that demonstrated the continuing influence of the traditional approaches while representing the major perspectives in the contemporary debate. Of course, authors' clarity of thought, and publishers' permissions fees also played a role in our decisions. But that is the mundane stuff of producing edited volumes.

The book focuses on ideas, but it also tells two parallel stories. One story is about political leaders and their visions for a united Europe. The other is about scholars seeking to understand the process of uniting nations. Both stories begin with a tremendous burst of idealism and optimism: the politicians think they can unite Europe and the social scientists think they can explain the process and predict its outcome. But both stories end on a sober, realistic note: the politicians are divided on who *should* rule—national governments or federal institutions—and scholars are divided on who *does* rule, national governments or federal institutions. So where does this leave the European Union? The politicians seem to have lost what vision they had, and the academy is no longer confident in its ability to explain the vast decisionmaking complex we call the European Union. But perhaps this is not the end. Theory seems to follow practice; if and when the EU experiences another spurt of integrating energy (as it did in 1985–1992, and as it may do as a result of the underestimated Amsterdam treaty), enthusiastic scholars will be right behind to explain it. Chances are, however, that they will be dipping into the same intellectual stew set over the fire by the likes of Altiero Spinelli, Jean Monnet, Ernst Haas, Stanley Hoffmann, and Bela Balassa.

. . .

As we stated in the first edition of this book, readers need to be aware of several protocols we employed when constructing the book. First, the introductions preceding each selection set the context and summarize the argument of that selection. These prologues are designed to amplify the dialogue among the authors of the texts. They should not substitute for a broader discussion of the historical or theoretical contexts, nor should they replace a close reading of each piece. Second, we have abridged each selection. Centered bullets mark significant abridgments; less significant abridgments (i.e., less than a paragraph) are marked with ellipses; very minor abridgments go unmarked; brackets [ ] mark editors' additions; and all notes are omitted. We have taken great care to preserve the core—and much more—of each author's argument, but readers should consider the original sources before making definitive (i.e., published) statements about the selections reprinted here.

. . .

The first edition of this reader was conceived and executed at Furman University (Greenville, South Carolina). The second edition is a cyber-age product of cross-continental e-mail exchanges between Greenville, Helsinki, London, and a number of other cities, which culminated in lively working sessions in the cafés around the London School of Economics and Political Science. We, of course, take full responsibility for the final product, but we could not have put this book together without the help of both European and North American friends and colleagues. In determining the content of the second edition we took valuable advice from Simon Bulmer, Maria Green Cowles, Kevin Featherstone, Cleveland Fraser, Robert Geyer, James Guth, Janne Haaland Matlary, Simon Hix, Christine Ingebritsen, Paulette Kurzer, Brigid Laffan, Leon Lindberg, Phil McGuin, Andrew Moravcsik, Rory O'Donnell, Donald Puchala, Martin Sæter, Ulf Sverdrup, Helen Wallace, and William Wallace. Valuable secretarial help was provided by Margaret Crisp, Sharon Dilworth, and (master proofreader) Timothy Hill. Lilli Ann Hall provided essential library support, and Nicolas Stubb's computer expertise was always appreciated. Finally, we owe a tremendous debt of gratitude to Lynne Rienner—who has backed our vision from the beginning and always offered treasured advice—and Sally Glover, who made sure the book made it to press.

The Duke Endowment and the Knight Foundation, via Furman University's Research and Professional Growth Program, provided generous financial support for this project. And as with our first edition, emotional support and personal sacrifices were freely offered by our long-suffering families. Their love and support provide the foundation on which we stand.

Brent F. Nelsen
Alexander C-G. Stubb

PART 1

Visions of a United Europe

The Ventotene Manifesto

ALTIERO SPINELLI AND ERNESTO ROSSI

Visions of a united Europe have their roots in the political unity of ancient Rome and the ideological solidarity of medieval Christendom.
In the twentieth century these visions grew to maturity in the harsh
climate of modern war. When the Allies began to turn back Hitler's
armies, Europeans of many political persuasions began arguing for a
united Europe as a means of eliminating the possibility of war and
preserving European civilization. The resistance movements fighting
fascist occupation were especially vocal in their criticism of the nation-state system and their support for a unified Europe. Leading the
way was a small group of left-wing intellectuals from the Italian Resistance Movement who illegally launched their drive for a federated
Europe from a political internment center on the island of Ventotene.

Altiero Spinelli (1907–1986), a former communist and future
academic and politician (see Chapter 12) and Ernesto Rossi
(1897–1967), an anti-fascist journalist, in consultation with several
other prisoners, drafted what came to be known as the Ventotene
Manifesto in June 1941. Ada Rossi smuggled the Manifesto to the Italian mainland, where the underground press published it in late
1941.[1] In August 1943 Spinelli founded the European Federalist
Movement, which adopted the Manifesto as its political program.

The Manifesto is ultimately a call to action. It begins with a critique of totalitarianism and its causes, then proceeds to call for a
movement of workers and intellectuals to seize the opportunity offered by the war to create a "European Federation" equipped to provide security and social justice for all Europeans. The section of the

Reprinted with permission from *Documents on the History of European
Integration, Vol. 1: Continental Plans for European Union, 1939–1945*, ed.
Walter Lipgens (Berlin: Walter de Gruyter, 1985), pp. 471–484. Notes
omitted.

Manifesto reprinted below—which appeared under the heading "Post-war Duties: European Unity"—assesses the coming postwar crisis and asserts that a European Federation would easily solve "the multiple problems which poison international life on the continent." Finally, the authors sketch the outline of a federal state that controls the armed forces of Europe, its economy, and its internal security, while leaving the states with sufficient autonomy to develop the political life of their people.

The version reproduced here is the 1981 Rome translation with further English clarifications inserted in brackets.

·   ·   ·

Germany's defeat would not automatically lead to the reformation of Europe according to our ideal of civilization.

In the brief, intense period of general crises (during which the fallen governments lie broken, during which the popular masses anxiously await a new message and are, meanwhile, like molten matter, burning, susceptible of being poured into new moulds, capable of welcoming the guidance of serious internationalists), the classes which were most privileged under the old national systems will attempt, underhandedly or violently, to quench the thirst, the sentiments, the passions groping towards internationalism, and they will ostentatiously [obstinately] begin to reconstruct the old state organ. And it is probable that the English leaders, perhaps in agreement with the Americans, will attempt to push things in this direction, in order to restore the policy of the balance of power, in the apparent immediate interests of their empire.

·   ·   ·

If this purpose were to be reached [achieved], the reaction would have won. In appearance, these states might well be broadly democratic and socialistic; [but] it would only be a question of time before power returned into the hands of the reactionaries. National jealousies would again develop, and [each] state would again express its satisfaction at its own existence in its armed strength. In a more or less brief space of time the most important duty would be to convert populations into armies. Generals would again command, the monopoly holders would again draw profits from autarchy, the bureaucracy would continue to swell, the priests would keep the masses docile. All the initial conquests would shrivel into nothing, in comparison to the necessity of once more preparing for war.

The question which must first be resolved, and if it is not then any other progress made up to that point is mere appearance, is that of the abolition of the division of Europe into national, sovereign states.

The collapse of the majority of the states of the continent under the German steam-roller has already placed the destinies of the European populations on common ground: either all together they will submit to Hitler's dominion, or all together they will enter a revolutionary crisis after his fall, and they will not find themselves adamantly distinct in solid, state structures.

The general spirit today is already far more [better] disposed than it was in the past to a federal reorganization of Europe. The hard experience of the last decades has opened the eyes even of those who would not see, and has matured many circumstances favorable to our ideal.

All reasonable men recognize that it is impossible to maintain a balance of power among European states with militarist Germany enjoying equal conditions, nor can Germany be broken up into pieces once it is conquered. We have seen a demonstration that no country within Europe can stay on the sidelines to naught. The uselessness, even harmfulness, of organizations like the League of Nations has been demonstrated: they pretend to guarantee an international law without a military force capable of imposing its decisions respecting the absolute sovereignty of the member states. The principle of non-intervention turned out to be absurd. According to it each population was left free to choose the despotic government it thought best, as if the constitution of each of the single states were not a question of vital interest for all the other European nations.

The multiple problems which poison international life on the continent have proved to be insoluble: tracing boundaries through areas inhabited by mixed populations, defence of alien minorities, seaports for landlocked countries, the Balkan question, the Irish problem, and so on. All matters which would find easy solutions in the European Federation.

.   .   .

And, once the horizon of the Old Continent is passed beyond, and all the peoples who make up humanity embrace in a grand vision of their common participation it will have to be recognized that European Federation is the single conceivable guarantee that relationships with American and Asiatic peoples can exist on the basis of peaceful cooperation; this while awaiting a more distant future, when the political unity of the entire globe becomes a possibility.

The dividing line between progressive and reactionary parties no longer follows the formal line of greater or lesser democracy, or of more or less socialism to be instituted; rather the division falls along the line, very new and substantial, that separates the party members into two groups. The first is made up of those who conceive of the essential purpose and goal of struggle as the ancient one, that is, the conquest of national political power—and who, although involuntarily, play into the hands of reactionary forces, letting the incandescent lava of popular passions set in the old moulds, and this allowing old absurdities to arise once again. The second are those who see as the main purpose the creation of a solid international state; they will direct popular forces toward this goal, and having won national power, use it first and foremost as an instrument for achieving international unity.

With propaganda and action, seeking to establish in every possible way the agreements and links among the single [similar] movements which are certainly being formed in the various countries, the foundation must be built now for a movement that knows how to mobilize all forces for the birth of the new organism which will be the grandest creation, and the newest, that has occurred in Europe for centuries; in order to constitute a steady federal state, that will have at its disposal a European armed service instead of national armies; to break decisively economic autarchies, the backbone of totalitarian regimes; [an organism] that will have sufficient means to see that its deliberations for the maintenance of common order are executed in the single federal states, while each state will retain the autonomy it needs for a plastic articulation and development of political life according to the particular characteristics of its people.

If a sufficient number of men in European countries understand this, then victory is shortly to be [will soon be] in their hands, because the situation and the spirit [people's minds] will be favourable to their work. They will have before them [as their adversaries] parties and factions that have already been disqualified by the disastrous experience of the last twenty years. It will be the moment of new men: the movement for a free and united Europe.

- **NOTES**

1. Walter Lipgens, *Documents on the History of European Integration, Vol. 1: Continental Plans for European Union 1939–1945*, ed. Walter Lipgens (Berlin: Walter de Gruyter, 1985), pp. 471–73.

2 The Tragedy of Europe

WINSTON S. CHURCHILL

Calls for a united Europe—like that of the Ventotene Manifesto—drew the attention of a wide range of political leaders and activists. Many were young idealists or politicians with limited influence; no leaders of undeniable political stature raised a strong voice in favor of a federated Europe—that is, until Winston Churchill (1874–1965) spoke from a platform in Zurich.

Churchill, the great wartime prime minister of Britain, found himself leader of the Conservative opposition in Parliament after Labour's victory in the 1945 general election. Despite his removal from office, Churchill remained a key architect of the postwar world by identifying the dangers facing the West and articulating a clear strategy for defending western interests and values.

Churchill's speech at Zurich University on 19 September 1946 profoundly influenced the shape of postwar Europe. He began this speech with the refrain common to all the postwar integrationists: Europe must unite before war destroys the continent, its glorious civilization, and perhaps much of the rest of the world. He called specifically for a "United States of Europe" led by Europe's former antagonists, France and Germany, but he did not outline a detailed program for achieving unity. Rather, he argued simply and powerfully for Europe to adopt an ideal to style its future. Interestingly, Churchill seems to exclude Britain from his grand European project, thus reflecting an ambiguity toward Europe that remains strong in Britain today.

Reprinted with permission from *Winston S. Churchill: His Complete Speeches, 1897–1963*, Vol. 7, 1943–1949, ed. Robert Rhodes James (Chelsea House Publishers, 1974). Copyright 1974 by Chelsea House Publishers.

Churchill's stature forced European leaders to take his Zurich call seriously. His efforts eventually led to the Hague Congress of May 1948 and the creation of the Council of Europe in 1949, both milestones in European integration.

I wish to speak to you today about the tragedy of Europe. This noble continent, comprising on the whole the fairest and the most cultivated regions of the earth, enjoying a temperate and equable climate, is the home of all the great parent races of the western world. It is the fountain of Christian faith and Christian ethics. It is the origin of most of the culture, arts, philosophy, and science both of ancient and modern times. If Europe were once united in the sharing of its common inheritance, there would be no limit to the happiness, to the prosperity and glory which its three or four hundred million people would enjoy. Yet it is from Europe that have sprung that series of frightful nationalistic quarrels, originated by the Teutonic nations, which we have seen even in this twentieth century and in our lifetime, wreck the peace and mar the prospects of all mankind.

And what is the plight to which Europe has been reduced? Some of the smaller states have indeed made a good recovery, but over wide areas a vast quivering mass of tormented, hungry, careworn and bewildered human beings gape at the ruins of their cities and homes, and scan the dark horizons for the approach of some new peril, tyranny or terror. Among the victors there is a babel of jarring voices; among the vanquished a sullen silence of despair. That is all that Europeans, grouped in so many ancient states and nations, that is all that the Germanic Powers have got by tearing each other to pieces and spreading havoc far and wide. Indeed, but for the fact that the great Republic across the Atlantic Ocean has at length realized that the ruin or enslavement of Europe would involve their own fate as well, and has stretched out hands of succor and guidance, the Dark Ages would have returned in all their cruelty and squalor. They may still return.

Yet all the while there is a remedy which, if it were generally and spontaneously adopted, would as if by a miracle transform the whole scene, and would in a few years make all Europe, or the greater part of it, as free and as happy as Switzerland is today. What is this sovereign remedy? It is to re-create the European Family or as much of it as we can, and provide it with a structure under which it can dwell in peace, in safety and in freedom. We must build a kind of United States of Europe. In this way only will hundreds of millions of toilers be able to regain the simple joys and hopes which make life worth living. The process is simple. All that is needed is the resolve of hundreds of millions of men and women to do right instead of wrong and gain as their reward blessing instead of cursing.

Much work has been done upon this task by the exertions of the Pan-European Union which owes so much to Count Coudenhove-Kalergi and which commanded the services of the famous French patriot and statesman, Aristide Briand. There is also that immense body of doctrine and procedure, which was brought into being amid high hopes after the first world war, as the League of Nations. The League of Nations did not fail because of its principles or conceptions. It failed because these principles were deserted by those states who had brought it into being. It failed because the governments of those days feared to face the facts, and act while time remained. This disaster must not be repeated. There is therefore much knowledge and material with which to build; and also bitter dear-bought experience.

I was very glad to read in the newspapers two days ago that my friend President Truman had expressed his interest and sympathy with this great design. There is no reason why a regional organization of Europe should in any way conflict with the world organization of the United Nations. On the contrary, I believe that the larger synthesis will only survive if it is founded upon coherent natural groupings. There is already a natural grouping in the Western Hemisphere. We British have our own Commonwealth of Nations. These do not weaken, on the contrary they strengthen, the world organization. They are in fact its main support. And why should there not be a European group which could give a sense of enlarged patriotism and common citizenship to the distracted peoples of this turbulent and mighty continent and why should it not take its rightful place with other great groupings in shaping the destinies of men? In order that this should be accomplished there must be an act of faith in which millions of families speaking many languages must consciously take part.

We all know that the two world wars through which we have passed arose out of the vain passion of a newly-united Germany to play the dominating part in the world. In this last struggle crimes and massacres have been committed for which there is no parallel since the invasions of the Mongols in the fourteenth century and no equal at any time in human history. The guilty must be punished. Germany must be deprived of the power to rearm and make another aggressive war. But when all this has been done, as it will be done, as it is being done, there must be an end to retribution. There must be what Mr. Gladstone many years ago called "a blessed act of oblivion." We must all turn our backs upon the horrors of the past. We must look to the future. We cannot afford to drag forward across the years that are to come the hatreds and revenges which have sprung from the injuries of the past. If Europe is to be saved from infinite misery, and indeed from final doom, there must be an act of faith in the European family and an act of oblivion against all the crimes and follies of the past.

Can the free peoples of Europe rise to the height of these resolves of the soul and instincts of the spirit of man? If they can, the wrongs and injuries which have been inflicted will have been washed away on all sides by the miseries which have been endured. Is there any need for further floods of agony? Is it the only lesson of history that mankind is unteachable? Let there be justice, mercy and freedom. The peoples have to will it, and all will achieve their hearts' desire.

I am now going to say something that will astonish you. The first step in the re-creation of the European family must be a partnership between France and Germany. In this way only can France recover the moral leadership of Europe. There can be no revival of Europe without a spiritually great France and a spiritually great Germany. The structure of the United States of Europe, if well and truly built, will be such as to make the material strength of a single state less important. Small nations will count as much as large ones and gain their honor by their contribution to the common cause. The ancient states and principalities of Germany, freely joined together for mutual convenience in a federal system, might each take their individual place among the United States of Europe. I shall not try to make a detailed program for hundreds of millions of people who want to be happy and free, prosperous and safe, who wish to enjoy the four freedoms of which the great President Roosevelt spoke, and live in accordance with the principles embodied in the Atlantic Charter. If this is their wish, they have only to say so, and means can certainly be found, and machinery erected, to carry that wish into full fruition.

But I must give you a warning. Time may be short. At present there is a breathing space. The cannon have ceased firing. The fighting has stopped; but the dangers have not stopped. If we are to form the United States of Europe or whatever name or form it may take, we must begin now.

In these present days we dwell strangely and precariously under the shield and protection of the atomic bomb. The atomic bomb is still only in the hands of a state and nation which we know will never use it except in the cause of right and freedom. But it may well be that in a few years this awful agency of destruction will be wide-spread and the catastrophe following from its use by several warring nations will not only bring to an end all that we call civilization, but may possibly disintegrate the globe itself.

I must now sum up the propositions which are before you. Our constant aim must be to build and fortify the strength of [the United Nations]. Under and within that world concept we must re-create the European family in a regional structure called, it may be, the United States of Europe. The first step is to form a Council of Europe. If at first all the states of Europe are not willing or able to join the union, we must nevertheless proceed to assemble and combine those who will and those who can. The salvation of the common people of every race and of every land from war or servitude must be established on solid foundations and must be guarded by the readiness of all men and women to die rather than submit to tyranny. In all this urgent work, France and Germany must take the lead together. Great Britain, the British Commonwealth of Nations, mighty America, and I trust Soviet Russia—for then indeed all would be well—must be the friends and sponsors of the new Europe and must champion its right to live and shine.

3 The Schuman Declaration

ROBERT SCHUMAN

Efforts in the 1940s to realize Churchill's vision of a united Europe led to increased economic and political cooperation but did not yield anything like a United States of Europe. European leaders needed a new strategy to achieve such a goal. On 9 May 1950, Robert Schuman (1886–1963), France's foreign minister, outlined a plan to unite under a single authority the coal and steel industries of Europe's bitterest enemies, France and Germany. The purpose of the plan, which was developed by Jean Monnet, was to begin building a peaceful, united Europe one step at a time. European governments would start with two industries essential to the making of war, coal and steel, then add other economic and political sectors until all major decisions were taken at a European level. This would create, in Schuman's words, a "de facto solidarity" that would ultimately make war between France and Germany "materially impossible." The practical approach of Schuman and Monnet won favor on the European continent; France, Germany, Italy, and the Benelux countries eventually responded by creating the European Coal and Steel Community in 1952.

World peace cannot be safeguarded without the making of creative efforts proportionate to the dangers which threaten it.

The contribution which an organized and living Europe can bring to civilization is indispensable to the maintenance of peaceful relations. In taking upon herself for more than 20 years the role of champion of a united Europe, France has always had as her essential aim the service of peace. A united Europe was not achieved and we had war.

Europe will not be made all at once, or according to a single plan. It will be built through concrete achievements which first create a *de facto* solidarity. The coming together of the nations of Europe requires the elimination of the age-old opposition of France and Germany. Any action taken must in the first place concern these two countries.

With this aim in view, the French government proposes that action be taken immediately on one limited but decisive point. It proposes that Franco-German production of coal and steel as a whole be placed under a common High Authority, within the framework of an organization open to the participation of the other countries of Europe.

The pooling of coal and steel production should immediately provide for the setting up of common foundations for economic development as a first step in the federation of Europe, and will change the destinies of those regions which have long been devoted to the manufacture of munitions of war, of which they have been the most constant victims.

The solidarity in production thus established will make it plain that any war between France and Germany becomes not merely unthinkable, but materially impossible. The setting up of this powerful productive unit, open to all countries willing to take part and bound ultimately to provide all the member countries with the basic elements of industrial production on the same terms, will lay a true foundation for their economic unification.

This production will be offered to the world as a whole without distinction or exception, with the aim of contributing to raising living standards and to promoting peaceful achievements.

In this way, there will be realized simply and speedily that fusion of interests which is indispensable to the establishment of a common economic system; it may be the leaven from which may grow a wider and deeper community between countries long opposed to one another by sanguinary divisions.

By pooling basic production and by instituting a new High Authority, whose decisions will bind France, Germany and other member countries, this proposal will lead to the realization of the first concrete foundation of a European federation indispensable to the preservation of peace.

.   .   .

4 Preambles to the Treaties Establishing the European Communities (Treaties of Paris and Rome)

In Rome on 25 March 1957, the six member countries of the European Coal and Steel Community (ECSC) signed treaties establishing the European Economic Community (EEC) and the European Atomic Energy Community (EURATOM). These two treaties are often called the "Treaties of Rome" (the ECSC treaty was signed in Paris). The EEC treaty is also sometimes referred to as the "Treaty of Rome."

The preambles to each of the three original treaties reflect the founders' vision for building, through economic integration, "an ever closer union among the peoples of Europe." The deep desire for peace on the Continent runs through each of the preambles and links them to the visions articulated by Spinelli and Rossi, Churchill, Schuman, Monnet, and many others. But the documents also represent a subtle shift in emphasis away from peace to economic prosperity as the driving motive for unity. We can detect the shift in the Schuman Declaration and its parallel, the preamble to the ECSC treaty, but it becomes more evident in the preamble to the EEC treaty, where "economic and social progress" seems to take precedence over preserving and strengthening "peace and liberty." European leaders, while mindful of the dangers of violent conflict in Western Europe, were becoming more concerned with the material improvement of life on a peaceful continent.

■ EUROPEAN COAL AND STEEL COMMUNITY

. . .

CONSIDERING that world peace can be safeguarded only by creative efforts commensurate with the dangers that threaten it,

CONVINCED that the contribution which an organized and vital Europe can make to civilization is indispensable to the maintenance of peaceful relations,

RECOGNIZING that Europe can be built only through practical achievements which will first of all create real solidarity, and through the establishment of common bases for economic development,

ANXIOUS to help, by expanding their basic production, to raise the standard of living and further the works of peace,

RESOLVED to substitute for age-old rivalries the merging of their essential interests; to create, by establishing an economic community, the basis for a broader and deeper community among peoples long divided by bloody conflicts; and to lay the foundations for institutions which will give direction to a destiny henceforward shared,

HAVE DECIDED to create a European Coal and Steel Community.

. . .

■ EUROPEAN ECONOMIC COMMUNITY

. . .

DETERMINED to lay the foundations of an ever closer union among the peoples of Europe,

RESOLVED to ensure the economic and social progress of their countries by common action to eliminate the barriers which divide Europe,

AFFIRMING as the essential objective of their efforts the constant improvement of the living and working conditions of their peoples,

RECOGNIZING that the removal of existing obstacles calls for concerted action in order to guarantee steady expansion, balanced trade and fair competition,

ANXIOUS to strengthen the unity of their economies and to ensure their harmonious development by reducing the differences existing between the various regions and the backwardness of the less favored regions,

DESIRING to contribute, by means of a common commercial policy, to the progressive abolition of restrictions on international trade,

INTENDING to confirm the solidarity which binds Europe and the overseas countries and desiring to ensure the development of their prosperity, in accordance with the principles of the Charter of the United Nations,

RESOLVED by thus pooling their resources to preserve and strengthen peace and liberty, and calling upon the other peoples of Europe who share their ideal to join in their efforts,

HAVE DECIDED to create a European Economic Community.

.   .   .

■ EUROPEAN ATOMIC ENERGY COMMUNITY

.   .   .

RECOGNIZING that nuclear energy represents an essential resource for the development and invigoration of industry and will permit the advancement of the cause of peace,

CONVINCED that only a joint effort undertaken without delay can offer the prospect of achievements commensurate with the creative capacities of their countries,

RESOLVED to create the conditions necessary for the development of a powerful nuclear industry which will provide extensive energy resources, lead to the modernization of technical processes and contribute, through its many other applications, to the prosperity of their peoples,

ANXIOUS to create the conditions of safety necessary to eliminate hazards to the life and health of the public,

DESIRING to associate other countries with their work and to cooperate with international organizations concerned with the peaceful development of atomic energy,

HAVE DECIDED to create a European Atomic Energy Community (EURATOM).

.   .   .

A Ferment of Change

JEAN MONNET

Jean Monnet (1888–1979) was the "father of Europe." No single individual influenced the shape of the European Union more than this French civil servant and diplomat. Monnet convinced Robert Schuman to propose the European Coal and Steel Community and became the first president of its High Authority. Monnet convinced Johan Willem Beyen and Paul-Henri Spaak to propose EURATOM and the EEC, and then established the influential Action Committee for a United States of Europe to pressure governments to accept the proposals. Monnet worked hard, and eventually successfully, to enlarge the Community by adding Britain, Ireland, and Denmark. And shortly before his death, Monnet persuaded EC governments to turn their regular summits into the European Council.[1]

Monnet was a pragmatic government official who quite naturally developed a strategy for uniting Europe that looked much like the step-by-step functionalism of David Mitrany (see Chapter 13). Monnet argued that problems of insecurity and human need in the world—and in Europe in particular—required radical changes in the way people thought. Nations, he believed, should adopt common rules governing their behavior and create common institutions to apply these rules. Such a strategy, even if applied on a small scale, would create a "silent revolution in men's minds" that would change the way people thought and acted. For Monnet, the European Communities of the early 1960s demonstrated that small collective steps set off "a chain reaction, a ferment where one change induces another." This ferment, he asserted, would not lead to another nineteenth-century–style great power—although a united Europe would be able to shoulder an equal burden of

Reprinted with permission from *Journal of Common Market Studies*, 1(1)(1962):203–211. Copyright 1962 by Blackwell Publishers.

leadership with the United States—nor would it be confined to Europe. Integration was a process that may have started in Europe but would soon have to include the broader West, then the rest of the world, if humanity was to "escape destruction."

This century has probably changed the manner of life more for every one of us than all the thousands of years of man's progress put together. In the past, men were largely at the mercy of nature. Today in our industrial countries of the Western world and elsewhere, we are acquiring an unprecedented mastery over nature. Natural resources are no longer a limitation now that we control more and more forms of energy and can use raw materials in more and more ways. We are entering the age of abundance where work, as we know it, will only be one of many human activities. For the first time we in the West are witnessing the emergence of a truly mass society marked by mass consumption, mass education and even mass culture.

We are moving, in the West, from a society where privilege was part of nature to one where the enjoyment of human rights and human dignity are common to all. Unfortunately, two-thirds of mankind have not shared in this process.

And now, on the very eve of creating unprecedented conditions of abundance, we are suddenly faced with the consequences of our extraordinary mastery over the physical forces of nature. Modern medicine is steadily increasing our prospects of life, so that the population of the world is increasing fantastically fast. This revolution is creating new explosive pressures of all kinds in the world. At the same time, science is repeatedly creating new powers of destruction. This faces us with the greatest threat humanity has ever had to deal with. The issue today is no longer peace or war, but the triumph or destruction of civilized life.

We cannot assume that we shall avoid such destruction. We have only to look back on the last fifty years to see how constant the risk of upheaval has become. No region of the world has escaped violence. One-third of mankind has become Communist, another third has obtained independence from colonialism, and even among the remaining third nearly all countries have undergone revolutions or wars. True, atomic bombs have made nuclear war so catastrophic that I am convinced no country wishes to resort to it. But I am equally convinced that we are at the mercy of an error of judgment or a technical breakdown, the source of which no man may ever know.

We are then in a world of rapid change, in which men and nations must learn to control themselves in their relations with others.

This, to my mind, can only be done through institutions; and it is this need for common institutions that we have learnt in Europe since the war.

We are used to thinking that major changes in the traditional relations between countries only take place violently, through conquest or revolution. We are so accustomed to this that we find it hard to appreciate those that are taking place peacefully in Europe even though they have begun to affect the world. We can see the communist revolution, because it has been violent and because we have been living with it for nearly fifty years. We can see the revolution in the ex-colonial areas because power is plainly changing hands. But we tend to miss the magnitude of the change in Europe because it is taking place by the constitutional and democratic methods which govern our countries.

Yet we have only to look at the difference between 1945 and today to see what an immense transformation has been taking place under our very eyes, here in what used to be called the old world. After the war, the nations of continental Europe were divided and crippled, their national resources were depleted and, in most of them, the peoples had little faith in the future. During the last fifteen years, these countries have lost their empires. It might have been expected they would be further depressed by what many considered the loss of past greatness and prestige.

And yet, after all these upheavals, the countries of continental Europe, which have fought each other so often in the past and which, even in peacetime, organized their economies as potential instruments of war, are now uniting in a Common Market which is laying the foundations for political union. Britain is negotiating to enter this European Community and by this very fact changing the tradition of centuries. And now the President of the United States is already asking Congress for powers to negotiate with the enlarged European Common Market.

To understand this extraordinary change in all its basic simplicity, we must go back to 1950, only five years after the war. For five years, the whole French nation had been making efforts to re-create the bases of production, but it became evident that to go beyond recovery towards steady expansion and higher standards of life for all, the resources of a single nation were not sufficient. It was necessary to transcend the national framework.

The need was political as well as economic. The Europeans had to overcome the mistrust born of centuries of feuds and wars. The governments and peoples of Europe still thought in the old terms of victors and vanquished. Yet, if a basis for peace in the world was to be established, these notions had to be eliminated. Here again, one had to go beyond the nation and the conception of national interest as an end in itself.

We thought that both these objectives could in time be reached if conditions were created enabling these countries to increase their resources by merging them in a large and dynamic common market; and if these same countries could be made to consider that their problems were no longer solely of national concern, but were mutual European responsibilities.

Obviously this could not be done all at once. It was not possible to create a large dynamic market immediately or to produce trust between recent enemies overnight. After several unsuccessful attempts, the French Government through its Foreign Minister, M. Robert Schuman, proposed in 1950 what many people today would regard as a modest beginning but which seemed very bold at the time; and the parliaments of France, Germany, Italy and Benelux voted that, for coal and steel, their countries would form a single common market, run by common institutions administering common rules, very much as within a single nation. The European Coal and Steel Community was set up. In itself this was a technical step, but its new procedures, under common institutions, created a silent revolution in men's minds. It proved decisive in persuading businessmen, civil servants, politicians and trade unionists that such an approach could work and that the economic and political advantages of unity over division were immense. Once they were convinced, they were ready to take further steps forward.

In 1957, only three years after the failure of the European Army, the six parliaments ratified the Treaty of Rome which extended the Common Market from coal and steel to an economic union embracing all goods. Today, the Common Market, with its 170 million people that will become 225 million when Britain joins, is creating in Europe a huge continental market on the American scale.

The large market does not prejudge the future economic systems of Europe. Most of the Six have a nationalized sector as large as the British and some also have planning procedures. These are just as compatible with private enterprise on the large market as they are within a single nation. The contribution of the Common Market is to create new opportunities of expansion for all the members, which make it easier to solve any problems that arise, and to provide the rest of the world with prospects of growing trade that would not exist without it. In Europe, an open society looking to the future is replacing a defensive one regretting the past.

The profound change is being made possible essentially by the new method of common action which is the core of the European Community. To establish this new method of common action, we adapted to our situation the methods which have allowed individuals to live together in society: common rules which each member is committed to respect, and common institutions to watch over the application of these rules. Nations have applied this method within their frontiers for centuries, but they have never yet been applied between them. After a period of trial and error, this method has become a permanent dialogue between a single European body, responsible for expressing the view of the general interest of the Community, and the national governments expressing the national views. The resulting procedure for collective decisions is something quite new and, as far as I know, has no analogy in any traditional system. It is not federal because there is no central government; the nations take their decisions together in the Council of Ministers. On the other hand, the independent European body proposes policies, and the common element is further underlined by the European Parliament and the European Court of Justice.

This system leads to a completely changed approach to common action. In the past, the nations felt no irrevocable commitment. Their responsibility was strictly to themselves, not to any common interest. They had to rely on themselves alone. Relations took the form either of domination if one country was much stronger than the others, or of the trading of advantages if there was a balance of powers between them. This balance was necessarily unstable and the concessions made in an agreement one year could always be retracted the next.

But in the European Communities, common rules applied by joint institutions give each a responsibility for the effective working of the Community as a whole. This leads the nations, within the discipline of the Community, to seek a solution to the problems themselves, instead of trading temporary advantages. It is this method which explains the dramatic change in the relations of Germany with France and the other Common Market countries. Looking forward to a common future has made them agree to live down the feuds of the past. Today people have almost forgotten that the Saar was ever a problem and yet from 1919 to 1950 it was a major bone of contention between France and Germany. European unity has made it seem an anachronism. And today, at French invitation, German troops are training on French soil.

· · ·

We have seen that Europe has overcome the attitude of domination which ruled state policies for so many centuries. But quite apart from what this means for us in the old continent, this is a fact of world importance. It is obvious that countries and peoples who are overcoming this state of mind between themselves will bring the same mentality to their relations with others, outside Europe. The new method of action developed in Europe replaces the efforts at domination of nation states by a constant process of collective adaptation to new conditions, a chain reaction, a ferment where one change induces another.

Look at the effect the Common Market has already had on world tariffs. When it was set up, it was widely assumed the member countries would want to protect themselves and become, as some put it, an inward-looking group. Yet everything that has happened since has shown this view to be wrong. The Six have reduced the tariffs between themselves and towards other countries faster than expected. Now President Kennedy proposes America and Europe should cut tariffs on manufactures by half, and the Common Market will certainly welcome it. This leads to a situation where tariffs throughout the major trading areas of the world will be lower than they have ever been.

These changes inside and outside Europe would not have taken place without the driving force of the Common Market. It opens new prospects for dealing with problems the solution of which was becoming increasingly urgent. I am thinking of world agriculture in a more and more industrial civilization; of links between the new and the long-established industrial regions, and in particular of the need for growing trade between Japan and the United States and Europe together.

Naturally, increasing trade will also benefit the Commonwealth. The prospect of Britain's future entry into the Common Market has already made the Continent more aware than ever before of the problems of the Commonwealth. Clearly, for countries whose major need is to obtain more capital for development, the fact that Britain is part of a rapidly developing Europe holds great promise of future progress.

Similarly, problems are arising that only Europe and the United States together have the resources to deal with. The need to develop policies of sustained growth, which in large part depend on maintaining international monetary stability, is an example. Increasing the aid of the West to the underdeveloped areas on a large scale is another. Separately, the European nations have inevitably taken divergent views of aid policies. But tomorrow, the nations of Europe by

acting together can make a decisive contribution. The r
condition of such a partnership between America and '
Europe should be united and thus be able to deploy re
same scale as America. This is what is in the course c
day.

That we have begun to cooperate on these affairs at the Atlantic level is a great step forward. It is evident that we must soon go
a good deal further towards an Atlantic Community. The creation of
a united Europe brings this nearer by making it possible for America
and Europe to act as partners on an equal footing. I am convinced
that ultimately, the United States too will delegate powers of effective
action to common institutions, even on political questions. Just as
the United States in their own day found it necessary to unite, just as
Europe is now in the process of uniting, so the West must move towards some kind of union. This is not an end in itself. It is the beginning on the road to the more orderly world we must have if we are to
escape destruction.

The discussions on peace today are dominated by the question
of disarmament. The world will be more and more threatened by destruction as long as bombs continue to pile up on both sides. Many
therefore feel that the hopes for peace in the world depend on as
early an agreement on armaments as possible, particularly an agreement on nuclear arms. Of course we must continue to negotiate on
these questions. But it is too simple to hope the problems that arise
out of philosophic conflicts could be settled without a change in the
view which people take of the future. For what is the Soviet objective? It is to achieve a Communist world, as Mr. Khrushchev has told
us many times. When this becomes so obviously impossible that nobody, even within a closed society, can any longer believe it—when
the partnership of America and a United Europe makes it plain to all
that the West may change from within but that others cannot change
it by outside pressures, then Mr. Khrushchev or his successor will accept the facts, and the conditions will at last exist for turning so-
called peaceful coexistence into genuine peace. Then at last real disarmament will become possible.

Personally, I do not think we shall have to wait long for this
change. The history of European unification shows that when people
become convinced a change is taking place that creates a new situation, they act on their revised estimate before that situation is established. After all, Britain has asked to join the Common Market before it was complete. The President of the United States is seeking
powers to negotiate with the European Community on steps to an
Atlantic partnership even before Britain has joined. Can we not ex-

pect a similar phenomenon in the future relations with the Soviet Union?

What conclusions can we draw from all these thoughts?

One impression predominates in my mind over all others. It is this: unity in Europe does not create a new kind of great power; it is a method for introducing change in Europe and consequently in the world. People, more often outside the European Community than within, are tempted to see the European Community as a potential nineteenth-century state with all the overtones of power this implies. But we are not in the nineteenth century, and the Europeans have built up the European Community precisely in order to find a way out of the conflicts to which the nineteenth-century power philosophy gave rise. The natural attitude of a European Community based on the exercise by nations of common responsibilities will be to make these nations also aware of their responsibilities, as a Community, to the world. In fact, we already see this sense of world responsibilities developing as unity in Europe begins to affect Britain, America and many other areas of the world. European unity is not a blueprint, it is not a theory, it is a process that has already begun, of bringing peoples and nations together to adapt themselves jointly to changing circumstances.

European unity is the most important event in the West since the war, not because it is a new great power, but because the new institutional method it introduces is permanently modifying relations between nations and men. Human nature does not change, but when nations and men accept the same rule and the same institutions to make sure that they are applied, their behavior towards each other changes. This is the process of civilization itself.

■ NOTE

1. Richard Mayne, "Gray Eminence," in *Jean Monnet: The Path to European Unity*, ed. Douglas Brinkley and Clifford Hackett (New York: St. Martin's Press, 1991), 114–116.

6 A Concert of European States

CHARLES DE GAULLE

Charles de Gaulle (1890–1970), French Resistance leader and first president of France's fifth republic, was above all a French national-ist. His overriding objective after the humiliation of World War II was to reestablish France as a great power, free from domination by the superpowers and once again the source of western civilization's cul-tural and spiritual strength. De Gaulle's vision of France profoundly shaped his vision of Europe, which differed markedly from the views held by the founders of the European Communities, most noticeably Jean Monnet.

De Gaulle believed in European unity, but he criticized the supranational vision of Europe as unrealistic and undesirable. He ar-gued instead for a "concert of European states" where national gov-ernments coordinated their policies extensively but did not give up their rights as sovereign entities to a European "superstate." De Gaulle's unwillingness to concede France's right to control its vital af-fairs led to the 1965 crisis in the Communities and eventually the Luxembourg Compromise, which in practice, gave every member state the right to veto Community decisions (although it has officially been invoked only a handful of times). In effect, the Six were forced to accept de Gaulle's vision of an intergovernmental Europe.

War gives birth and brings death to nations. In the meantime, it never ceases to loom over their existence. For us French, the develop-

Reprinted from "Europe," in *Memoirs of Hope: Renewal and Endeavor*, trans. Terence Kilmartin (Simon and Schuster, 1971).

ment of our national life, our political regimes and our world position from 1815 to 1870 was determined by the hostile coalition
which united the nations of Europe against the Revolution, the dazzling victories and then the downfall of Napoleon, and finally the
disastrous treaties which sanctioned so many battles. Thereafter, during the forty-four years of the "armed truce," it was our defeat, our
secret desire to avenge it, but also the fear that a united Germany
might inflict another on us, that dominated our actions at home and
abroad. Although the gigantic effort put forth by our people in the
First World War opened the way to renewal, we closed it upon ourselves by failing to consolidate our military victory, by forgoing the
reparations which would have provided us with the means of indus-
trializing our country and thus compensating for our enormous human and material losses, and, finally, by withdrawing into a passive
strategic and foreign policy which left Europe a prey to Hitler's ambitions. Now, in the aftermath of the last conflict in which she had all
but perished, on what premises was France to base her progress and
her actions?

The first of these premises was that, in spite of everything, she
was alive, sovereign and victorious. That was undoubtedly a marvel.
Who would have thought that, after suffering an unparalleled disaster,
after witnessing the subjection of her rulers to the authority of the enemy, after undergoing the ravages of the two greatest battles of the
war and, in the meantime, prolonged plundering by the invader, after
enduring the systematic abasement inflicted on her by a regime
founded on surrender and humiliation, she would ever heal the
wounds inflicted on her body and her soul? Who would not have
sworn that her liberation, if it was to come, would be due to foreigners alone and that they would decide what was to become of her at
home and abroad? Who, in the almost total extinction of her resistance, had not condemned as absurd the hope that one day the enemy
would surrender to her at the same time as to her allies? Nevertheless,
in the end she had emerged from the struggle with her frontiers and
her unity intact, in control of her own affairs, and in the ranks of the
victors. There was nothing, therefore, to prevent her now from being
what she intended to be and doing what she wished to do.

This was all the more true because, for the first time in her history, she was unhampered by any threat from her immediate neighbors. Germany, dismembered, had ceased to be a formidable and
domineering power. Italy regretted having turned her ambitions
against us. The alliance with England, preserved by Free France, and
the process of decolonization which had removed old grievances, ensured that the wind of mistrust no longer blew across the English

Channel. Bonds of affection and common interest were bringing a serene France and a pacified Spain closer together across the Pyrenees. And what enmities could possibly spring up from the friendly lands of Belgium, Luxembourg, Holland or neutral Switzerland? Thus we were relieved of the state of constant tension in which dangerous neighbors once held us and which gravely hampered our activities.

It is true that, while France had lost her special vocation of being constantly in danger, the whole world was now haunted by the permanent fear of global conflict. Two empires, the American and the Soviet, now became giants in comparison with the old powers, confronted each other with their forces, their hegemonies and their ideologies. Both were in possession of nuclear armaments which could at any moment shake the entire world, and which made each of them omnipotent protectors in their respective camps. This perilous balance was liable to tip over eventually into limitless war unless it evolved into a general *détente*. For France, reduced in wealth and power by the conflicts in which she had been engaged over the past two centuries, dangerously exposed by her geographical position at the edge of the Old World and facing the New, mortally vulnerable by reason of her size and population, peace was obviously of vital importance. And, as it happened, circumstances now ordained that she should appoint herself its champion. For she was in the singular position of having no claims on what others possessed while they had nothing to claim from her, and of harboring no grievances on her own behalf against either of the giants, for whose peoples she cherished a traditional friendship confirmed by recent events, while they felt an exceptional attachment to her. In short, if there was a voice that might be listened to and a policy that might be effective with a view to setting up a new order to replace the Cold War, that voice and that policy were pre-eminently those of France. But only on condition that they were really her own and that the hand she held out in friendship was free.

At the same time, France now enjoyed a vast fund of interest and trust among peoples whose future was in gestation but who refused to pay allegiance to either of the rival dominations. China, endowed with such reserves of manpower and resources that limitless possibilities were open to her for the future; Japan, re-creating an independent world role on the basis of economic strength; India, at grips with problems of subsistence as vast as her size, but ultimately destined to turn towards the outside world; a great number of old and new states in Africa, Asia and Latin America which accepted aid from either or both of the two camps for the immediate needs of their development, but refused to align themselves—all these now looked by choice towards France. True, until she had completed the process of decolonization, they bitterly criticized her, but the criticisms soon ceased when she had liberated her former possessions. It remained for her to exploit the potential of respect, admiration and prestige which existed in her favor over a large part of the globe provided that, as the world expected of her, she served the universal cause of human dignity and progress.

Thus the same destiny which had enabled France to survive the terrible crisis of the war, offered to her afterwards, in spite of all she had lost over the past two centuries in terms of relative power and wealth, a leading international role which suited her genius, responded to her interests and matched her means. I was naturally determined that she should play this role, the more so since I believed that the internal transformation, the political stability and the social progress without which she would unquestionably be doomed to disorder and decline demanded that she should once again feel herself invested with world responsibility. Such was my philosophy. What was my policy to be as regards the practical problems that faced our country abroad?

Apart from that of Algeria and our colonies, which was for us to settle on our own, these problems were of such scope and range that their solution would be a very lengthy undertaking, unless a new war should chance to come and cut the Gordian knots tied by the previous one. Hence a sustained and continuous policy was required to deal with them, and this was precisely what, in contrast to the unending shifts and changes of the past, our new institutions made possible.

But what exactly were these problems? First of all there was Germany, divided into three by the existence of a parliamentary republic in the West, a Communist dictatorship in the East, and a special status for Berlin, a prey to the internal strains imposed by this state of affairs and the principal pawn in the rivalry between the two camps. There was Europe, impelled by reason and sentiment towards unification after the terrible convulsions which had torn it apart but radically divided by the Iron Curtain, the Cold War and the enforced subjection of its eastern half to Soviet domination. There was the organization imposed on the Atlantic alliance, which amounted to the military and political subordination of Western Europe to the United States of America. There was the problem of aid for the development of the Third World, which was used by Washington and Moscow as a battleground for their rivalry. There were crises in the East, in Africa, in Asia and in Latin America, which the rival interventions of the two giants rendered chronic and incurable. And there were the international institutions in which the two opposing camps polarized judgments on all subjects and prohibited impartiality.

In each of these fields, I wanted France to play an active part. In this poor world which deserved to be handled gently and each of whose leaders was weighed down with grave difficulties, we had to advance step by step, acting as circumstances demanded and respecting the susceptibilities of all. I myself had struck many a blow in my time, but never at the pride of a people nor at the dignity of its leaders. Yet it was essential that what we did and said should be independent of others. From the moment of my return to power, that was our rule—such a complete change of attitude on the part of our country that the world political scene was suddenly and profoundly transformed.

It is true that the Eastern camp at first confined itself to watching to see what new attitude emerged in Paris. But our Western partners, among whom up till then official France had submissively taken its place under the hegemony known as Atlantic solidarity, could not help being put out. However, they would eventually resign themselves to the new situation. It must be said that the experience of dealing with de Gaulle which some of them had had during the war, and all of them after it, meant that they did not expect this Republic to be as easy to handle as the previous one. Still, there was a general feeling in their chancelleries, their parliaments and their newspapers that the ordeal would be a brief one, that de Gaulle would inevitably disappear after a while, and that everything would then be as it had been before. On the other hand, there was no lack of people in these countries, especially among the masses, who were not at all displeased by France's recovery and who felt a certain satisfaction, or envy perhaps, when they saw her shaking off a supremacy which weighed heavily on the whole of the Old World. Added to this were the feelings which foreign crowds were kind enough to entertain for me personally and which, each time I came in contact with them, they demonstrated with a fervor that impressed their governments. On the whole, in spite of the annoyance that was felt, the malicious remarks that were made, the unfavorable articles and aggressive caricatures that proliferated, the outside world would soon accommodate itself to a France who was once more behaving like a great power, and henceforth would follow her every action and her every word with an attention that had long been lacking.

I was to find rather less resignation in what was said and written in quarters which had hitherto been looked upon as the fountainhead of French political thought. For there it had long been more or less taken for granted that our country should take no action that

was not dictated to it from outside. No doubt this attitude of mind
dated from the time when the dangers which threatened France
forced her continually to seek support from abroad, and when the instability of the political regime prevented the government from taking upon itself the risks of major decisions. Even before the First
World War, in its alliance with Russia, the Third Republic had had to
undertake to respect the Treaty of Frankfurt and let St. Petersburg
lead the way rather than Paris. It is true that, during the long battle
subsequently fought on our soil in alliance with the English, the Bel-
gians and finally the Americans, the leading role and then the
supreme command fell to the French, who in fact provided the principal effort. But was it not primarily the Anglo-Saxons' cry of
"Halt!" that brought the sudden cessation of hostilities on 11 November 1918, at the very moment when we were about to pluck the
fruits of victory? Were not the wishes and promises of the American
President the dominant factor in the Treaty of Versailles, which admittedly restored Alsace and Lorraine to us but left the enemy's unity,
territory and resources intact? And afterwards, was it not to gratify
the wishes of Washington and London that the government in Paris
surrendered the guarantees we had secured and renounced the reparations which Germany owed us in exchange for specious schemes
offered to us by America? When the Hitlerian threat appeared and
the Führer ventured to move his troops into the Rhineland, and preventive or repressive action on our part would have been enough to
bring about his retreat and discomfiture at a time when he was still
short of armaments, did not our ministers remain passive because
England failed to take the initiative? At the time of the Austrian Anschluss, then the dismemberment and annexation of Czechoslovakia
by the Reich, from whence did French acquiescence stem if not from
the example of the English? In the surrender of Vichy to the invader's
law and in the "collaboration" designed to make our country participate in a so-called European order which in fact was purely Germanic, was there not a trace of this long inurement to satellite status?
At the same time, even as I strove to preserve France's sovereign
rights in relation to our allies while fighting the common enemy,
whence sprang the reprobation voiced by even those closest to me, if
not from the idea that we should always give way?

      After so many lessons, it might have been thought that once the
war was over, those who claimed to lead public opinion would be
less inclined towards subordination. Far from it: for the leading
school of thought in each political party, national self-effacement had
become an established and flaunted doctrine. While for the Communists it was an absolute rule that Moscow is always right, all the old

party formations professed the doctrine of "supranationalism," in other words France's submission to a law that was not her own. Hence the support for "Europe" seen as an edifice in which technocrats forming an "executive" and parliamentarians assuming legislative powers—the great majority of both being foreigners—would have the authority to decide the fate of the French people. Hence, too, the passion for the Atlantic organization which would put the security and therefore the policy of our country at the disposal of another. Hence, again, the eagerness to submit the acts of our government to the approval of international organizations in which, under a semblance of collective deliberation, the authority of the protector reigned supreme in every field, whether political, military, economic, technical or monetary, and in which our representatives would never dare to say "we want" but simply confine themselves to "pleading France's cause." Hence, finally, the constant fury aroused among the party-political breed by my actions in the name of an independent nation.

Nevertheless, I was to find no lack of support. Emotionally, I would have the backing of the French people, who, without being in the least inclined to arrogance, were determined to preserve their own identity, all the more so because they had nearly lost it and because others everywhere were ardently affirming theirs, whether in terms of sovereignty, language, culture, production or even sport. Whenever I expressed myself in public on these matters I felt a quiver of response. Politically, the organization which had been formed to follow me above and beyond all the old parties, and which had had a numerous and compact group elected to parliament, was to accompany me through thick and thin. Practically, I would have a stable government at my side, whose Prime Minister was convinced of France's right and duty to act on a world scale, and whose Foreign Minister displayed in his field an ability which few have equalled in the course of our arduous history.

Maurice Couve de Murville had the required gifts. Amid a welter of interlocking problems and tangled arguments he was immediately able to distinguish the essential from the accessory, so that he was clear and precise in matters which others deliberately made as obscure and ambiguous as possible. He had the experience, having dealt with many of the issues of the day and known most of the men in command in the course of a distinguished career. He had the confidence, certain as he was that the post to which I had nominated him would be his for a long time. He had the manner, being skillful at making contact by listening, observing and taking note, and then excelling, at the critical moment, in the authoritative formulation of a position from which he would never be deflected. He had the necessary faith, convinced as he was that France could survive only in the first rank of nations, that de Gaulle could put her back there, and that nothing in life was more important than working towards this goal.

This was what we were aiming for in the vast arena of Europe. I myself had always felt, and now more than ever, how much the nations which peopled it had in common. Being all of the same white race, with the same Christian origins and the same way of life, linked to one another since time immemorial by countless ties of thought, art, science, politics and trade, it was natural that they should come to form a whole, with its own character and organization in relation to the rest of the world. It was in pursuance of this destiny that the Roman emperors reigned over it, that Charlemagne, Charles V and Napoleon attempted to unite it, that Hitler sought to impose upon it his crashing domination. But it is a fact of some significance that not one of these federators succeeded in inducing the subject countries to surrender their individuality. On the contrary, arbitrary centralization always provoked an upsurge of violent nationalism by way of reaction. It was my belief that a united Europe could not today, any more than in previous times, be a fusion of its peoples, but that it could and should result from a systematic *rapprochement*. Everything prompted them towards this in an age of proliferating trade, international enterprises, science and technology which know no frontiers, rapid communications and widespread travel. My policy therefore aimed at the setting up of a concert of European states which in developing all sorts of ties between them would increase their interdependence and solidarity. From this starting point, there was every reason to believe that the process of evolution might lead to their confederation, especially if they were one day to be threatened from the same source.

In practice this led us to put the European Economic Community into effect; to encourage the Six to concert together regularly in political matters; to prevent certain others, in particular Great Britain, from dragging the West into an Atlantic system which would be totally incompatible with a European Europe, and indeed to persuade these centrifugal elements to integrate themselves with the Continent by changing their outlook, their habits and their customers; and finally to set an example of *détente* followed by understanding and cooperation with the countries of the Eastern bloc, in the belief that beyond all the prejudices and preconceptions of ideology and propaganda, it was peace and progress that answered the needs and desires of the inhabitants of both halves of an accidentally divided Europe.

At the heart of the problem and at the center of the continent lay Germany. It was her destiny to be the keystone of any European edifice, and yet her misdeeds had contributed more than anything else to tearing the Old World apart. True, now that she was sliced into three segments, with the forces of her conquerors stationed in each, she was no longer a direct threat to anyone. But how could the memory of her ambition, her audacity, her power and her tyranny be effaced from people's memories—an ambition which only yesterday had unleashed a military machine capable of crushing with one blow the armies of France and her allies; an audacity which, thanks to Italy's complicity, had carried her armies as far as Africa and the Nile basin; a power which, driving across Poland and Russia with Italian, Hungarian, Bulgarian and Rumanian aid, had reached the gates of Moscow and the foothills of the Caucasus; a tyranny whose reign had brought oppression, plunder and crime wherever the fortune of war took the German flag? Henceforth, every precaution must be taken to prevent Germany's evil genius from breaking loose again. But how could a real and lasting peace be built on foundations that were unacceptable to this great people? How could a genuine union of the continent be established without Germany being a part of it? How could the age-old threat of ruin and death be finally dispelled on either side of the Rhine as long as the old enmity remained?

On the all-important question of Germany's future, my mind was made up. First of all, I believed that it would be unjust and dangerous to revise the *de facto* frontiers which the war had imposed on her. This meant that the Oder-Neisse line which separates her from Poland should remain her definitive boundary, that nothing should remain of her former claims in respect of Czechoslovakia, and that a new Anschluss in whatever form must be precluded. Furthermore, the right to possess or to manufacture atomic weapons—which in any case she had declared her intention to renounce—must in no circumstances be granted to her. This being so, I considered it essential that she should form an integral part of the organized system of cooperation between states which I envisaged for the whole of our continent. In this way the security of all nations between the Atlantic and the Urals would be guaranteed, and a change brought about in circumstances, attitudes and relationships which would doubtless ultimately permit the reunion of the three segments of the German people. In the meantime, the Federal Republic would have an essential role to play within the Economic Community and, should it ever materialize, in the political concert of the Six. Finally, I intended that France should weave a network of preferential ties with Germany, which would gradually lead the two peoples towards the mutual understanding and

appreciation to which their natural instinct prompts them when they
are no longer using up their energies in fighting each other.

. . .

Cooperation between the two former enemies [France and Germany]
was a necessary but by no means a sufficient precondition for organized European cooperation. It is true that, judging merely by the
spate of speeches and articles on the subject, the unification of our
Continent might well appear to be a matter as simple as it was fore-
ordained. But when the realities of needs, interests and preconceptions came into play, things took on an altogether different aspect.
While fruitless bargaining with the British showed the fledgling Community that good intentions are not enough to reconcile the irreconcilable, the Six found that even in the economic sphere alone the adjustment of their respective positions bristled with difficulties which
could not be resolved solely in terms of the treaties concluded to that
end. It had to be acknowledged that the so-called executives installed
at the head of common institutions by virtue of the delusions of integration which had prevailed before my return, were helpless when it
came to making and enforcing decisions, that only governments were
in a position to do this, and then only as a result of negotiations carried out in due form between ministers or ambassadors.

In the case of the European Coal and Steel Community, for example, once it had used up the birthday presents bestowed upon it by
its member states, none of them, be it said, for our benefit—French
relinquishment of coke from the Ruhr, deliveries of coal and iron to
Italy, financial subventions to the Benelux mines—the High Authority, although vested with very extensive theoretical powers and considerable resources, was soon overwhelmed by the problems presented by competing national requirements. Whether it was a matter
of fixing the price of steel, or regulating fuel purchases from outside,
or converting the collieries of the Borinage, the areopagus enthroned
in Luxembourg was powerless to legislate. The result was a chronic
decline in that organization, whose prime mover, Jean Monnet, had
moreover resigned the presidency.

At the same time, in the case of EURATOM, there seemed an
irremediable disparity between the situation of France, equipped for
some fifteen years past with an active Atomic Energy Commissariat,
provided with numerous installations and already engaged in precise
and far-reaching programs of research and development, and that of
the other countries which, having done nothing on their own account, now wanted to use the funds of the common budget to obtain
what they lacked by placing orders with American suppliers.

Lastly, in the case of the Economic Community, the adoption of the agricultural regulations in conjunction with the lowering of industrial tariffs raised obstacles which the Brussels Commission was unable to overcome on its own. It must be said that in this respect the spirit and terms of the Treaty of Rome did not meet our country's requirements. The industrial provisions were as precise and explicit as those concerning agriculture were vague. This was evidently due to the fact that our negotiators in 1957, caught up in the dream of a supranational Europe and anxious at any price to settle for something approaching it, had not felt it their duty to insist that a French interest, no matter how crucial, should receive satisfaction at the outset. It would, therefore, be necessary either to obtain it *en route*, or to liquidate the Common Market. Meanwhile, determined though it was to have its way in the end, the French government was able to allow the machinery of the Treaty of Rome to be set in motion thanks to the recovery of our balance of payments and the stabilization of the franc. In December 1958 it announced that it would implement the inaugural measures which were scheduled for New Year's Day, in particular a 10 percent tariff cut and a 20 percent quota increase.

Once initiated, the implementation of the Common Market was to give rise to a vast outgrowth of not only technical but also diplomatic activity. For, irrespective of its very wide economic scope, the operation proved to be hedged about with specifically political intentions calculated to prevent our country from being its own master. Hence, while the Community was taking shape, I was obliged on several occasions to intervene in order to repel the threats which overshadowed our cause.

The first arose from the original ambivalence of the institution. Was its objective—in itself momentous enough—the harmonization of the practical interests of the six states, their economic solidarity in face of the outside world and, if possible, their cooperation in foreign policy? Or did it aim to achieve the total fusion of their respective economies and policies in a single entity with its own government, parliament and laws, ruling in every respect its French, German, Italian, Dutch, Belgian and Luxembourg subjects, who would become fellow citizens of an artificial motherland, the brainchild of the technocrats? Needless to say, having no taste for make believe, I adopted the former conception. But the latter carried all the hopes and illusions of the supranational school.

For these champions of integration, the European executive was already alive and kicking: it was the Commission of the Economic Community, made up, admittedly, of representatives nominated by the six states but, thereafter, in no way dependent on them. Judging by the chorus of those who wanted Europe to be a federation, albeit without a federator, all the authority, initiative and control of the exchequer which are the prerogatives of government in the economic sphere must in future belong to this brigade of experts, not only within the Community but also—and this could be indefinitely extensible—from the point of view of relations with other countries. As for the national ministers, who could not as yet be dispensed with in their executive capacity, they had only to be summoned periodically to Brussels, where they would receive the Commission's instructions in their specialized fields. At the same time, the mythmongers wanted to exhibit the Assembly in Strasbourg, consisting of deputies and senators delegated by the legislatures of the member countries, as a "European parliament" which, while having no effective power, provided the Brussels "executive" with a semblance of democratic responsibility.

Walter Hallstein was the Chairman of the Commission. He was ardently wedded to the thesis of the superstate, and bent all his skillful efforts towards giving the Community the character and appearance of one. He had made Brussels, where he resided, into a sort of capital. There he sat, surrounded with all the trappings of sovereignty, directing his colleagues, allocating jobs among them, controlling several thousand officials who were appointed, promoted and remunerated at his discretion, receiving the credentials of foreign ambassadors, laying claim to high honors on the occasion of his official visits, concerned above all to further the amalgamation of the Six, believing that the pressure of events would bring about what he envisaged. But after meeting him more than once and observing his activities, I felt that although Walter Hallstein was in his way a sincere European, he was first and foremost a German who was ambitious for his own country. For in the Europe that he sought lay the framework in which his country could first of all regain, free of charge, the respectability and equality of rights which the frenzy and defeat of Hitler had cost it, then acquire the preponderant influence which its economic strength would no doubt earn it, and finally ensure that the cause of its frontiers and its unity was backed by a powerful coalition in accordance with the doctrine to which, as Foreign Minister of the Federal Republic, he had formerly given his name. These factors did not alter my esteem and regard for Walter Hallstein, but the goals I was pursuing on behalf of France were incompatible with such projects.

The fundamental divergence between the way the Brussels Commission conceived its role and my own government's insistence, while looking to the Commission for expert advice, that important measures should be subordinated to the decisions of the individual states, nurtured an atmosphere of latent discord. But since the Treaty specified that during the inaugural period no decision was valid unless unanimous, it was enough to enforce its application to ensure that there was no infringement of French sovereignty. So during this period the institution took wing in what was and must remain the economic sphere without being subjected to any mortal political crisis, in spite of frequent clashes. Moreover, in November 1959, at the initiative of Paris, it was decided that the six foreign ministers should meet at three-monthly intervals to examine the overall situation and its various implications and to report back to their own governments, which would have the last word if the need arose. It may be imagined that ours did not allow itself to be led.

But it was not only from the political angle that the newfledged Community had to undergo the truth test. Even in the economic sphere two formidable obstacles, secreting all kinds of contradictory interests and calculations, threatened to bar its way. These were, of course, the external tariff and agriculture, which were closely bound up with each other. True, on signing the Treaty, our partners had seemed to accept that common taxes should be imposed upon foreign goods as customs duties were reduced within the Community. But although they all recognized in principle that this procedure was essential to their solidarity, some of them were nonetheless irked by it because it deprived them of trade facilities which had hitherto been intrinsic to their existence. They therefore wanted the common external tariff to be as low as possible and in any case so elastic that their habits would not be disturbed. The same countries, for the same reasons, were in no hurry to see the Six take upon themselves the consumption and, therefore, the cost of continental farm products, nearly half of which happened to be French. For instance, Germany, nearly two-thirds of whose food was imported cheaply from outside the Community in exchange for manufactured goods, would have liked to see a Common Market for industrial goods only, in which case the Federal Republic would inevitably have had an overwhelming advantage. This was unacceptable to France. We therefore had to put up a fight in Brussels.

The battle was long and hard. Our partners, who bitterly regretted our having changed Republics, had been counting on us once again to sacrifice our own cause to "European integration," as had happened successively with the Coal and Steel Community, in which all the advantages went to others at our expense; with EURATOM, for which our country put up practically the entire stake without a *quid pro quo,* and, moreover, submitted her atomic assets to foreign supervision; and with the Treaty of Rome, which did not settle the agricultural question which was of paramount importance to ourselves. But now France was determined to get what she needed, and in any case her demands were consistent with the logic of the Community system. So her requirements were eventually met.

In May 1960, at our urgent insistence, the Six agreed to establish the external tariff and to adopt a timetable for the decisions to be taken on agricultural policy. In December of the same year, while urging an acceleration of the process of lowering customs barriers between them, they agreed that all imports of foodstuffs from elsewhere should be liable to an enormous financial levy at the expense of the purchasing state. And in January 1962 they adopted the decisive resolutions.

For at this date, now that the first phase of application was completed, it had to be decided whether or not, in pursuance of the terms of the Treaty, to proceed to the second phase, a kind of point of no return, involving a 50 percent reduction in customs duties. We French were determined to seize the opportunity to tear aside the veil and induce our partners to make formal commitments on what we regarded as essential. When they proved reluctant to give way, and indeed showed signs of some disquieting reservations, I judged that now or never was the moment to take the bull by the horns. Our ministers in Brussels, Couve de Murville, Baumgartner and Pisani, made it quite clear that we were prepared to withdraw from the Community if our requirements were not met. I myself wrote in similar terms to Chancellor Adenauer, whose government was our principal antagonist in this matter, and repeated it by formal telegram on the evening of the final debate. Feeling ran high in the capitals of the Six. In France, the parties and most of the newspapers, echoing foreign opinion, were disturbed and scandalized by the attitude of General de Gaulle, whose intransigence was threatening "the hopes of Europe." But France and common sense prevailed. During the night of 13–14 January 1962, after some dramatic exchanges, the Council of Ministers of the six states formally decided to admit agriculture into the Common Market, laid down then and there a broad basis for its implementation, and made the necessary arrangements to establish the agricultural regulations on the same footing and at the same time as the rest. Whereupon the implementation of the Treaty was able to enter its second phase.

But how far could it go, in view of the difficulties which the British were doing their utmost to raise, and the tendency of our five partners to submit to their influence? It was not surprising that Great Britain should be radically opposed to the whole venture, since by virtue of her geography, and therefore her policy, she has never been willing to see the Continent united or to merge with it herself. In a sense it might almost be said that therein lay the whole history of Europe for the past eight hundred years. As for the present, our neighbors across the Channel, adapted to free trade by the maritime nature of their economic life, could not sincerely agree to shut themselves up behind a continental tariff wall, still less to buy their food dear from us rather than import it cheap from everywhere else, for example the Commonwealth. But without the common tariff and agricultural preference, there could be no valid European Community. Hence at the time of the preliminary studies and discussions that led up to the Treaty of Rome, the London government, which was represented at the outset, had soon withdrawn. Then, with the intention of undermining the project of the Six, it had proposed that they should join a vast European free trade area with itself and various others. Things had reached this stage when I returned to power.

As early as 29 June 1958, Prime Minister Harold Macmillan had come to see me in Paris. In the midst of our friendly discussions which touched upon a great many topics, he suddenly declared with great feeling: "The Common Market is the Continental System all over again. Britain cannot accept it. I beg you to give it up. Otherwise, we shall be embarking on a war which will doubtless be economic at first but which runs the risk of gradually spreading into other fields." Ignoring the overstatement, I tried to pacify the English premier, at the same time asking him why the United Kingdom should object to seeing the Six establish a system of preference such as existed inside the Commonwealth. Meanwhile, his minister, Reginald Maudling, was actively engaged inside the so-called Organization for European Economic Cooperation, to which Britain belonged, in negotiations which were keeping the Six in suspense, and delaying the launching of the Community by proposing that the latter should be absorbed and, consequently, dissolved in a free trade area. Harold Macmillan wrote me a number of very pressing letters in an effort to obtain my compliance. But my government broke the spell, and made it clear that it would not agree to anything which did not include the common external tariff and an agricultural arrangement. London then appeared to abandon its policy of obstruction and, suddenly changing course, set up its own European Free Trade Association, with the Scandinavians, Portugal, Switzerland and Austria. At once, our Brussels partners dropped all their hesitations and set about launching the Common Market.

But the match had merely been postponed. In the middle of 1961 the British returned to the offensive. Having failed from without to prevent the birth of the Community, they now planned to paralyze it from within. Instead of calling for an end to it, they now de-

clared that they themselves were eager to join, and proposed examining the conditions on which they might do so, "provided that their
special relationships with the Commonwealth and their associates in
the free trade area were taken into consideration, as well as their special interests in respect of agriculture." To submit to this would obviously have meant abandoning the Common Market as originally
conceived. Our partners could not bring themselves to do so. But, on
the other hand, it was beyond their power to say "No" to England.
So, affecting to believe that the squaring of the circle was a practical
proposition, they proceeded to discuss a series of projects and
counter-projects in Brussels with the British minister, Edward Heath,
which threw nothing but doubt on the future of the Community. I
could see the day approaching when I should either have to remove
the obstruction and put an end to the tergiversation, or else extricate
France from an enterprise which had gone astray almost as soon as it
had begun. At all events, as could have been foreseen, it was now
clear to all that in order to achieve the unification of Europe, individual states are the only valid elements, that when their national interest is at stake nothing and nobody must be allowed to force their
hands, and that cooperation between them is the only road that will
lead anywhere.

In this respect what is true of economics is even truer of politics. And this is no more than natural. What depths of illusion or
prejudice would have to be plumbed in order to believe that European nations forged through long centuries by endless exertion and
suffering, each with its own geography, history, language, traditions
and institutions, could cease to be themselves and form a single entity? What a perfunctory view is reflected in the parallel often naively
drawn between what Europe ought to do and what the United States
have done, when the latter was created from nothing in a completely
new territory by successive waves of uprooted colonists? For the Six
in particular, how was it conceivable that their external aims should
suddenly become identical when their origins, situations and ambitions were so very different? In the matter of decolonization, which
France was about to bring to a conclusion, what part could her
neighbors play? If, from time immemorial, it had been in her nature
to accomplish "God's work," to disseminate freedom of thought, to
be a champion of humanity, why should it *ipso facto* become the
concern of her partners? Germany, balked by defeat of her hopes of
supremacy, divided at present and suspected by many of seeking her
revenge, was now a wounded giant. By what token should her
wounds automatically be shared by others? Given the fact that Italy,
having ceased to be an annex of the Germanic or the French empires,

and thwarted of her Balkan ambitions, remained a peninsular power confined to the Mediterranean and naturally located within the orbit of the maritime nations, why should she throw in her lot with the Continentals? By what miracle would the Netherlands, which had always owed its livelihood to shipping and its independence to overseas resources, allow itself to be swallowed up by the land powers? How could Belgium, hard put to it to maintain the juxtaposition of Flemings and Walloons in a single entity ever since a compromise between rival powers had turned her into a State, genuinely devote herself to anything else? With Luxembourg lying at the center of the territorial arrangements which had succeeded the rivalries of the two great countries bordering on the Moselle, what major concern could its people have other than the survival of Luxembourg?

On the other hand, while recognizing that each of these countries had its own national personality which it must preserve, there was no reason why they should not organize concerted action in every sphere, arrange for their ministers to meet regularly and their Heads of State or Government periodically, set up permanent organs to discuss politics, economics, culture and defense, have these subjects debated in the normal way by an assembly of delegates from their respective parliaments, acquire the taste and habit of examining together problems of common interest, and as far as possible adopt a united attitude towards them. Linked with what was already being practiced in the economic sphere in Brussels and Luxembourg, might not this general cooperation lead to a European policy as regards progress, security, influence, external relations, aid to the developing countries, and finally and above all as regards peace? Might not the grouping thus formed by the Six gradually attract the other states of the Continent into joining in on the same terms? And perhaps in this way, by opposing war, which is the history of men, that united Europe which is the dream of the wise might ultimately be achieved.

. . .

In the course of a press conference on 5 September [1960], after saying that "to build Europe, which means to unite Europe, is an essential aim of our policy," I declared that to this end it was necessary "to proceed, not on the basis of dreams, but in accordance with realities. Now, what are the realities of Europe? What are the pillars on which it can be built? The truth is that those pillars are the states of Europe . . . states each of which, indeed, has its own genius, history and language, its own sorrows, glories and ambitions; but states that are the only entities with the right to give orders and the power to be obeyed." Then, while recognizing "the technical value of certain

more or less extranational or supranational organisms," I pointed
out that they were not and could not be politically effective, as was
proved by what was happening at that very moment in the European
Coal and Steel Community, EURATOM and the Brussels Community. I insisted that, "although it is perfectly natural for the states of
Europe to have specialist bodies available to prepare and whenever
necessary to follow up their decisions, those decisions must be their
own." Then I outlined my plan: "To arrange for the regular cooperation of the states of Western Europe in the political, economic and
cultural spheres, as well as that of defense, is an aim that France
deems desirable, possible and practical. . . . It will entail organized,
regular consultations between the governments concerned and the
work of specialist bodies in each of the common domains, subordinated to those governments. It will entail periodic deliberations by an
assembly made up of delegates of the national parliaments. It must
also, in my view, entail as soon as possible a solemn European referendum, in order to give this new departure for Europe the popular
backing which is essential to it." I concluded: "If we set out on this
road . . . links will be forged, habits will be developed, and, as time
does its work, it is possible that we will come to take further steps towards European unity."

·   ·   ·

7 Preamble to the Single European Act

Representatives of the twelve members of the European Community signed the Single European Act (SEA) in February 1986 and saw it implemented in July 1987. The SEA, the first major revision of the Treaties of Rome, brought together in one "single" act a treaty on European cooperation in the area of foreign policy and institutional and procedural reforms (such as the increased use of qualified majority voting and the introduction of the cooperation procedure) designed to facilitate the completion of the Single Market. The SEA, while not universally recognized as significant at the time, marked a milestone in the attempt by Community leaders to bury the legacy of Charles de Gaulle and "relaunch" Europe. The success of the SEA in facilitating the single market opened the way for further institutional reforms in the early 1990s.

The preamble to the SEA differs significantly from its predecessors. Gone is the vision of a united Europe as an alternative to war. In its place is a vision of an evolving European Union ready to act in the world as a single entity to protect the common interests of its members, promote democracy and human rights, contribute to the "preservation of international peace," and "improve the economic and social situation in Europe." The preamble assumed the European Communities now resembled a sovereign entity more than a mere collection of individual states, an evolution the signatories believed corresponded to the "wishes of the democratic peoples of Europe."

. . .

MOVED by the will to continue the work undertaken on the basis of the Treaties establishing the European Communities and to transform relations as a whole among their States into a European Union, in accordance with the Solemn Declaration of Stuttgart of 19 June 1983,

RESOLVED to implement this European Union on the basis, firstly, of the Communities operating in accordance with their own rules and, secondly, of European Cooperation among the Signatory States in the sphere of foreign policy and to invest this union with the necessary means of action,

DETERMINED to work together to promote democracy on the basis of the fundamental rights recognized in the constitutions and laws of the Member States, in the Convention for the Protection of Human Rights and Fundamental Freedoms and the European Social Charter, notably freedom, equality and social justice,

CONVINCED that the European idea, the results achieved in the fields of economic integration and political cooperation, and the need for new developments correspond to the wishes of the democratic peoples of Europe, for whom the European Parliament, elected by universal suffrage, is an indispensable means of expression,

AWARE of the responsibility incumbent upon Europe to aim at speaking ever increasingly with one voice and to act with consistency and solidarity in order more effectively to protect its common interests and independence, in particular to display the principles of democracy and compliance with the law and with human rights to which they are attached, so that together they may make their own contribution to the preservation of international peace and security in accordance with the undertaking entered into by them within the framework of the United Nations Charter,

DETERMINED to improve the economic and social situation by extending common policies and pursuing new objectives, and to ensure a smoother functioning of the Communities by enabling the institutions to exercise their powers under conditions most in keeping with Community interests,

WHEREAS at their Conference in Paris from 19 to 21 October 1972 the Heads of State or of Government approved the objective of the progressive realization of Economic and Monetary Union,

HAVING REGARD to the Annex to the conclusions of the Presidency of the European Council in Bremen on 6 and 7 July 1978 and the Resolution of the European Council in Brussels on 5 December 1978 on the introduction of the European Monetary System (EMS) and related questions, and noting that in accordance with that

Resolution, the Community and the Central Banks of the Member States have taken a number of measures intended to implement monetary cooperation,

HAVE DECIDED to adopt this Act.

. . .

8   A Family of Nations

MARGARET THATCHER

Margaret Thatcher served as Britain's prime minister from 1979 to 1990. During her eleven years in office, she attempted to reduce the role of government in British society, particularly the economy. Her distrust of big government extended to the institutions of the European Community, which she considered a threat to prosperity in Europe and her policy successes in Britain. While prime minister, Thatcher raised the ire of most EC leaders by working tirelessly and unapologetically for Britain's particular interests and by resisting, often alone, most attempts to expand the powers of EC institutions. After her elevation to the House of Lords, she furthered her reputation as a virulent Euroskeptic by leading a small group of parliamentarians in a loud but unsuccessful fight to block Britain's ratification of the Maastricht treaty in 1993.

Prime Minister Thatcher outlined her views on European integration in a speech at the College of Europe in Bruges, Belgium, on 20 September 1988. There she placed Britain firmly in Europe but rejected the notion that "Europe" meant the absorption of Britain—and all the other member states—into a single, bureaucratized European "superstate." The European Community, she argued, would succeed only if each member state was allowed to maintain its own identity. Her vision of Europe as a "family of nations"—which mirrors de Gaulle's—represents well the traditional British approach to integration, but challenges the federalist vision of the founders and continental builders of the Community. For this reason, Margaret Thatcher's Bruges speech proved highly controversial.

Reprinted with permission from Lady Thatcher.

Mr Chairman, you have invited me to speak on the subject of Britain and Europe. Perhaps I should congratulate you on your courage. If you believe some of the things said and written about my views on Europe, it must seem rather like inviting Genghis Khan to speak on the virtues of peaceful coexistence!

I want to start by disposing of some myths about my country, Britain, and its relationship with Europe. And to do that I must say something about the identity of Europe itself. Europe is not the creation of the Treaty of Rome. Nor is the European idea the property of any group or institution. We British are as much heirs to the legacy of European culture as any other nation. Our links to the rest of Europe, the continent of Europe, have been the dominant factor in our history. For three hundred years we were part of the Roman Empire and our maps still trace the straight lines of the roads the Romans built. Our ancestors—Celts, Saxons and Danes—came from the continent. Our nation was—in that favorite Community word—"restructured" under Norman and Angevin rule in the eleventh and twelfth centuries. This year we celebrate the three hundredth anniversary of the Glorious Revolution in which the British crown passed to Prince William of Orange and Queen Mary. Visit the great churches and cathedrals of Britain, read our literature and listen to our language: all bear witness to the cultural riches which we have drawn from Europe—and other Europeans from us.

We in Britain are rightly proud of the way in which, since Magna Carta in 1215, we have pioneered and developed representative institutions to stand as bastions of freedom. And proud too of the way in which for centuries Britain was a home for people from the rest of Europe who sought sanctuary from tyranny. But we know that without the European legacy of political ideas we could not have achieved as much as we did. From classical and medieval thought we have borrowed that concept of the rule of law which marks out a civilized society from barbarism. And on that idea of Christendom—for long synonymous with Europe—with its recognition of the unique and spiritual nature of the individual, we still base our belief in personal liberty and other human rights.

Too often the history of Europe is described as a series of interminable wars and quarrels. Yet from our perspective today surely what strikes us most is our common experience. For instance, the story of how Europeans explored and colonized and—yes, without apology—civilized much of the world is an extraordinary tale of talent, skill and courage.

We British have in a special way contributed to Europe. Over the centuries we have fought to prevent Europe from falling under the dominance of a single power. We have fought and we have died for her freedom. Only miles from here in Belgium lie the bodies of 120,000 British soldiers who died in the First World War. Had it not been for that willingness to fight and to die, Europe would have been united long before now—but not in liberty, not in justice. It was British support to resistance movements throughout the last War that helped to keep alive the flame of liberty in so many countries until the day of liberation. It was from our island fortress that the liberation of Europe itself was mounted. And still today we stand together. Nearly 70,000 British servicemen are stationed on the mainland of Europe. All these things alone are proof of our commitment to Europe's future.

The European Community is one manifestation of that European identity. But it is not the only one. We must never forget that east of the Iron Curtain peoples who once enjoyed a full share of European culture, freedom and identity have been cut off from their roots. We shall always look on Warsaw, Prague and Budapest as great European cities. Nor should we forget that European values have helped to make the United States of America into the valiant defender of freedom which she has become.

This is no arid chronicle of obscure facts from the dust-filled libraries of history. It is the record of nearly two thousand years of British involvement in Europe, cooperation with Europe and contribution to Europe, a contribution which today is as valid and as strong as ever. Yes, we have looked also to wider horizons—as have others—and thank goodness for that because Europe never would have prospered and never will prosper as a narrow-minded, inward-looking club.

The European Community belongs to all its members. It must reflect the traditions and aspirations of all its members. And let me be quite clear. Britain does not dream of some cozy isolated existence on the fringes of the European Community. Our destiny is in Europe, as part of the Community. That is not to say that our future lies only in Europe. But nor does that of France or Spain or indeed any other member.

The Community is not an end in itself. Nor is it an institutional device to be constantly modified according to the dictates of some abstract intellectual concept. Nor must it be ossified by endless regulation. The European Community is the practical means by which Europe can ensure the future prosperity and security of its people in a world in which there are many other powerful nations and groups of nations. We Europeans cannot afford to waste our energies on internal disputes or arcane institutional debates. They are no substitute for effective action. Europe has to be ready both to contribute in full measure to its own security and to compete commercially and industrially, in a world in which success goes to the countries which encourage individual initiative and enterprise, rather than to those which attempt to diminish them.

This evening I want to set out some guiding principles for the future which I believe will ensure that Europe does succeed, not just in economic and defence terms but also in the quality of life and the influence of its peoples.

My first guiding principle is this: willing and active cooperation between independent sovereign states is the best way to build a successful European Community. To try to suppress nationhood and concentrate power at the center of a European conglomerate would be highly damaging and would jeopardize the objectives we seek to achieve. Europe will be stronger precisely because it has France as France, Spain as Spain, Britain as Britain, each with its own customs, traditions and identity. It would be folly to try to fit them into some sort of identikit European personality.

Some of the founding fathers of the Community thought that the United States of America might be its model. But the whole history of America is quite different from Europe. People went there to get away from the intolerance and constraints of life in Europe. They sought liberty and opportunity; and their strong sense of purpose has, over two centuries, helped create a new unity and pride in being American—just as our pride lies in being British or Belgian or Dutch or German.

I am the first to say that on many great issues the countries of Europe should try to speak with a single voice. I want to see us work more closely on the things we can do better together than alone. Europe is stronger when we do so, whether it be in trade, in defense, or in relations with the rest of the world. But working more closely together does not require power to be centralized in Brussels or decisions to be taken by an appointed bureaucracy. Indeed, it is ironic that just when those countries such as the Soviet Union, which have tried to run everything from the center, are learning that success depends on dispersing power and decisions away from the center, some in the Community seem to want to move in the opposite direction. We have not successfully rolled back the frontiers of the state in Britain, only to see them reimposed at a European level, with a European superstate exercising a new dominance from Brussels.

Certainly we want to see Europe more united and with a greater sense of common purpose. But it must be in a way which preserves the different traditions, parliamentary powers and sense of national pride in one's own country; for these have been the source of Europe's vitality through the centuries.

My second guiding principle is this: Community policies must tackle present problems in a practical way, however difficult they may be. If we cannot reform those Community policies which are patently wrong or ineffective and which are rightly causing public disquiet, then we shall not get the public's support for the Community's future development.

.   .   .

My third guiding principle is the need for Community policies which encourage enterprise. If Europe is to flourish and create the jobs of the future, enterprise is the key. The basic framework is there: the treaty of Rome itself was intended as a Charter for Economic Liberty. But that is not how it has always been read, still less applied.

The lesson of the economic history of Europe in the 1970s and 1980s is that central planning and detailed control don't work, and that personal endeavor and initiative do. That a state-controlled economy is a recipe for low growth; and that free enterprise within a framework of law brings better results. The aim of a Europe open to enterprise is the moving force behind the creation of the Single European Market by 1992. By getting rid of barriers, by making it possible for companies to operate on a Europewide scale, we can best compete with the United States, Japan and the other new economic powers emerging in Asia and elsewhere. And that means action to free markets, action to widen choice, action to reduce government intervention. Our aim should not be more and more detailed regulation from the center: it should be to deregulate and to remove the constraints on trade.

.   .   .

My fourth guiding principle is that Europe should not be protectionist. The expansion of the world economy requires us to continue the process of removing barriers to trade, and to do so in the multilateral negotiations in the GATT [General Agreement on Tariffs and Trade]. It would be a betrayal if, while breaking down constraints on trade within Europe, the Community were to erect greater external protection. We must ensure that our approach to world trade is consistent with the liberalization we preach at home.

We have a responsibility to give a lead on this, a responsibility which is particularly directed towards the less developed countries.

They need not only aid; more than anything they need improved trading opportunities if they are to gain the dignity of growing economic strength and independence.

. . .

I believe it is not enough just to talk in general terms about a European vision or ideal. If we believe in it, we must chart the way ahead and identify the next steps. That is what I tried to do this evening.

This approach does not require new documents: they are all there, the North Atlantic Treaty, the Revised Brussels Treaty, and the Treaty of Rome, texts written by far-sighted men. However far we may want to go, the truth is that we can only get there one step at a time.

What we need now is to take decisions on the next steps forward rather than let ourselves be distracted by Utopian goals. Utopia never comes, because we know we should not like it if it did. Let Europe be a family of nations, understanding each other better, appreciating each other more, doing more together but relishing our national identity no less than our common European endeavor.

Let us have a Europe which plays its full part in the wider world, which looks outward not inward, and which preserves that Atlantic Community—that Europe on both sides of the Atlantic—which is our noblest inheritance and our greatest strength.

9   A Necessary Union

JACQUES DELORS

Jacques Delors assumed the presidency of the Commission of the European Community in January 1985 and served for ten years. Prior to his appointment to the Commission, he was elected to the European Parliament (1979) and served as minister of finance (1981–1984) in France. Delors's energetic and visionary leadership contributed significantly to the revival of the Community in the 1980s and early 1990s. Under his watch, the Community took several significant steps, including the creation of the Single Market and the European Economic Area, and the negotiation and implementation of the Single European Act and the Maastricht treaty.

On 17 October 1989, one year after Margaret Thatcher made her Bruges speech, Jacques Delors traveled to the same spot and offered an alternative vision. His purpose was to convince the Community to seize the moment afforded by history and take a dramatic leap toward federalism. World events, particularly those in the East, and global interdependence necessitated the strengthening of EC institutions and the expansion of the "joint exercise of sovereignty." But true federalism, he asserted, included the principle of subsidiarity: "never entrust to a bigger unit anything that is best done by a smaller one." Subsidiarity, he argued in response to Margaret Thatcher, made federalism the savior of pluralism, diversity, patriotism, and national identity in Europe. Indeed, the rejection of federalism, he warned, would mean the return of ugly nationalism.

Two years later, in Maastricht, EC leaders heeded Delors's Bruges call.

I am speaking to you today at the invitation of your Rector, Professor Lukaszewski, as the College of Europe celebrates its fortieth birthday. European integration has had its ups and downs over those forty years, its high seasons of hope and progress and its long winters of despondency and stagnation. But here, in Bruges, faith in the European ideal has never wavered. Your Rector affirmed this, ten years ago, in an exacting, pluralist conception of Europe. He wrote:

> Shaping European awareness, fostering attachment to Europe as a community of civilization and destiny, is totally in keeping with the great university tradition of the West.

It is a happy coincidence that this year your College has chosen to pay tribute to Denis de Rougemont, an all too little-known figure, whose lifework and writings are a precious legacy. I would like to speak in more personal terms of Denis de Rougemont. I never had the good fortune to work with him, but I would like to tell you why I think so much of him, why I draw on his intellectual and political contribution.

First of all, as a militant European, I, like many others, am carrying on the work he began in his time. He was an ardent federalist. For him federalism was a many-splendored thing; he saw it as a method, an approach to reality, a view of society. I often find myself invoking federalism as a method, with the addition of the principle of subsidiarity. I see it as a way of reconciling what for many appears to be irreconcilable: the emergence of a United Europe and loyalty to one's homeland; the need for a European power capable of tackling the problems of our age and the absolute necessity to preserve our roots in the shape of our nations and regions; and decentralization of responsibilities, so that we never entrust to a bigger unit anything that is best done by a smaller one. This is precisely what subsidiarity is about.

[I speak] as a personalist, a disciple of Emmanuel Mounier, whose influence will, I am convinced, revive as Europeans become aware of the quandaries of frenzied individualism, just as, for some years now, they have been rejecting collectivism and, in its attenuated form, the benevolent State.

I am pleased therefore to pay tribute today to a man who, throughout his life, kept on tilling the fields of hope. It is significant that, at the 1948 Congress in The Hague, Denis de Rougemont was asked to help draft and then read the Message to Europeans. He declared:

> Europe's mission is to unite her peoples in accordance with their genius of diversity and with the conditions of modern community life, and to open the way towards organized freedom for which the world is seeking. . . . Human dignity is Europe's finest achievement, freedom her true strength. Both are at stake in our struggle. The union of our continent is now needed not only for the salvation of the liberties we have won, but also for the extension of their benefits to all mankind. Upon this union depend Europe's destiny and the world's peace.

Were he with us here today, I would want to discuss two points with him which have a bearing on our common future.

Denis de Rougemont believed in what I would call working from the bottom up, rebuilding from below, from small entities rooted naturally in a solidarity of interests and a convergence of feeling. That is of course essential, but it is not enough. Others, and I am one of them, must at the same time work from the top down, viewing the paths of integration from above. Otherwise the small streams of solidarity will never converge to form a wide river.

And de Rougemont abhorred power. Let me quote him again: "My philosophy comes down to this: power is the authority one would wield over others; freedom is the authority one can wield over oneself." Although I would not deny the philosophical value of this statement, I would beg to disagree with it from a political standpoint.

Politically speaking, power is not necessarily the obverse of freedom. Neither the European Community—nor the peoples and nations that form it—will truly exist unless it is in a position to defend its values, to act on them for the benefit of all, to be generous. Let us be powerful enough to command respect and to uphold the values of freedom and solidarity. In a world like ours, there is no other way.

I would link power with the necessity I have so often invoked to promote the revitalization of European integration. Today I would like to get power working for the ideal. Where would necessity take us had we no vision of what we want to achieve? And, conversely, what impact can an ideal have without the resolve and the means to act? The time has come, I feel, to reconcile necessity and the ideal.

We can do so by drawing on our own experiences, on our national heritages, and on the strength of our institutions. Let me underline the importance of this at a time when people can appreciate the limits of any action implemented with national resources alone. Our present concerns—be it the social dimension or the new frontier represented by economic and monetary union—offer a golden opportunity for the joint exercise of sovereignty, while respecting diversity and hence the principles of pluralism and subsidiarity.

There is a need for urgency, for history does not wait. As upheavals shake the world, and the other "Europe" in particular, our reinvigorated Community must work for increased cohesion and set objectives commensurate with the challenges thrown down by history.

History is only interested in the far-sighted and those who think big, like Europe's founding fathers. They are still with us today in the inspiration they provided and the legacy they left.

By "thinking big," I mean taking account of worldwide geopolitical and economic trends, the movement of ideas and the development of the fundamental values which inspire our contemporaries. The founding fathers wanted to see an end to internecine strife in Europe. But they also sensed that Europe was losing its place as the economic and political center of the world. Their intuition was confirmed before our very eyes, to the point in the 1970s when we had to choose between survival and decline. I shocked many people at that time by constantly arguing this point. Gradually, though, the need for a quantum leap became apparent and created a climate in which a single European market by 1992 could be accepted as an objective. The same dynamism led to revision of the Treaty of Rome—the Single Act—and to what is known as the Delors package, in other words the financial reforms necessary to pay for our ambitious plans. Necessity woke Europe from its slumbers.

By "far-sighted," I mean being simultaneously capable of drawing on our historical heritage and looking to the future. Futurology has a part to play but so has a code of ethics for the individual, society and the human adventure. This, frankly, is what we most lack today. I can say, with both feet on the ground, that the theory of the bogeyman-nation has no place in the life of our Community if it wants to be a Community worthy of the name. The inevitable conflicts of interest between us must be transcended by a family feeling, a sense of shared values. These include the enhancement of personality through mutual knowledge and exchange. The younger generation is very conscious of this new horizon. It rejects isolation, it wants to experience other ideas, to explore new territory. The time has come, my friends, to revive the ideal.

To get there, however, we must take the path of necessity. At a time when the Community is being courted by some, threatened by others; at a time when there are those who, with scant regard for the mortar which already binds us, advocate a headlong dash in the name of a greater Europe, or offer us as an ultimate reference nothing more than the laws of the market; to these we must say that our

Community is the fruit not only of history and necessity, but also of political will.

Let us consider necessity for a moment. Since the turn-around of 1984–85 our achievements are there for all to see. The threat of a decline is receding. Businessmen and manufacturers are more aware of this than politicians, many of whom still underestimate the way in which the gradual achievement of the single European market and common policies have supported national efforts to adapt to the new world economic order. Yet all we need to do to see how far we have come is look beyond our frontiers: Europe is once again a force to be reckoned with and is arousing interest everywhere: in America, in Asia, in Africa, in the North and in the South.

Then there is political will. I know that the term has sometimes been abused, as a sort of incantation, but it is precisely political will that led first six, then nine, ten, twelve countries to decide to unite their destiny, with their eyes wide open. The contract binding them is clear, involving both rights and obligations.

Last of all, history. The Twelve cannot control history but they are now in a position to influence it once again. They did not want Europe to be cut in two at Yalta and made a hostage in the Cold War. They did not, nor do they, close the door to other European countries willing to accept the terms of the contract in full.

The present upheavals in Eastern Europe are changing the nature of our problems. It is not merely a matter of when and how all the countries of Europe will benefit from the stimulus and the advantages of a single market. Our times are dominated by a new mercantilism and our young people expect something better of us. Are we going to turn away?

Make no mistake about it. Behind triumphant nationalism and excessive individualism, ethics are making a comeback in the wake of scientific progress. How far, for example, are we prepared to allow genetic manipulation to go? We need a code of ethics for man, we need to promote our concept of the individual and his integrity. Nature, whether pillaged or neglected, strikes back with disturbances and upheavals. So we also need a code of ethics governing the relationship between man and nature. With millions of young people knocking in vain on the door of adult society, not least to find their place in the world of work, with millions of pensioners—still in the prime of life—cut off from any real role in society, we must ask ourselves what kind of society are we building? A society in which the door is always closed?

Europe has always been the continent of doubt and questioning, seeking a humanism appropriate to its time, the cradle of ideas which ultimately encircle the globe. The time has come to return to ideals, to let them penetrate our lives. Let us continue to consider, in everything we do in the field of politics, economics and social and cultural life, what will enable every man, every woman, to achieve their full potential in an awareness not only of their rights, but also of their obligations to others and to society as a whole. We must sustain our efforts to create a humane society in which the individual can blossom through contact and cooperation with others.

Of course any reference to humanism is bound to unleash a debate among Europeans. People will hold conflicting views, but a synthesis will emerge to the benefit of democracy and Europe itself. For the Community is a concept charged with significance. "Where there is no big vision, the people perish," as Jean Monnet said, making this saying of President Roosevelt's [and Prov. 29:18] his own.

In this respect we are engaged in a unique adventure. We are creating a model, admittedly by reference to inherited principles, but in circumstances so extraordinary that the end result will be unique, without historical precedent. We owe much to the strength of our institutions because our Community is a Community based on the rule of law. And the condition for success is the joint, transparent exercise of sovereignty.

Let us consider the strength of our institutions for a moment, beginning with legitimacy. Without legitimacy—as earlier attempts to unite nations have shown—no progress, no permanence is possible. In the Community the progress of history is there for all to see. We have the Treaty duly ratified by all national parliaments, an expression of national will. The Court of Justice plays a vital role in dealing with differences of interpretation. The European Council—now institutionalized—allows Heads of State and Government to monitor progress, to pinpoint delays and failures to honor the contract that unites and binds us, to provide impetus and to make good any deficiencies. A new development is that the Commission now presents a balance sheet at each meeting of what has been accomplished and what remains to be done. The Commission takes the European Council's pronouncements very seriously and does not hesitate to remind the Twelve of undertakings given. In this way the Community is demonstrating more and more clearly that it has little in common with organizations that produce worthy resolutions that are rarely if ever acted upon.

· · ·

But effectiveness is another measure of the strength of our institutions. We must never underestimate the inspired approach of the authors of the Treaty of Rome. What demands it makes on us!

First of all on the Commission, which is responsible for seeing to it that the ground rules are observed, for ensuring that commitments are honored, for implementing Council decisions when the Council see fit to allow it to do so. From this point of view we are wide of the mark, more precisely of the targets set by the Single Act. But it is above all in exercising its right of initiative that the Commission shoulders its responsibilities. And everyone gives it credit for having defined goals and proposed ways and means of revitalizing European integration.

The Commission intends to retain this dynamic approach, assuming it can come up with new ideas and options. Let us be quite clear here. The Commission must never get drunk on its own powers. It must be strict in applying the principle of subsidiarity. It must be aware of the conditions for a dynamic compromise between the Twelve and to that end endeavor to understand each nation and its people. It must draw conclusions from this and be tireless in the pursuit of consensus. It must have the courage to say no when there is a danger of the letter and the spirit of the Treaty being ignored. And most important of all, it must have the courage to take a back seat whenever this can serve the European cause.

The strength of the law is illustrated in turn by the European Parliament. I know that there is a debate on the democratic deficit and I have no doubt whatsoever that, before too long, the powers of the Strasbourg assembly will be strengthened further. But we cannot ignore the influence that today's Parliament has had on European integration. Let me just ask you this: do you think that it would have been possible to convene the Intergovernmental Conference that produced the Single Act had Parliament not thrown its weight behind the idea on the basis of the draft European Union Treaty which it had adopted at the initiative of that great European, Altiero Spinelli?

Many envy us our Community based on the rule of law and this explains its growing influence. What a model our institutions, which allow every country irrespective of its size to have its say and make its contribution, offer the nations of Eastern Europe. They, and many other nations besides, admire the practical, forward-looking application of pluralist democracy within our borders. In the circumstances how can anyone expect us to accept absorption into a larger, looser structure along intergovernmental lines? We would be abandoning a bird in the hand for two in the bush. It would be a tragic mistake for Europe.

Despite the success of our Community based on the rule of law, disputes about sovereignty continue. We need to face the issues squarely.

A dogmatic approach will get us nowhere. It will merely complicate the difficult discussions that lie ahead and make it even harder to remove the remaining obstacles on the road to the single European market and 1992.

The facts speak for themselves. Each nation needs to consider how much room for manoeuvre it genuinely has in today's world. The growing interdependence of our economies, the internationalization of the financial world, the present or growing influence of the main protagonists on the world stage—all point to a dual conclusion. Firstly, nations should unite if they feel close to each other in terms of geography, history, values—and also necessity. Secondly—and ideally at the same time—cooperation should develop at world level to deal with such matters as international trade, the monetary system, underdevelopment, the environment and drugs. The two are complementary rather than concurrent, because in order to exist on a global level and to influence events, not only the trappings of power are needed, but also a strong hand—that is, a capacity for generosity which is essential to any great undertaking. Europe has little clout as yet, although, as I have said, our economic performance is impressing our partners and reassuring our own people. It is quite clear that the fault lies in the deliberately fostered fiction of full national sovereignty and hence of the absolute effectiveness of national policies.

We are all familiar with the expression "speaking with a single voice." This is a reality rather than a formula. It is a reality that strengthens our institutions, a reality reflected in the results achieved when we do agree to the joint exercise of sovereignty. The consequences of the opposite approach prove the point. Think of the shortcomings of our common commercial policy—enshrined though it is in the Treaty—often explained by countries acting alone or failing to identify their own interests correctly. Think of our inability to make a constructive contribution to the problems of indebtedness and underdevelopment, when joint action could move mountains of egoism and hegemony. May I remind you of what Sir Geoffrey Howe said on July 19 last: "The sovereign nations of the European Community, sharing their sovereignty freely, are building for themselves a key role in the power politics of the coming century."

This brings me back to our institutions. You will all remember the decision-making debate which paralysed the Community in the 1960s and led ultimately to the pseudo-compromise reached in Luxembourg. Since the Single Act and increased recourse to majority voting, there is a new dynamic. Sometimes the Council takes a vote, sometimes it considers it wiser not to force countries into a minority position and adopts a decision without a vote. Thanks to this progress on the institutional front, the Community is advancing rapidly towards the single European market and strengthening its rules and common policies. To the advantage of some? No, to the advantage of all: in a sort of positive-sum game.

To put it another way, the old "inequality-unanimity-immobility" triangle has been replaced by a new "equality-majority-dynamism" triangle, the key to success. We will need to draw conclusions from this experiment when the time comes to make further improvements to our institutional apparatus.

And that time is not far off. By its very nature, economic and monetary union is the interface between economic integration and political integration. It is the political crowning of economic convergence. It is a perfect illustration of the joint exercise of sovereignty because a single market for capital and financial services in a world dominated by matters financial calls for a monetary policy which is sufficiently coordinated and sufficiently tight to allow us to make the most of it. Without such a policy, we would be prey to international speculation and the instability of dominant currencies.

Monetary union will be acceptable and feasible only if there is parallel progress towards increased convergence of our economies so that policies are more consistent and harnessed to agreed objectives. There is consensus on economic expansion against a background of stability, on qualitative growth to generate new jobs. In a democratic society objectives can only be defined by political authorities which have democratic legitimacy. We therefore need to combine an independent monetary authority—the guarantor of stability—with the subsidiarity which is vital if each nation is to pursue its own policies in areas which are a matter for it alone, and control by our elected representatives in the shape of the European Parliament, our governments and our national parliaments.

Let me remind you before I go any further that the decision on economic and monetary union has been taken. The report of the committee which I had the honor of chairing was recognized as an essential basis for discussion by the European Council. What we need now is an institutional framework compatible with the principles discussed above and adapted to the new tasks entrusted to the Community.

Subsidiarity is central to future discussions. The principle is clear, but we need to define how it will apply in this particular case. The committee's report is quite specific. A new monetary institution would formulate a common policy valid inside and outside the union. Its federal structure would guarantee that each central bank had a hand in the formulation of decisions and implemented joint guidelines nationally with substantial margins for manoeuvre. The Council would concentrate on the convergence of objectives and the tools of economic policy, but each nation would retain the resources necessary to finance its own policies on security at home and abroad, justice, education, health, social security, regional planning and so on.

. . .

Where does this rather cursory explanation leave those who argue that economic and monetary union will lead to excessive centralization and dirigisme? The fact of the matter is that realistic application of the principle of subsidiarity leaves them without a leg to stand on. The debate—and a debate there must be—should concentrate rather on what economic and monetary union will bring, what it will add in economic and social terms to the expected benefits of the single European market. And at a time when political leaders seem to be vacillating between further development of the Community and its absorption into a larger configuration, economic and monetary union is a necessary step which will strengthen European integration and guarantee political dynamism.

Acceptance of subsidiarity implies respect for pluralism and, by implication, diversity. This is evident not only in the discussions on economic and monetary union, but also in what we call the Community's social dimension.

The facts are clear. Our twelve countries have differing traditions in the area of industrial relations. Major disparities persist in terms of living standards, although our common policies are designed to reduce these gradually. There can be no question, therefore, of artificially forcing standards upwards, or, conversely, of provoking the export of social problems. Last but not least, our governments have differing, and in some cases opposing points of view. There are enormous problems to be overcome, then, if we are to make progress on the social dimension. But it is equally important whether our concern is regional development, town and country planning, or the need for common standards.

The social dimension permeates all our discussions and everything we do: our efforts to restore competitiveness and cooperate on macroeconomic policy to reduce unemployment and provide all young Europeans with a working future; common policies designed to promote the development of less-prosperous regions and the regeneration of regions hit by industrial change; employment policy and the concentration of efforts on helping young people to gain a foothold in the labor market and combating long-term unemployment; and the development of rural regions threatened by the decline in the number of farms, desertification and demographic imbalances. Think what a boost it would be for democracy and social justice if we could demonstrate that we are capable of working together to create a better-integrated society open to all.

. . .

In this area, as in others, the Commission has no intention of getting embroiled in insidious tactical manoeuvering designed to lead the member states in a direction they do not wish to take. Let me repeat that our Community is a community based on the rule of law, where we work by the book with complete openness. Indeed, this is the first rule for success. Everyone must acknowledge this in good faith. If I turn to the principles of federalism in a bid to find workable solutions, it is precisely because they provide all the necessary guarantees on pluralism and the efficiency of the emergent institutional machinery. Here, there are two essential rules:

1. the rule of autonomy, which preserves the identity of each member state and removes any temptation to pursue unification regardless;
2. the rule of participation, which does not allow one entity to be subordinated to another, but on the contrary, promotes cooperation and synergy, on the basis of the clear and well-defined provisions contained in the Treaty.

This is the starting point for an original experiment which resists comparison with any other models, such as the United States of America, for instance. I have always shied away from such parallels, because I know that our task is to unite old nations with strong traditions and personalities. There is no conspiracy against the nation state. Nobody is being asked to renounce legitimate patriotism. I want not only to unite people, as Jean Monnet did, but also to bring nations together. As the Community develops, as our governments emphasize the need for a people's Europe, is it heresy to hope that all Europeans could feel that they belong to a Community which they see as a second homeland? If this view is rejected, European integration will founder and the specter of nationalism will return to haunt us, because the Community will have failed to win the hearts and minds of the people, the first requirement for the success of any human venture.

The success of the Community is such that it is attracting interest from all quarters. It cannot ignore this without abandoning its claim to a universal dimension. But here again the question of "what should be done" is inseparable from the question of "how do we go about it."

History will not wait for the Single Act to work through the system. It is knocking at our door even now.

.   .   .

Communist Europe is exploding before our eyes. Gorbachev has launched Perestroika and Glasnost. Poland and Hungary are carrying out political reforms, ushering in an era of greater freedom and democracy. East Germany totters as tens of thousands of its people flee to the West. The virus of freedom has reached Leipzig and East Berlin.

As early as 1984 François Mitterrand, in a speech to the European Parliament, voiced his presentiment of a radical new departure in Europe. "It is clear," he said, "that we are moving away from the time when Europe's sole destiny was to be shared out and divided up by others. The two words 'European independence' now sound different. This is a fact that our century, which is nearing its end, will, I am sure, remember."

As many European leaders have already stressed, it is our Community, a Community based on the rule of law, a democratic entity and a buoyant economy, that has served as the model and the catalyst for these developments. The West is not drifting eastward, it is the East that is being drawn towards the West. Will the Community prove equal to the challenges of the future? This is the question we should ask ourselves today, whether we mean helping the countries of Eastern Europe to modernize their economies—a precondition for the success of political reforms—or getting to grips with the German question when the time comes, in other words, extending the right of self-determination to everyone.

I have no doubt that if we refuse to face up to these new challenges, not only will we be shirking our responsibilities but the Community will disintegrate, stopped in its tracks by the weight of unresolved contradictions. When I look around me now, as these events unfold, I see too much despondency, too much defeatist thinking, too much willingness paralyzed by passive acquiescence. Let me remind these pessimists of a statement by Hans-Dietrich Genscher which goes to the heart of the German question:

> The German people, in the heart of Europe, must never be seen as an obstacle to the prosperity of the people of Europe. On the contrary. It should behave in such a way that its existence is seen

as a piece of good fortune, or indeed a necessity, for the whole.
That is the best possible guarantee of its survival.

How are we to find a solution except by strengthening the federalist
features of the Community which, to paraphrase Hans-Dietrich Genscher, offer the best possible guarantee of survival to all concerned?
There, I am quite sure, lies the only acceptable and satisfactory solution to the German question.

How are we to shoulder our international responsibilities and
at the same time pave the way for the emergence of a greater Europe,
except by pressing ahead with European integration? Only a strong,
self-confident Community, a Community which is united and determined, can truly hope to control that process.

The pace of change is gathering momentum and we must try to
keep up. If our institutions are to adapt to the new situation, we cannot afford to shilly-shally about economic and monetary union.
There is no question of shortening the time we need to test wide-
ranging cooperation and move on to successive stages. That would
be unrealistic. But time is running out for the political decision which
will generate the dynamism necessary for success and lead to the creation of institutions with the capacity to face up to the demands imposed by our international responsibilities.

                         .   .   .

I have always favored the step-by-step approach—as the experiment
we are embarked upon shows. But today I am moving away from it
precisely because time is short. We need a radical change in the way
we think of the Community and in the way we act on the world
stage. We need to overcome whatever resistance we encounter, if only
to adapt the instruments we already have, so that we can, for example, inject more substance into the Lomé Convention or make a success of our aid program for Poland and Hungary. We need to give
countries that depend on exports for survival more access to our
markets to prevent their plunging deeper into debt. We need financial
instruments which will help these countries to adapt and modernize
their economies.

I am concerned that we will never achieve all this with our present decision-making procedures. Thanks to the Single Act, the Council, Parliament and the Commission are a more efficient institutional
troika than they were a few years ago. But this is not enough to enable us to keep pace with events.

For the honor of your generation and mine, I hope that in two
years' time we will be able to repeat the very words which another

great European, Paul-Henri Spaak, spoke at the signing of the Treaty of Rome: "This time the people of the West have not lacked daring and have not acted too late."

It is time, then, for a new political initiative. The Commission is ready for it and will play its full part in pointing the way. It will propose answers to the questions raised by another quantum leap: who takes the decisions; how do the various levels of decisionmaking intermesh (subsidiarity again!); who puts decisions into practice; what resources will be available; what will it mean in terms of democracy?

There is no doubt that we are living in exciting times, but they are dangerous times too. The Community is faced with the challenge of making a telling contribution to the next phase of our history.

As I stand before a predominantly young audience, I find myself dreaming of a Europe which has thrown off the chains of Yalta, a Europe which tends its immense cultural heritage so that it bears fruit, a Europe which imprints the mark of solidarity on a world which is far too hard and too forgetful of its underdeveloped regions.

I say to these young people: If we can achieve this Europe you will be able to stretch yourselves to the utmost, you will have all the space you need to achieve your full potential. For you are being invited to play your part in a unique venture, one which brings peoples and nations together for the better, not for the worse. It will bring you back to your philosophical and cultural roots, to the perennial values of Europe. But you will need to give of yourselves and insist that those who govern you display boldness tempered with caution, a fertile imagination and a clear commitment to making the Community a necessity for survival and an ideal towards which to work.

10 Preamble to the Treaty on European Union (The Maastricht Treaty)

Several factors, including the success of the Single Market program and the collapse of communism, increased momentum for integration as the European Community entered the 1990s. In December 1990, the member states opened negotiations to complete economic and monetary union, reform EC institutions, and expand Community competence in foreign and security policy. Final negotiations took place in December 1991 in Maastricht, The Netherlands, and the Maastricht treaty was signed there on 7 February 1992. Ratification seemed certain until Danish voters rejected the treaty on 2 June 1992 and opened a debate in Europe over the merits of integration. Public dissatisfaction with the complex treaty combined with a currency crisis and a severe economic recession to sap popular and elite enthusiasm for the European project. Nevertheless, all twelve countries finally ratified the treaty, which came into force in late 1993.

The preamble to the Maastricht treaty reflects the essence of Jacques Delors's thinking: The need to construct a new Europe out of a formerly divided continent requires a leap to a new stage of integration through the creation of a European Union. The institutions of the Union will have responsibility for issue areas previously reserved for national governments. But respect for Europe's core values, increased accountability, and faithful application of the principle of subsidiarity will, according to the treaty, preserve democracy and diversity within the new Europe.

. . .

RESOLVED to mark a new stage in the process of European integration undertaken with the establishment of the European Communities,

RECALLING the historic importance of the ending of the division of the European continent and the need to create firm bases for the construction of the future Europe,

CONFIRMING their attachment to the principles of liberty, democracy and respect for human rights and fundamental freedoms and the rule of law,

DESIRING to deepen the solidarity between their peoples while respecting their history, their culture and their traditions,

DESIRING to enhance further the democratic and efficient functioning of the institutions so as to enable them better to carry out, within a single institutional framework, the tasks entrusted to them,

RESOLVED to achieve the strengthening and the convergence of their economies and to establish an economic and monetary union including, in accordance with the provisions of this Treaty, a single and stable currency,

DETERMINED to promote economic and social progress for their peoples, within the context of the accomplishment of the internal market and of reinforced cohesion and environmental protection, and to implement policies ensuring that advances in economic integration are accompanied by parallel progress in other fields,

RESOLVED to establish a citizenship common to nationals of their countries,

RESOLVED to implement a common foreign and security policy including the eventual framing of a common defence policy, which might in time lead to a common defence, thereby reinforcing the European identity and its independence in order to promote peace, security and progress in Europe and in the world,

REAFFIRMING their objective to facilitate the free movement of persons, while ensuring the safety and the security of their peoples, by including provisions on justice and home affairs in this Treaty,

RESOLVED to continue the process of creating an ever closer union among the peoples of Europe, in which decisions are taken as closely as possible to the citizen in accordance with the principle of subsidiarity,

IN VIEW of further steps to be taken in order to advance European integration,

HAVE DECIDED to establish a European Union.

. . .

11

Reflections on European Policy

WOLFGANG SCHÄUBLE AND KARL LAMERS

The Maastricht treaty created a European Union (EU); the post-Maastricht debate explored the nature and purpose of this union. Attention focused on three immediate issues: the revision of the treaties through the 1996–1997 Intergovernmental Conference (IGC), Economic and Monetary Union, and enlargement. But a more fundamental question lurked beneath the surface: how could the EU reconcile the apparent contradiction between widening (enlargement) and deepening (further integration)?

On 1 September 1994 Wolfgang Schäuble, the leader of the Christian Democratic Union/Christian Social Union party group in the German Bundestag, and the party's foreign policy spokesman, Karl Lamers, addressed the deepening versus widening question in their pre-IGC position paper, Reflections on European Policy. *The document, which seems to have enjoyed Chancellor Helmut Kohl's tacit approval, first explained why it was in Germany's interest to be part of a wider and deeper EU, then proposed a solution to the deepening-widening contradiction: build a larger, more flexible Union around a "hard core" of member states both willing and able to pursue deeper integration. The idea contradicted the principle that all member states will abide by the same rules, thus drawing criticism for advocating a two-track Europe that might leave some members permanently behind. The Amsterdam treaty (signed on 2 October 1997), nevertheless, institutionalized flexible integration—especially in the*

Reprinted with permission from Karl Lamers, *A German Agenda for the European Union* (Federal Trust for Education and Research and the Konrad Adenauer Foundation, 1994).

first and third "pillars" established by the Maastricht treaty—ensuring that the next millennium will witness a wider but more differentiated Union.

■ THE SITUATION

The process of European unification has reached a critical juncture in its development. If, in the next two to four years, no solution to the causes of this critical development is found, the Union, contrary to the goal of ever closer union invoked in the Maastricht treaty, will in essence become a loosely knit grouping of states restricted to certain economic aspects and composed of various sub-groupings. It would then be no more than a "sophisticated" free-trade area incapable of overcoming either the existential internal problems of the European societies, or the external challenges they face.

. . .

■ GERMANY'S INTERESTS

Owing to its geographical location, its size and its history, Germany has a special interest in preventing Europe from drifting apart. If Europe were to drift apart, Germany would once again find itself caught in the middle between East and West, a position which throughout its history has made it difficult for Germany to give a clear orientation to its internal order and to establish a stable and lasting balance in its external relations. Germany's attempts to overcome its position at the center of Europe's conflicts through hegemony failed. The military, political and moral catastrophe of 1945—the consequence of the last such attempt—not only made Germany realize that it lacked the necessary resources; in particular, it led to the conviction that security could only be achieved by radically transforming the system of states in Europe into one in which hegemony appeared neither possible nor desirable. This conviction became the cornerstone of German policy. In this way, the problem of security "against" Germany was solved in the West by creating a system of security "with" Germany. This new system combined control over Germany by its partners with control over these partners by Germany. A condition for its establishment was that the western part of Germany became indispensable for the security of the West vis-à-vis the Soviet Union and that in the military field NATO, under American leadership, assumed this dual task of integrating Germany. In the economic and also increasingly in the political sphere, the solution was to integrate Germany into the European Community (EC)/European Union (EU). This was in line with the need to establish joint institutions to handle the increasingly dense network of relations among the countries of (Western) Europe. Within this system, Germany's relative economic superiority did not have a dominating effect but proved beneficial for all. In this way, Germany—or at least its larger part—for the first time in its history clearly became a part of the West with regard both to its internal order and to the orientation of its foreign policy. For Germany, there was no alternative to this extraordinarily stable and successful post-war system since, as a result of the East-West confrontation and Germany's total defeat in 1945, the option of pursuing an independent policy towards the East, or indeed of seeking alignment with the East, simply did not exist.

Now that the East-West conflict has come to an end, a stable order must be found for the eastern half of the continent too. This is in the interest of Germany in particular since, owing to its position, it would suffer the effects of instability in the East more quickly and directly than others. The only solution which will prevent a return to the unstable pre-war system, with Germany once again caught in the middle between East and West, is to integrate Germany's Central and Eastern European neighbors into the (West) European post-war system and to establish a wide-ranging partnership between this system and Russia. Never again must there be a destabilizing vacuum of power in central Europe. If (West) European integration were not to progress, Germany might be called upon, or be tempted by its own security constraints, to try to effect the stabilization of Eastern Europe on its own and in the traditional way. However, this would far exceed its capacities and, at the same time, erode the cohesion of the European Union, especially since everywhere memories are still very much alive that historically German policy towards the East concentrated on closer cooperation with Russia at the expense of the countries in between. Hence, Germany has a fundamental interest both in widening the Union to the East and in strengthening it through further deepening. Indeed, deepening is a precondition for widening. Without such further internal strengthening, the Union would be unable to meet the enormous challenge of eastward expansion. It might fall apart and once again become no more than a loose grouping of states unable to guarantee stability. Only if the new system set up after 1945 to regulate conflicts, to effect a balancing of interests, to promote mutual development and to ensure Europe's self-assertion in its external relations can be further developed and expanded to take in Germany's neighbors in Central and Eastern Europe, will Germany have a chance of becoming a center of stability in the heart of Europe. This German interest in stability is essentially identical with that of Europe.

Owing to its position, its size and its close relations with France, Germany bears a special responsibility and has a major opportunity to play a leading part in promoting a course of development which will benefit both it and Europe.

· · ·

■ **WHAT MUST BE DONE? PROPOSALS**

The above goal can only be achieved through a combination of measures in the institutional sphere and in a number of policy fields. The following five proposals are mutually dependent and reinforcing, and form an integrated whole:

- further develop the EU's institutions and put subsidiarity into effect, including the retransfer of powers;
- further strengthen the EU's hard core;
- raise the quality of Franco-German relations to a new level;
- improve the Union's capacity for effective action in the field of foreign and security policy;
- expand the Union towards the East.

It goes without saying that, especially with a view to enhancing public acceptance of European integration, these measures must be accompanied by efforts to combat organized crime, establish a common policy on migration, fight unemployment, establish a common social policy, ensure Europe's continued competitiveness and protect the environment.

☐   *Further Developing the EU's Institutions*

The further development of the EU's institutions . . . should be based on the following principles:

- The goal must be to strengthen the EU's capacity to act and to make its structures and procedures more democratic and federal.
- To this end, the question of who does what must be answered. This should be done in a quasi-constitutional document which, in a clear language, describes the division of

powers between the EU, the nation-states and the regions, and defines the fundamental values on which the Union is based.

- This document must be oriented to the model of a "federal state" and to the principle of subsidiarity. This applies not only to the division of powers but also to the question of whether public authorities, including those of the Union, should perform certain functions or should leave them to groups in society. Germany, at whose request the principle of subsidiarity was incorporated in the Maastricht treaty, and which has experience in applying it, is called upon to put forward recommendations not only on how the principle of subsidiarity can be applied to future measures of the EU but also on how existing regulations can be adapted to it.

- All existing institutions—the Council, the Commission, the Presidency and the European Parliament—must be reformed. Numerous reform proposals have been put forward, among others by the CDU/CSU [Christian Democratic Union/Christian Social Union] parliamentary group. The reforms must be geared to concepts for a new institutional balance, according to which the European Parliament will increasingly become a genuine lawmaking body with the same rights as the Council; the Council, in addition to performing tasks in the intergovernmental field in particular, will assume the functions of a second chamber, i.e., a chamber of the member states; and the Commission will take on features of a European government.

   In addition to greater efficiency, democratization must be acknowledged as the guiding principle of all reforms. Naturally, this applies first and foremost to the European Parliament. . . . This should be accompanied—not preceded—by efforts to enhance participation by national parliaments in the decision-making process within the EU. With regard to the Council, democratization means striking a better balance between the basic equality of all member states, on the one hand, and the ratio of population size to number of votes in the Council, on the other.

- The further development of the EU's institutions must combine coherence and consistency with elasticity and flexibility. On the one hand, they must be flexible enough to absorb and compensate for the tensions inherent in a Community stretching from the North Cape to Gibraltar and differentiated enough to cope with differences in member countries' ability (and willingness) to pursue further integration. On the other, they must be strong enough to ensure that, even in the face of tremendous challenges, the Union retains its ability to act. To achieve this, the "variable geometry" or "multi-speed" approach should as far as possible be sanctioned and institutionalized in the Union Treaty or the new quasiconstitutional document, despite the considerable legal and practical difficulties involved. Otherwise, this approach will continue to be limited to intergovernmental cooperation, which might well encourage a trend towards a "Europe à la carte." It must therefore be decided whether, in the case of amendments to the Maastricht treaty, the principle of unanimity laid down in Article N should be replaced by a quorum yet to be more clearly specified. It is essential that no country should be allowed to use its right of veto to block the efforts of other countries more able and willing to intensify their cooperation and deepen integration.

Developing flexible approaches to integration, as envisaged for monetary union in the Maastricht treaty and as already practiced outside the Treaty within the framework of the Schengen Agreement, appears all the more imperative in view of the immense difficulties the above institutional changes will cause even with membership at its present level. As the negotiations on the accession of the EFTA [European Free Trade Association] countries showed, these difficulties are unlikely to diminish in the future. Just preventing a standstill in the process of integration, which would in fact constitute a step backwards, would be a major achievement.

□ *Further Strengthening the EU's Hard Core*

In addition to ensuring that the decision-making process within the European Union becomes more efficient and democratic, the existing hard core of countries oriented to greater integration and closer cooperation must be further strengthened. At present, the core comprises five or six countries. This core must not be closed to other member states; rather, it must be open to every member state willing and able to meet its requirements. The task of the hard core is, by giving the Union a strong center, to counteract the centrifugal forces generated by constant enlargement and, thereby, to prevent a South-West grouping, more inclined to protectionism and headed in a certain sense by France, drifting apart from a North-East grouping, more in favor of free world trade and headed in a certain sense by Germany.

To this end, the countries of the hard core must not only participate as a matter of course in all policy fields, but should also be recognizably more Community-spirited in their joint action than others, and launch common initiatives aimed at promoting the development of the Union. Belgium, Luxemburg and the Netherlands must therefore be more closely involved in Franco-German cooperation—especially since the Netherlands, too, has revised its earlier skeptical attitude towards the essential function of these two countries as the driving force behind European integration. Cooperation among the core countries must focus in particular on the new policy fields added to the Treaty of Rome by the Maastricht treaty.

In the monetary field, too, there are strong signs that a hard core of five countries is emerging. They (together with Denmark and Ireland) are the ones which come closest to meeting the convergence criteria stipulated in the Maastricht treaty. This is especially important since monetary union is the cornerstone of political union (and not, as is often believed in Germany, an additional element of integration alongside political union).

The core countries must convince all the other members of the EU . . . of their unreserved willingness to involve them more closely as soon as they have overcome their current problems and insofar as they themselves are willing to work towards the common objectives. The formation of a core group of countries is not an end in itself but a means of reconciling the two ostensibly conflicting goals of widening and deepening the European Union.

□   *Raising the Quality of Franco-German Relations
to a New Level*

The quality of Franco-German relations must be raised to a new level if the historic process of European unification is not to peter out before its reaches its political goal. Therefore, no significant action in the foreign or EU policy fields should be taken without prior consultation between France and Germany. Following the end of the East-West conflict, the importance of Franco-German cooperation has not diminished; on the contrary, it has increased yet further.

Germany and France form the core of the hard core. From the outset, they were the driving force behind European unification. Their special relationship faces a stiff test because it too is beginning to show signs of the above-mentioned differentiation of interests and perceptions, which might cause them to drift apart as well. In France there are fears that the process of enlargement, taking in first the Scandinavian countries (as well as, in particular, Austria) and later the countries of Central and Eastern Europe, could transform the Union into a loose grouping of states in which Germany might acquire far greater power and thus assume a dominant position. For France, therefore, the issue of deepening the Union prior to enlargement is of vital importance. Now that Germany is reunited and—more importantly in this context—now that it can once again pursue an active foreign policy in the East and enjoys the same freedom of action as its partners in the West, the old question of how to integrate a powerful Germany into European structures, which arose when the process of European unification—limited initially to western Europe—began, assumes a new, if not in fact its real, meaning.

It is important for Franco-German relations in particular that this question be addressed frankly in order to avoid misunderstandings and mistrust.

An initial answer can be given by pointing to the fact—important for Germany too—that a desire not to become too dependent on Germany is, to a not inconsiderable degree, the reason why its eastern neighbors (like the EFTA countries before them) are keen to join the EU. However, this can only be achieved in a community which is more than just a free-trade area. It is vital, of course, that precisely at this point in time Germany should, through its policies, demonstrate its unwavering commitment to the goal of a strong and integrated Europe capable of effective action. . . .

If Germany puts forward clear and unequivocal proposals, then France must make equally clear and unequivocal decisions. It must rectify the impression that, although it allows no doubt as to its basic will to pursue European integration, it often hesitates in taking concrete steps towards this objective—the notion of the unsurrenderable sovereignty of the *"État nation"* still carries weight, although this sovereignty has long since become an empty shell.

. . .

More than ever before, Germany's relations with France are the yardstick by which to measure its sense of belonging to the West's community of shared political and cultural values, as opposed to the tendency, gaining ground once again especially among intellectuals, to seek a "German special path." This is especially important since, now that the East-West conflict has come to an end, the USA can no longer play its traditional role in the same way. Conducting a serious and open dialogue on the attitudes which underpin such tendencies, and on the mutual sentiments and resentments in the Franco-German relationship, is just as important as enhancing the quality of political cooperation between the two countries.

☐ *Improving the Union's Capacity for Effective Action
in the Field of Foreign and Security Policy*

Giving the Union the capacity to take even more effective action in the field of foreign and security policy is of vital importance for the future.

The nation-states of Europe are no longer capable of guaranteeing their external security individually, especially in view of the fact that other security problems [thought] to have been overcome in Europe have reemerged and that, following the end of the East-West confrontation, the USA's assistance in resolving every kind of conflict is no longer certain.

A state's ability to guarantee its external security—its ability to defend itself—is, however, the precondition for, and the quintessence of, sovereignty. This applies in turn to the EU as a community of states inasmuch as only within the community can nation-states preserve their sovereignty. Moreover, because a nation's awareness of its sovereignty determines not only its self-perception but also its relations with other nations, the common defense capability of this European community of states constitutes an indispensable factor in endowing the EU with an identity of its own, an identity which, however, at the same time leaves room for the sense of identity of each individual state.

In the few years since the end of the East-West conflict, a common foreign and security policy has become more important and more urgent than envisaged in the Maastricht treaty. Not even the larger member states are capable of addressing the new external challenges alone. All opinion polls show that a large majority of citizens would like to see a common foreign and security policy. The inadequacy of the Union's response to the dramatic developments in the eastern part of Europe has led to a clear drop in public support for the process of European unification. The question of the security status of future members is of decisive importance for the political make-up of Europe, and for its entire political order.

.   .   .

To propose the formation of a hard core in Europe and the further intensification of Franco-German cooperation does not, however, imply the abandoning of hopes that Great Britain will assume its role "in the heart of Europe" and thus in its core. Rather, these proposals are born of the conviction that determined efforts to spur on the further development of Europe are the best means of exerting a positive influence on the clarification of Great Britain's relationship to Europe and on its willingness to participate in further steps towards integration.

□   *Enlarging the EU Towards the East*

Poland, the Czech and Slovak Republics, Hungary (and Slovenia) should become Members of the European Union around the year 2000. Their accession should depend on the implementation of the measures outlined above and also be their objective.

The certain prospect of EU membership, and membership itself even more so, is more likely to promote the political and economic development of these countries than any form of external assistance. Apart from the clear political and psychological advantages, accession at that time, would, however, impose such a serious economic strain on members old and new that it will only be possible through a combination of measures. They include not only the approximation of laws in the acceding countries, already provided for in the Europe agreements, but also changes in various fields of EU policy, above all with regard to agriculture. In addition, to allow for economic adjustment there must be very long transitional periods (probably varying, in length from country to country), which will be a case for the applications of the concept of "variable geometry." The result must be that the costs for both sides are no higher than would be the case if accession were to take place at a later date. It must be borne in mind that the later accession takes place, the higher the costs are likely to be.

·   ·   ·

The integration of the Central and Eastern European countries into the European Union must be accompanied by the establishment of a wide-ranging partnership between the EU and Russia. As far as it is possible from outside, this policy must give Russia the certainty that, alongside the EU, it is acknowledged as the other center of the political order in Europe. The agreement on partnership and cooperation with Russia is a first major step in this direction. It must be followed by security agreements in connection with the accession of the Central and Eastern European countries to the EU/WEU [West European Union] and NATO.

Implementation of the program proposed above offers the best chance of overcoming the current uncertainties among our citizens with regard to the process of European unification. Unlike some intellectuals—and occasionally politicians too—who express views and opinions which are not only ill-considered and ill-informed but also far removed from reality, purely theoretical and legalistic, and politically dangerous, the large majority of citizens clearly recognize the need for European unity. They quite rightly, however, expect more democracy, openness and transparency, and, above all, successful policies by the EU in the above fields. Basically, our citizens know full well that Germany's interests can only be realized in, with and through Europe, and that, far from posing a threat to the nation, this in fact safeguards its essence because it safeguards its future.

PART 2

Early Currents in
Integration Theory

12

Altiero Spinelli and the Strategy for the United States of Europe

SERGIO PISTONE

Integration theory describes and explains the process of unifying separate nation-states. Early theories of integration also contained a strong prescriptive element. Thus, Altiero Spinelli (Chapter 1), founder of the European Federalist Movement, Italian Deputy, member of the European Parliament, and ardent federalist, was dedicated not just to understanding the integration process but even more to the actual uniting of Europe. Spinelli criticized the slow and, in his view, undemocratic process that characterized postwar integration in Europe. He longed for a revolutionary leap to a federal state.

Spinelli elaborated his federalist vision of European integration in the years after the Ventotene Manifesto. His goal, like most federalists, was a new European state composed of individual states that had ceded their sovereignty to common democratic institutions. What made his brand of federalism more than just a description of a European federation, however, was his strategy for achieving a united Europe, here summarized by Sergio Pistone (University of Torino). In Spinelli's view, overcoming resistance from national governments required a popular pan-European movement that demanded an American-style constitutional convention. This constituent assembly would command such democratic legitimacy that national governments would have to concede to its wishes and ratify the new European con-

Reprinted with permission from *Altiero Spinelli and Federalism in Europe and the World*, ed. Lucio Levi (Franco Angeli, 1990). Copyright 1990 by Franco Angeli. Notes omitted.

stitution. Spinelli believed that only a dramatic leap to federalism would succeed in unifying Europe; functionalism's step-by-step approach would never create institutions strong enough to solve major problems or be democratic enough to respond to the people.

Spinelli eventually saw the directly elected European Parliament (EP) as a possible constituent assembly and, as a member of parliament, set about writing a new constitution for Europe. Shortly before his death he saw this document passed by the EP as the Draft Treaty on European Union (1984). Although the Draft Treaty was not ratified by the member states, many of the ideas contained in it found their way into the Maastricht and Amsterdam treaties.

What distinguishes Spinelli's approach to European federalism from that of its former supporters is his commitment to turn it into an active movement with a political program. That is why his ideas about a campaign strategy for the United States of Europe, which he had always considered as a first stage in the process of unifying the whole world, are amongst the most important, if not the most important contributions to federalism. To illustrate the essential elements of these ideas is, in my view, a contribution to a clearer understanding of the problems of the struggle for European unification (still in progress), but also to help in the fight for world unity (now in its initial stages).

For the purposes of synthesis, my case will follow a logical rather than chronological course. In other words I will not trace the origins of Spinelli's strategic concepts, but the basic theses that emerged from his ideas and actions. In my view these boil down to three:

1. The autonomous nature of the movement for the European federation;
2. The European Constituent Assembly;
3. The exploitation of the contradictions of the functional approach to European unification.

The arguments in favor of the autonomy of the movement for the European federation stem from the belief that the national democratic governments are, simultaneously, the means and the obstacles to European unification.

They are the means because unification can only be achieved as a result of freely arrived at decisions by democratic governments. This implies the rejection of two other ways forward. Spinelli rejects any attempts to unite Europe by force, as Hitler tried, and against which European federalists fought in the Resistance during the Second World War. As a matter of principle he also rejects unification by illegal and violent means from below, because the federalist struggle takes place in Western Europe within democratic political systems which provide legal means for even the most radical change. Moreover such unification stems from the historical development of European democracy.

Whilst European unification can only be achieved by the free decisions of democratic national governments, by their very nature they represent obstacles to its attainment. As a direct consequence of the Second World War, which led to the collapse of the European nation states, they are obliged to face the alternative of "either unite or perish." Yet, at the same time, they are inclined to reject a genuine European federation involving the irreversible transfer of substantial parts of their sovereignty to a supranational authority.

With regard to this obstacle one must clarify Spinelli's important distinction between the permanent agents of executive power, such as diplomats, civil servants and the military, and those who wield political power temporarily, such as heads of governments and their ministers. The strongest opposition to the transfer of sovereignty usually comes from the former because they would suffer immediate and substantial loss of power and status. After all, the permanent agents of executive power were originally created to put into effect the unfettered sovereignty of the state, and they thus became the natural defenders of nationalist traditions. For the latter, wielders of temporary power, the situation is rather more complex for three reasons: (1) without permanent positions of power they have much greater opportunities of playing a role within a wider European political framework; (2) they represent democratic parties with international programs which usually include support for a European federation; (3) they are in direct touch with public opinion which, in countries suffering from the decline and crisis of the nation state, is generally favorable to European unification. This distinction is of great importance, as we shall see later, in considering procedures for the creation of institutions for European unity. Nevertheless, there remains the fact that democratic national governments, by the very nature of their structures, are unfavorably inclined towards federal unification. In the absence of ulterior reasons they are only likely to favor the type of unification which does not involve the irrevocable transfer of power.

A direct consequence springs from these structural problems: namely, that an essential condition for exercising pressure on govern-

ments and political parties in favor of genuine federal unification is
the existence of an independent movement for a European federation, which is able to persuade them in favor of action they would
not, otherwise, take readily on their own.

According to Spinelli, the basic features of such a movement
must be:

1. it should not be a political party, but an organization aimed
   at uniting all supporters of a European federation, irrespective of their political beliefs or social background. This is because a political party seeking national power to achieve European unification would be fatally weakened by intending
   to transfer to supranational institutions substantial parts of
   the national power for which it would be competing;
2. it has to be a supranational organization uniting all federalists beyond their national allegiance, so as to imbue them
   with a supranational loyalty and enable them to organize
   political action at European level;
3. it must seek to establish direct influence on public opinion,
   outside national electoral campaigns, which would help it to
   exert effective pressure on the European policies of governments. One should remember that these have been the guiding principles of the Italian European Federalist Movement
   from its inception in 1943, even when Spinelli ceased to be
   its leader and continued to cooperate with the MFE [Euro-
   pean Federalist Movement] as an ordinary member, while
   working in the European Commission or Parliament.

The existence of a European federal movement with these characteristics represents for Spinelli merely a subjective condition for effective federalist action. There is, however, also need for objective
conditions for a successful struggle, such as those provided by crises
within national political systems.

During periods of relative stability of national political systems,
when governments appear able to deal with the principal political,
economic or social problems, the movement for a European federation is unable to influence national governments effectively, because
public opinion tends to support the latter and their policies. Only at
times of acute crisis, when governments are unable to cope and this
fact is generally evident, will public opinion be able to share the federalist point of view. At such times the federalist movement ought to
be able to mobilize support for federal solutions and persuade governments in favor of them. Spinelli was always convinced that such

crises were bound to arise because we are living during a historically critical stage for nation states which, after periods of relative and apparent stability, will be subject to intense crises of their political systems. And this is also true for policies of European unification based on the maintenance of absolute national sovereignty, because intergovernmental cooperation does not provide adequate means for facing such crises, which stem from an irreversible decline of national power of European states.

I will now deal with the second main theme of Spinelli's strategy—the concept of a European constituent assembly.

The fact that national governments are simultaneously the means and the obstacles to the federal unification of Europe carries important implications for the procedure needed to establish European institutions: if one wants federal institutions then one must proceed by way of a constituent assembly and not by the use of intergovernmental or diplomatic conferences.

In other words, Spinelli was always convinced that the creation of European institutions, being entrusted to representatives of national governments, and diplomats in particular, or if they have the last word over the constituent procedure, cannot bring about federal solutions, because the tendency of all such diplomatic negotiations will be the maintenance of absolute national sovereignty at the expense of effective unification. In contrast, in a constituent assembly, composed of people representing public opinion, a favorable attitude towards federal institutions is likely to be incomparably stronger than nationalist tendencies. This is for a number of reasons: (1) the great majority of public opinion (especially in countries first committed to European unification) is in favor of genuine unification and its representatives have to take account of this; (2) the parties and the principal democratic political trends have an international orientation which, by its very nature, would be favorable to a European federation, and would, therefore, back the creation of transnational groups within a European assembly working to strengthen pro-European attitudes; (3) those representing public opinion, unlike the diplomats, do not hold positions of power which are directly dependent on the maintenance of absolute national sovereignty.

Thus, in the event of a critical situation, the pre-eminent task of the movement for a European federation will be to persuade governments (which, at such moments, are susceptible to persuasion by the federalists) to initiate a constituent democratic procedure under which the ultimate responsibility for proposing the nature of the European institutions will be entrusted to the representatives of public opinion, and whose draft of the European constitution will then be

directly submitted for ratification to the appropriate constitution organs of the member states, without being subjected to prior diplomatic negotiations.

The concept of a constituent European assembly was patterned
by Spinelli on the way the first federal constitution in history was
drawn up, namely that of the American constitution, worked out by
the Philadelphia Convention in 1787. The example of Philadelphia
which, according to him, should provide the model for a European
constituent procedure contains three essential elements:

1. governments of individual states have the basic responsibility for initiating the process by conferring the constituent
   mandate upon the convention, but refrain from interfering
   in its deliberations;
2. the convention acts by majority votes in drawing up the constitution;
3. the ratification of the constitution is entrusted to the appropriate constitutional organs of individual states, and it comes
   into force once ratified by a majority of them (in the American case it required ratification by 9 out of the 13 states).

Throughout his federalist campaign Spinelli never ceased to
press for the adoption of a constituent procedure on these lines. One
needs to stress that for him the essence lay not in the form but the
substance of the procedure, namely to give the last word on the constitutional project to a parliamentary assembly. During the various
stages of his campaign he proposed various forms of political action,
each adapted to prevailing circumstances, to advance the constituent
procedure:

1. a constituent assembly elected by universal suffrage with the
   sole mandate of drawing up a European constitution;
2. the transformation of the consultative parliamentary assembly into a constituent one, either by its own action or by
   mandate conferred upon it by national governments;
3. by the direct election of a European parliament with a specific constituent mandate;
4. by a popular referendum which would confer the constituent
   mandate upon the European parliament.

But the substance remained unchanged.

Spinelli's constituent concept stemmed from his belief that the
functional approach to European unification will not achieve pro-

found and irreversible unity. He never shared the conviction of the supporters of the functional approach that one can integrate selected sectors of national activity without a federalist constitutional framework from the very start. And this for two fundamental reasons:

1. by refusing to start with a supranational authority of a democratic character, the principle of the national veto is retained (even with a formal acceptance of majority voting). This would deprive European institutions of the capacity to overcome special interests that arise from the exercise of unfettered national sovereignty, and to ensure the supremacy of the common European interest;
2. the chaos and inefficiency which result from the lack of common management of the interdependent economies of modern states and of their foreign and defense policies.

One needs to recognize, however, that Spinelli accepted that unification could start with effective supranational powers being first confined to economic issues, while postponing their immediate adoption in matters of foreign and security policies (as provided in the draft treaty for European Union). And this from the consideration that convergence in the latter sectors was already being influenced by American leadership. But he always stressed the need for genuine federal institutions which would ensure the ultimate extension of supranational powers from economic to defense and foreign policies. That is why he never ceased to insist on the constitutional approach, in place of the functional one, by calling for a federal constitution from the start, obtained by a democratic constituent procedure.

Spinelli's criticism of the functional method was not confined to a dialectical and doctrinaire preference for the constitutional approach. First he was clearly aware that the functional approach stemmed largely from the contradictory nature of the attitudes of national governments to European unification. As objective historical circumstances force them to face the need for supranational unification, whilst they resist giving up their sovereignty, it is natural that they prefer an approach that postpones indefinitely the establishment of an authentic supranational authority. At the same time he recognized that the functional approach could assist the constitutional process by exposing, due to its inadequacy, the contradictions of the former, that could be exploited in the course of the federalist struggle.

These contradictions boil down to two. The first stems from the precariousness and inefficiency of functional unification. Functional institutions established by the unanimous decisions of national governments have shown themselves to be weak and incapable of acting decisively at critical moments when particularly grave problems face them. As a consequence, positive results obtained in more favorable circumstances tend to be compromised or abandoned in time of crisis. This leads to the disappointment of expectations in the development of European integration and can lead to support for federal solutions. The second contradiction stems from the democratic deficit which arises when important responsibilities and powers are transferred to the supranational level without subjecting them to effective democratic control. This causes uneasiness among political parties and to democratically sensitive public opinion which can be thus influenced to favor the concept of supranational democracy. Spinelli's federalist campaign had always aimed at exploiting these contradictions in order to initiate the democratic constituent procedure.

.   .   .

13 A Working Peace System

DAVID MITRANY

David Mitrany (1888–1975) was a Romanian-born academic who spent most of his adult life in Britain and the United States. During World War II, Mitrany thought seriously about the shape of the post-war world and how to prevent future wars. The result of his reflection was a pamphlet entitled A Working Peace System, *which he published in London in the summer of 1943, two years before the end of the war. In this pamphlet, Mitrany argued for a transformation of the way people think about international relations, particularly the prevention of war. His "functional alternative" aimed at world, not European, unity. Nevertheless, it had a profound effect on European activists and early integration theorists, especially the neofunctionalists (see Chapters 15 and 16).*

Mitrany saw the division of the world into "competing political units" as the root of international conflict. A world federal government, he argued, would eliminate these divisions but would be impossible to establish given the modern "disregard for constitutions and pacts" and continuing nationalism. Mitrany called, instead, for a functional approach that would "overlay political divisions with a spreading web of international activities and agencies, in which and through which the interests and life of all the nations would be gradually integrated." Functional integration would be pragmatic, technocratic, and flexible; it would deliberately blur distinctions between national and international, public and private, and political and nonpolitical. As functional agencies were formed and joined, national divisions would become less and less important. Ultimately, a central authority might coordinate the various agencies, but such a government would not be

Reprinted from *A Working Peace System* (Quadrangle Books, 1966). Copyright 1966 by The Society for a World Service Federation. Notes omitted.

necessary to successful international relations, and might not be desirable. Here Mitrany parted with many other functionalists (such as Monnet) and the neofunctionalists who believed federal institutions were essential to the success of functional integration.

■ **THE GENERAL PROBLEM**

The need for some new kind of international system was being widely canvassed before the Second World War, in the measure in which the League of Nations found itself frustrated in its attempts to prevent aggression and to organize peace. Some blamed this failure on the irresponsibility of small states; others rather the egoism of the Great Powers. Still others imputed the League's failure more directly to weaknesses in its own constitution and machinery: the proper ingredients were there, but the political dosage was inadequate. It was especially among those who held this view that the idea of a wide international federation began to be embraced as a new hope.

Federation seemed indeed the only alternative to a League tried so far for linking together a number of political units by democratic methods. It would mean an association much closer than was the League, and its advocacy therefore takes it for granted that the League failed because it did not go far enough. In what way would federation go further? Federation would be a more intensive union of a less extensive group; the constitutional ties would be closer. Second, certain activities would be more definitely and actively tied together. More definite common action is clearly the end; the formal arrangements which the federalists put in the forefront would be merely a necessary adjunct, to ensure the reliable working of the federal undertakings. And that is as it should be for, leaving formal arguments aside, it is plain that the League failed not from overstrain but from inanition. It might have done more about sanctions, but that would not have been enough. Even if the League's action for "security" had been more fearless, that would not by itself have sufficed to give vitality to an international system that was to last and grow. To achieve that end, such a system must in some important respects take over and coordinate activities hitherto controlled by the national state, just as the state increasingly has to take over activities which until now have been carried on by local bodies; and like the state, any new international authority could under present conditions not be merely a police authority.

We realize now that the League failed because, whatever the reasons, it could not further that process of continuous adjustment and settlement which students of international affairs call "peaceful change." But they themselves, taking the form for the substance, all too often thought of it mainly as a matter of changing frontiers. We shall have to speak of this again, but what peaceful change should mean, what the modern world, so closely interrelated, must have for its peaceful development, is some system that would make possible automatic and continuous social action, continually adapted to changing needs and conditions, in the same sense and of the same general nature as any other system of government. Its character would be the same for certain purposes; only the range would be new. It is in that sense that the League's work has in truth been inadequate and ineffective, as one may readily see if one reflects whether a change of frontiers now and then would really have led to a peaceful and cooperative international society.

A close federation is supposed to do just what the League proved unable to do, and in a set and solid way. But to begin with, can we take a system which has worked well in one field and simply transplant it to another, so much wider and more complex? Federations have still been national federations; the jump from national states to international organization is infinitely more hazardous than was the jump from provincial units to national federations. None of the elements of neighborhood, of kinship, of history are there to serve as steps. The British Empire is bound closely by old ties of kinship and history, but no one would suggest that there is among its parts much will for federation. Yet apart from this matter of whether the federal idea has any great prospects, there is the more important question whether it would have any great virtues in the international sphere. If the evil of conflict and war springs from the division of the world into detached and competing political units, will it be exorcised simply by changing or reducing the lines of division? Any political reorganization into separate units must sooner or later produce the same effects; any international system that is to usher in a new world must produce the opposite effect of subduing political division. As far as one can see, there are only two ways of achieving that end. One would be through a world state which would wipe out political divisions forcibly; the other is the way discussed in these pages, which would rather overlay political divisions with a spreading web of international activities and agencies, in which and through which the interests and life of all the nations would be gradually integrated. That is the fundamental change to which any effective international system must aspire and contribute: to make international government coextensive with international activities. A League would be too loose to be able to do it; a number of sectional federations would, on the contrary, be too tight to be welded into something like it. Therefore when the need is so great and pressing, we must have the vision to break away from traditional political ideas, which in modern times have always linked authority to a given territory, and try some new way that might take us without violence toward that goal. The beginnings cannot be anything but experimental; a new international system will need, even more than national systems, a wide freedom of continuous adaptation in the light of experience. It must care as much as possible for common needs that are evident, while presuming as little as possible upon a global unity which is still only latent and unrecognized. As the late John Winant well said in a lecture at Leeds in October 1942: "We must be absolute about our principal ends (justice and equality of opportunity and freedom), relative and pragmatic about the mechanical means used to serve those ends."

The need for a pragmatic approach is all the greater because we are so clearly in a period of historical transition. When the state itself, whatever its form and constitution, is everywhere undergoing a deep social and political sea-change, it is good statesmanship not to force the new international experiments into some set familiar form, which may be less relevant the more respectable it seems, but to see above all that these experiments go with and fit into the general trend of the time.

When one examines the general shape of the tasks that are facing us, one is, to begin with, led to question whether order could be brought into them by the device of formal written pacts. Why did written constitutions, declarations of rights, and other basic charters play such a great role during the nineteenth century? The task of that time, following the autocratic period, was to work out a new division of the sphere of authority, to determine new relationships between the individual and the state, to protect the new democracy. These relationships were meant to be fixed and final, and they had to rest on general principles, largely of a negative character. It was natural and proper that all that should be laid down in formal rules, meant to remain untouched and permanent. In much the same way the new nation state was in world society what the new citizen was in municipal society; and with the increase in their number, the liberal growth in international trade and cultural and social intercourse, the resulting international rules and a host of written treaties and pacts sought, like the national constitutions, to fix the formal relationship between the sovereign individual states and their collectivity; which in this case also was expected to be fixed and final, with international law as a gradually emerging constitution for that political cosmos.

Viewed in this light, the Covenant of the League is seen to have continued that nineteenth-century tradition. It was concerned above all with fixing in a definite way the formal relationship of the member states and in a measure also of non-members, and only in a very secondary way with initiating positive common activities and action. The great expectation, security, was a vital action, but a negative one; its end was not to promote the active regular life of the peoples but only to protect it against being disturbed. Broadly one might say that the Covenant was an attempt to universalize and codify the rules of international conduct, gradually evolved through political treaties and pacts, and to give them general and permanent validity. It was neither unnatural nor unreasonable to follow up that nineteenth-century trend and try to steady international relations by bringing them within the framework of a written pact, one provided with set rules for its working. But when it came to going beyond that, the League could not be more or do more than what its leading members were ready to be and do, and they were ready to do but little in a positive way. It was indeed characteristic of the post-Armistice period 1918–19 that even the victors hastened to undo their common economic and other machinery, such as the Allied Shipping Control, which had grown and served them well during the war. And that was at a time when within each country government action and control were spreading fast, causing many a private international activity also to be cut down or cut off. In other words, the incipient common functions, as well as many old connections, were disbanded in the international sphere at the very time when a common constitution was being laid down for it. It was that divorce between life and form that doomed the League from the outset, and not any inadequacy in its written rules.

Hence it is pertinent to ask: Would another written pact, if only more elaborate and stringent, come to grips more closely with the problems of our time? Let us by way of a preliminary answer note two things: First, the lusty disregard for constitutions and pacts, for settled rules and traditional rights, is a striking mark of the times. In the pressure for social change no such formal ties are allowed to stand in the way, either within the several countries or between them. It is a typical revolutionary mood and practice. If it does not always take the outward form of revolution, that is because the governments themselves act as spearheads of the trend, and not only in countries ruled by dictatorships. Those who lead in this rush for social change pride themselves indeed on their disregard for forms and formalities. The appeal which communism, fascism, and nazism had for youth in particular and for the masses in general lies in no small degree in that political iconoclasm. At the turn of the nineteenth century the radical masses were demanding settled rules and rights, and Napoleon could play the trump card of constitutional nationalism against the autocratic rulers. Now the masses demand social action without regard to established "rights," and the totalitarian leaders have been playing the strong card of pragmatic socialism against constitutional democracy.

That universal pressure for social reform, in the second place, has utterly changed the relation of nationalism to internationalism, in a way that could be promising if rightly used. In constitution-making there was a parallel between the two spheres, but nothing more, for they belonged politically to different categories. The nineteenth-century nationalism rested mainly on cultural and other differential factors, and the creation of the nation state meant inevitably a breaking up of world unity. A cosmopolitan outlook spread rapidly, but the nations at the same time balked at international political organization and control, and they could justify that refusal by seemingly good principle. At present the new nationalism rests essentially on social factors; these are not only alike in the various countries, thus paradoxically creating a bond even between totalitarian groups, but often cannot make progress in isolation. At many points the life of the nation state is overflowing back into that common world which existed before the rise of modern nationalism. At present the lines of national and international evolution are not parallel but converging, and the two spheres now belong to the same category and differ only in dimensions.

In brief, the function of the nineteenth century was to restrain the powers of authority; that led to the creation of the "political man" and likewise of the "political nation," and to the definition through constitutional pacts of their relation to the wider political group. The Covenant (and the Locarno and Kellogg pacts) was still of that species essentially, with the characteristic predominance of rules of the "thou shall not" kind. The function of our time is rather to develop and coordinate the social scope of authority, and that cannot be so defined or divided. Internationally it is no longer a question of defining relations between states but of merging them—the work-day sense of the vague talk about the need to surrender some part of sovereignty. A constitutional pact could do little more than lay down certain elementary rights and duties for the members of the new community. The community itself will acquire a living body not through a written act of faith but through active organic development. Yet there is in this no fundamental dispute as to general principles and ultimate aims. The only question is, which is the more immediately practicable and promising way: whether a general political framework should be provided formally in advance, on some theoretical pattern, or left to grow branch by branch from action and experience and so find its natural bent.

■ THE FUNCTIONAL ALTERNATIVE

Can these vital objections be met, and the needs of peace and social advance be satisfied, through some other way of associating the nations for common action? The whole trend of modern government indicates such a way. That trend is to organize government along the lines of specific ends and needs, and according to the conditions of their time and place, in lieu of the traditional organization on the basis of a set constitutional division of jurisdiction and of rights and powers. In national government the definition of authority and the scope of public action are now in a continuous flux, and are determined less by constitutional norms than by practical requirements. The instances are too many and well known to need mentioning; one might note only that while generally the trend has been toward greater centralization of services, and therefore of authority, under certain conditions the reverse has also occurred, powers and duties being handed over to regional and other authorities for the better performance of certain communal needs. The same trend is powerfully at work in the several federations, in Canada and Australia, and especially in the United States, and in these cases it is all the more striking because the division of authority rests on written constitutions which are still in being and nominally valid in full. Internationally, too, while a body of law had grown slowly and insecurely through rules and conventions, some common activities were organized through ad hoc functional arrangements and have worked well. The rise of such specific administrative agencies and laws is the peculiar trait, and indeed the foundation, of modern government.

A question which might properly be asked at the outset in considering the fitness of that method for international purposes is this: Could such functions be organized internationally without a comprehensive political framework? Let it be said, first, that the functional method as such is neither incompatible with a general constitutional framework nor precludes its coming into being. It only follows Burke's warning to the sheriffs of Bristol that "government is a practical thing" and that one should beware of elaborating constitutional forms "for the gratification of visionaries." In national states and federations the functional development is going ahead without much regard to, and sometimes in spite of, the old constitutional divisions.

If in these cases the constitution is most conveniently left aside, may not the method prove workable internationally without any immediate and comprehensive constitutional framework? If, to cite Burke again, it is "always dangerous to meddle with foundations," it is doubly dangerous now. Our political problems are obscure, while the political passions of the time are blinding. One of the misfortunes of the League experiment was that a new institution was devised on what have proved to be outworn premises. We might also recollect that of the constitutional changes introduced in Europe after the First World War, fine and wise though they may have been, none has survived even a generation. How much greater will that risk of futility be in Europe after the Second World War, when the split within and between nations will be much worse than in 1919? We know now even less about the dark historical forces which have been stirred up by the war, while in the meantime the problems of our common society have been distorted by fierce ideologies which we could not try to bring to an issue without provoking an irreconcilable dogmatic conflict. Even if an action were to be to some extent handicapped without a formal political framework, the fact is that no obvious sentiment exists, and none is likely to crystallize for some years, for a common constitutional bond.

In such conditions any pre-arranged constitutional framework would be taken wholly out of the air. We do not know what, if anything, will be in common—except a desperate craving for peace and for the conditions of a tolerable normal life. The peoples may applaud declarations of rights, but they will call for the satisfaction of needs. That demand for action could be turned into a historic opportunity. Again we might take to heart what happened to the U.S. in 1932–33 and think of what chances the Roosevelt administration would have to have had to achieve unity, or indeed to survive, if instead of taking immediate remedial action it had begun by offering constitutional reforms—though a common system was already in being. A timid statesman might still have tried to walk in the old constitutional grooves; Mr. Roosevelt stepped over them. He grasped both the need and opportunity for centralized practical action. Unemployment, the banking collapse, flood control, and a hundred other problems had to be dealt with by national means if they were to be dealt with effectively and with lasting results.

The significant point in that emergency action was that each and every problem was tackled as a practical issue in itself. No attempt was made to relate it to a general theory or system of government. Every function was left to generate others gradually, like the functional subdivision of organic cells; and in every case the appropriate authority was left to grow and develop out of actual performance. Yet the new functions and the new organs, taken together, have revolutionized the American political system. The federal government has become a national government, and Washington for the first time is really the capital of America. In the process, many improvements in the personnel and machinery of government have come about, and many restrictive state regulations have melted away. More recently there has been heard the significant complaint that the ties between cities and their states are becoming looser, while those with the national government become ever stronger. No one has worked to bring this about, and no written act has either prescribed it or confirmed it. A great constitutional transformation has thus taken place without any changes in the Constitution. There have been complaints, but the matter-of-course acceptance has been overwhelming. People have gladly accepted the service when they might have questioned the theory. The one attempt at direct constitutional revision, to increase and liberalize the membership of the Supreme Court, was bitterly disputed and defeated. Yet that proposal involved in effect much less of a constitutional revolution than has the experiment of the Tennessee Valley Authority. The first would not have ensured any lasting change in the working of the American government, whereas the second has really introduced into the political structure of the United States a new regional dimension unknown to the Constitution.

In many of its essential aspects—the urgency of the material needs, the inadequacy of the old arrangements, the bewilderment in outlook—the situation at the end of the Second World War will resemble that in America in 1933, though on a wider and deeper scale. And for the same reasons the path pursued by Mr. Roosevelt in 1933 offers the best, perhaps the only, chance for getting a new international life going. It will be said inevitably that in the United States it was relatively easy to follow that line of action because it was in fact one country, with an established Constitution. Functional arrangements could be accepted, that is, because in many fields the federal states had grown in the habit of working together. That is no doubt true, but not the most significant point of the American experiment; for that line was followed not because the functional way was so easy but because the constitutional way would have been so difficult. Hence the lesson for unfederated parts of the world would seem to be this: If the constitutional path had to be avoided for the sake of effective action even in a federation which already was a working political system, how much less promising must it be as a starting mode when it is a matter of bringing together for the first time a number of varied, and sometimes antagonistic, countries? But if the constitutional approach, by its very circumspectness, would hold up the start of a working international system, bold initiative during the period of emergency at the end of the war might set going lasting instruments and habits of a common international life. And though it may appear rather brittle, that functional approach would in fact be more solid and definite than a formal one. It need not meddle with foundations; old institutions and ways may to some extent hamper reconstruction, but reconstruction could begin by a common effort without a fight over established ways. Reconstruction may in this field also prove a surer and less costly way than revolution. As to the new ideologies, since we could not prevent them we must try to circumvent them, leaving it to the growth of new habits and interests to dilute them in time. Our aim must be to call forth to the highest possible degree the active forces and opportunities for cooperation, while touching as little as possible the latent or active points of difference and opposition.

There is one other aspect of the post-war period which has been much discussed and has a bearing on this point, and which helps to bring out the difference in outlook between the two methods contrasted here. Much has been heard of a suggestion that when the war ends we must have first a period of convalescence and that the task of permanent reorganization will only come after that. It is a useful suggestion, insofar as it may help to clear up certain practical problems. But it could also be misleading and even dangerous if the distinction were taken to justify either putting off the work of international government or differentiating between the agencies by which the new international activities are to be organized, into nurses for convalescence and mentors for the new life. A clean division in time between two such periods in any case is not possible, for the period of convalescence will be different for different activities and ends; but, above all, except for such direct and exceptional consequences of the war as demobilization and the rebuilding of damaged areas, the needs of society will be the same at once after the war as later on. The only difference will be the practical one of a priority of needs, the kind of difference which might be brought about by any social disturbance—an epidemic or an earthquake or an economic crisis—and the urgency of taking action. For the rest, one action and period will merge into the other, according to circumstances. Seed and implements will be as urgent for ensuring the food supply of Europe and Asia as the actual distribution of relief, and indeed more urgent if the war should end after a harvest. Again, both relief and reconstruction will depend greatly on the speedy reorganization and proper use of transport, and so on.

Both circumstances point again to the advantage of a functional practice and to the disadvantage, if not the impossibility, of a comprehensive attempt at political organization. To obtain sufficient agreement for some formal general scheme would, at best, not be possible without delay; at the same time, action for relief and reconstruction will have to start within the hour after the ceasefire. The alternatives would be, if a comprehensive constitutional arrangement is desired and waited for, either to put the immediate work in the hands of temporary international agencies or to leave it to the individual states. The one, in fact, would prepare for the other. Except in matters of relief—the distribution of food, fuel, and clothing and also medical help—*ad hoc* temporary agencies could have no adequate authority or influence; all of what one might call the society-building activities, involving probably considerable planning and reorganization within and between the several countries, would fall upon the individual states again, as in 1919, when they competed and interfered rather than cooperated with each other, to the loss of them all. Yet it is vital that international activity should be from the outset in the same hands and move in the same direction after the war as later; otherwise the chances of building up an international system would be gravely prejudiced. It is certain that one of the chief reasons for the failure of the League was that it was given a formal authority and promissory tasks for the future, while the immediate, urgent, and most welcome tasks of social reconstruction and reform were left to be attended to by national agencies. Later efforts to retrieve that mistake only led to a series of barren economic conferences, as by that time the policy of each country was set hard in its own mold. It is inevitable with any scheme of formal organization that the national states should have to re-start on their own, and natural therefore that refuge should be sought in the idea of a period of convalescence while the full-fledged scheme is worked out and adopted. But functional authorities would not need such political hospitalization, with its arbitrary and dangerous division of stages; they would merely vary, like any other agency anywhere and at any time, the emphasis of their work in accordance with the changing condition of their task, continuing to control and organize transport, for instance, after they had rebuilt it, and in the same way taking each task in hand with a plan and authority for continuing it. The simple fact is that all the re-starting of agriculture and industry and transport will either be done on some pre-arranged common program or it will have to be done, for it could not wait, on disjointed local plans; it will be done either by pre-established international agencies or it will have to be done by local national agencies—and the agencies which will act in the supposed convalescence period will also be those to gather authority and acceptance unto themselves.

.   .   .

□   *The Broad Lines of Functional Organization*

The problem of our generation, put very broadly, is how to weld together the common interests of all without interfering unduly with the particular ways of each. It is a parallel problem to that which faces us in national society, and which in both spheres challenges us to find an alternative to the totalitarian pattern. A measure of centralized planning and control, for both production and distribution, is no longer to be avoided, no matter what the form of the state or the doctrine of its constitution. Through all that variety of political forms there is a growing approximation in the working of government, with differences merely of degree and of detail. Liberal democracy needs a redefinition of the public and private spheres of action. But as the line of separation is always shifting under the pressure of fresh social needs and demands, it must be left free to move with those needs and demands and cannot be fixed through a constitutional re-instatement. The only possible principle of democratic confirmation is that public action should be undertaken only where and when and insofar as the need for common action becomes evident and is accepted for the sake of the common good. In that way controlled democracy could yet be made the golden mean whereby social needs might be satisfied as largely and justly as possible, while still leaving as wide a residue as possible for the free choice of the individual.

That is fully as true for the international sphere. It is indeed the only way to combine, as well as may be, international organization with national freedom. We have already suggested that not all interests are common to all, and that the common interests do not concern all countries in the same degree. A territorial union would bind together some interests which are not of common concern to the group, while it would inevitably cut asunder some interests of common concern to the group and those outside it. The only way to avoid that twice-arbitrary surgery is to proceed by means of a natural selection, binding together those interests which are common, where they are common, and to the extent to which they are common. That functional selection and organization of international needs would extend, and in a way resume, an international development which has been gathering strength since the latter part of the nineteenth century. The work of organizing international public services and activities was taken a step further by the League, in its health and drug-control work, in its work for refugees, in the experiments with the transfer of minorities and the important innovations of the League loan system, and still more through the whole activity of the ILO [International Labour Organisation]. But many other activities and interests in the past had been organized internationally by private agencies—in finance and trade and production, etc., not to speak of scientific and cultural activities. In recent years some of these activities have been brought under public national control in various countries; in totalitarian countries indeed all of them. In a measure, therefore, the present situation represents a retrogression from the recent past: the new turn toward self-sufficiency has spread from economics to the things of the mind; and while flying and wireless were opening up the world, many old links forged by private effort have been forcibly severed. It is unlikely that most of them could be resumed now except through public action, and if they are to operate as freely as they did in private hands they cannot be organized otherwise than on a nondiscriminating functional basis.

What would be the broad lines of such a functional organization of international activities? The essential principle is that activities would be selected specifically and organized separately—each according to its nature, to the conditions under which it has to operate, and to the needs of the moment. It would allow, therefore, all freedom for practical variation in the organization of the several functions, as well as in the working of a particular function as needs and conditions alter. Let us take as an example the group of functions which fall under communications, on which the success of post-war reconstruction will depend greatly. What is the proper basis for the international organization of *railway* systems? Clearly it must be European, or rather *continental*, North American, and so on, as that gives the logical administrative limit of coordination. A division of the Continent into separate democratic and totalitarian unions would not achieve the practical end, as political division would obstruct that necessary coordination; while British and American participation would make the organization more cumbersome without any added profit to the function. As regards shipping, the line of effective organization which at once suggests itself is *international*, or intercontinental, but not universal. A European union could not solve the problem of maritime coordination without the cooperation of America and of certain other overseas states. *Aviation* and *broadcasting*, a third example in the same group, could be organized effectively only on a *universal* scale, with perhaps subsidiary regional arrangements for more local services. Such subsidiary regional arrangements could in fact be inserted at any time and at any stage where that might prove useful for any part of a function. Devolution according to need would be as easy and natural as centralization, whereas if the basis of organization were political every such change in dimension would involve an elaborate constitutional re-arrangement. Similarly, it could be left safely to be determined by practical considerations whether at the points where functions cross each other—such as rail and river transport in Europe and America—the two activities should be merely coordinated or put under one control.

These are relatively simple examples. The functional coordination of production, trade, and distribution evidently would be more complex, especially as they have been built up on a competitive basis. But the experience with international cartels, with the re-organization of the shipping, cotton, and steel industries in England, not to speak of the even wider and more relevant experience with economic coordination in the two world wars—all shows that the thing can be done and that it has always been done on such functional lines. No fixed rule is needed, and no rigid pattern is desirable for the organization of these working functional strata.

A certain degree of fixity would not be out of place, however, in regard to more *negative* functions, especially those related to law and order, but also to any others of a more formal nature which are likely to remain fairly static. Security, for instance, could be organized on an interlocking regional basis, and the judicial function likewise, with a hierarchy of courts, as the need may arise—the wider acting as courts of appeal from the more local courts. Yet, even in regard to security, and in addition to regional arrangements, the elasticity inherent in functional organization may prove practicable and desirable, if only in the period of transition. Anglo-American naval cooperation for the policing of the seas may prove acceptable for a time, and it would cut across physical regions. Agreement on a mineral sanction would of necessity mean common action by those countries which control the main sources; and other such combinations might be found useful for any particular task in hand. That is security only for defense; security arrangements were conceived usually on a geographical basis because they were meant to prevent violence, and that would still be the task of sanctions, etc., based on some regional devolution. But in addition there is a growing functional devolution in the field of social security in connection with health, with the drug and white slave traffic, with crime, etc. In all that important field of social policing it has been found that coordination and cooperation with the police of other countries on functional lines, varying with each task, was both indispensable and practicable. There is no talk and no attempt in all this to encroach upon sovereignty, but only a detached functional association which works smoothly and is already accepted without question.

However that may be, in the field of more *positive* active functions—economic, social, cultural—which are varied and ever changing in structure and purpose, any devolution must, like the main organization, follow functional lines. Land transport on the Continent would need a different organization and agencies should the railways after a time be displaced by roads; and a Channel tunnel would draw England into an arrangement in which she does not at present belong, with a corresponding change in the governing organ.

Here we discover a cardinal virtue of the functional method—what one might call the virtue of technical self-determination. The functional *dimensions*, as we have seen, determine its appropriate *organs*. It also reveals through practice the nature of the action required under given conditions, and in that way the *powers* needed by the respective authority. The function, one might say, determines the executive instrument suitable for its proper activity, and by the same process provides a need for the reform of the instrument at every stage. This would allow the widest latitude for variation between functions, and also in the dimension or organization of the same function as needs and conditions change. Not only is there in all this no need for any fixed constitutional division of authority and power, prescribed in advance, but anything beyond the original formal definition of scope and purpose might embarrass the working of the practical arrangements.

☐   *The Question of Wider Coordination*

The question will be asked, however, in what manner and to what degree the various functional agencies that may thus grow up would have to be linked to each other and articulated as parts of a more comprehensive organization. It should be clear that each agency could work by itself, but that does not exclude the possibility of some of them or all being bound in some way together, if it should be found needful or useful to do so. That indeed is the test. As the whole sense of this particular method is to let activities be organized as the need for joint action arises and is accepted, it would be out of place to lay down in advance some formal plan for the coordination of various functions. Coordination, too, would in that sense have to come about functionally. Yet certain needs and possibilities can be foreseen already now, though some are probable and others only likely, and it may help to round off the picture if we look into this aspect briefly.

1. *Within the same group* of functions probably there would have to be coordination either simply for technical purposes or for wider functional ends, and this would be the first stage toward a wider integration. To take again the group concerned with communications—rail, road, and air transport in Europe would need *technical* coordination in regard to timetables, connections, etc. They may need also a wider *functional* coordination if there is to be some distribution of passenger and freight traffic for the most economic performance—whether that is done by a superior executive agency or by some arbitral body, perhaps on the lines of the Federal Commerce Commission in America. Sea and air traffic across the Atlantic or elsewhere, though separately organized, probably would also benefit from a similar type of coordination. Again, various mineral controls, if they should be organized separately, would need some coordination, though this arbitrary grouping of "minerals" would be less to the point that the coordination of specific minerals and other products with possible substitutes—of crude oil with synthetic oil, of crude rubber with synthetic rubber, and so on.

2. The next degree or stage might be, if found desirable, the coordination of *several groups* of functional agencies. For instance, the communications agencies may not only work out some means of acting together in the distribution of orders for rolling stock, ships, etc., but they could or should work in this through any agencies that may have come into being for controlling materials and production, or through some intermediary agency as a clearinghouse. There is no need to prescribe any pattern in advance, or that the pattern adopted in one case should be followed in all the others.

3. The coordination of such working functional agencies with any *international planning* agencies would present a third stage, and one that brings out some interesting possibilities, should the ideas for an international investment board or an international development commission, as an advisory organ, come to fruition. One can see how such a development commission might help to guide the growth of functional agencies into the most desirable channels, and could watch their inter-relations and their repercussions. And an investment board could guide, for instance, the distribution of orders for ships, materials, etc., not only according to the best economic use but also for the purpose of ironing out cyclical trends. It could use, ac-

cording to its nature, its authority or its influence to make of such orders a means additional to international public works, etc., for dealing with periods or pockets of unemployment. Coordination of such a general kind may in some cases amount almost to arbitration of differences between functional agencies; regional boards or councils like those of the Pan-American Union might be used to adjust or arbitrate regional differences.

4. Beyond this there remains the habitual assumption, as we have already said, that international action must have some overall *political authority* above it. Besides the fact that such a comprehensive authority is not now a practical possibility, it is the central view of the functional approach that such an authority is not essential for our greatest and real immediate needs. The several functions could be organized through the agreement, given specifically in each case, of the national governments chiefly interested, with the grant of the requisite powers and resources; whereas it is clear, to emphasize the previous point, that they could not allow such organizations simply to be prescribed by some universal authority, even if it existed. For an authority which had the title to do so would in effect be hardly less than a world government; and such a strong central organism would inevitably tend to take unto itself rather more authority than that originally allotted to it, this calling in turn for the checks and balances which are used in federal systems, but which would be difficult to provide in any loose way. If issues should arise in any functional system which would call either for some new departure or for the reconsideration of existing arrangements, that could be done only in council by all the governments concerned. Insofar as it may be desired to keep alive some general view of our problems, and perhaps a general watch over the policies of the several joint agencies, some body of a representative kind, like the League Assembly or the governing body of the ILO, could meet periodically, perhaps elected by proportional representation from the assemblies of the member states. Such an assembly, in which all the states would have a voice, could discuss and ventilate general policies, as an expression of the mind and will of public opinion; but it could not actually prescribe policy, as this might turn out to be at odds with the policy of governments. Any line of action recommended by such an assembly would have to be pressed and secured through the policy-making machinery of the various countries themselves.

These, then, are the several types and grades of coordination which might develop with the growth of functional activities. But there is, finally, in the political field also the problem of security, admittedly a crucial problem, for on its being solved effectively the successful working of the other activities will depend. At the same time, the general discussion of functional organization will have served to bring out the true place and proportion of security, as something indispensable but also as something incapable by itself of achieving the peaceful growth of an international society. It is in fact a separate function like the others, not something that stands in stern isolation, overriding all the others. Looking at it in this way, as a practical function, should also make it clear that we would not achieve much if we handled it as a one-sided, limited problem—at present too often summed up in "German aggression." German aggression was a particularly vicious outgrowth of a bad general system, and only a radical and general change of the system itself will provide continuous security for all. In this case also it would be useful to lay down some formal pledges and principles as a guiding line, but the practical organization would have to follow functional, perhaps combined with regional, lines. That is all the more necessary as we know better now how many elements besides the purely military enter into the making of security. The various functional agencies might, in fact, play an important role in that wide aspect of security; they could both watch over and check such things as the building of strategic railways or the accumulation of strategic stocks in metals or grains. Possibly they could even be used, very properly and effectively, as a first line of action against threatening aggression, by their withholding services from those who are causing the trouble. They could apply such preventive sanctions more effectively than if this were to wait upon the agreement and action of a number of separate governments; and they could do so as part of their practical duties, and therefore with less of the political reactions caused by political action.

□   *Representation in Controls*

One aspect likely to be closely examined is that of the structure of the functional controls, and here again the initial difficulty will be that we shall have to break away from attractive traditional ideas if we are to work out the issue on its merits. It is not in the nature of the method that representation on the controlling bodies should be democratic in a political sense, full and equal for all. Ideally it may seem that all functions should be organized on a worldwide scale and that all states should have a voice in control. Yet the weight of reality is on the side of making the jurisdiction of the various agencies no wider than the most effective working limits of the function; and while it is understandable that all countries might wish to have a voice in control, that would be really to hark back to the outlook of political sovereignty. In no functional organization so far have the parties interested had a share in control as "by right" of their separate existence—neither the various local authorities in the London Transport Board, nor the seven states concerned in the TVA [Tennessee Valley Authority]. An in any case, in the transition from power politics to a functional order we could be well satisfied if the control of the new international organs answered to some of the merits of each case, leaving it to experience and to the maturing of a new outlook to provide in time the necessary correctives.

. . .

■ THROUGH FUNCTIONAL ACTION TO INTERNATIONAL SOCIETY

□ The Way of Natural Selection

One cannot insist too much that such gradual functional developments would not create a new system, however strange they might appear in the light of our habitual search for a unified formal order. They would merely rationalize and develop what is already there. In all countries social activities, in the widest sense of the term, are organized and reorganized continually in that way. But because of the legalistic structure of the state and of our political outlook, which treat national and international society as two different worlds, social nature, so to speak, has not had a chance so far to take its course. Our social activities are cut off arbitrarily at the limit of the state and, if at all, are allowed to be linked to the same activities across the border only by means of uncertain and cramping political ligatures. What is here proposed is simply that these political amputations should cease. Whenever useful or necessary the several activities would be released to function as one unit throughout the length of their natural course. National problems would then appear, and would be treated, as what they are—the local segments of general problems.

. . .

□ Epilogue

Peace will not be secured if we organize the world by what divides it. But in the measure in which such peace-building activities develop and succeed, one might hope that the mere prevention of conflict, crucial as that may be, would in time fall to a subordinate place in the scheme of international things, while we would turn to what are the real tasks of our common society—the conquest of poverty and of disease and of ignorance. The stays of political federation were needed when life was more local and international activities still loose. But now our social interdependence is all-pervasive and all-embracing, and if it be so organized the political side will also grow as part of it. The elements of a functional system could begin to work without a general political authority, but a political authority without active social functions would remain an empty temple. Society will develop by our living it, not by policing it. Nor would any political agreement survive long under economic competition, but economic unification would build up the foundation for political agreement, even if it did not make it superfluous. In any case, as things are, the political way is too ambitious. We cannot start from an ideal plane but must be prepared to make many attempts from many points, and build things and mend things as we go along. The essential thing is that we should be going together, in the same direction, and that we get into step now.

· · ·

Cooperation for the common good is the task, both for the sake of peace and of a better life, and for that it is essential that certain interests and activities should be taken out of the mood of competition and worked together. But it is not essential to make that cooperation fast to a territorial authority, and indeed it would be senseless to do so when the number of those activities is limited, while their range is the world. "Economic areas do not always run with political areas," wrote the *New York Times* (February 26, 1943) in commenting on the Alaska Highway scheme, and such cross-country cooperation would simply make frontiers less important. "Apply this principle to certain European areas and the possibilities are dazzling." If it be said that all that may be possible in war but hardly in peace, that can only mean that practically the thing is possible but that we doubt whether in normal times there would be the political will to do it. Now, apart from everything else, the functional method stands out as a solid touchstone in that respect. Promissory covenants and charters may remain a headstone to unfulfilled good intentions, but the functional way is action itself and therefore an inescapable test of where we stand and how far we are willing to go in building up a new international society. It is not a promise to act in a crisis, but itself the action that will avoid the crisis. Every activity organized in that way would be a layer of peaceful life; and a sufficient addition of them would create increasingly deep and wide strata of peace—not the forbidding peace of an alliance, but one that would suffuse the world with a fertile mingling of common endeavor and achievement.

This is not an argument against any ideal of formal union, if that should prove a possible ultimate goal. It is, above all, a plea for the creation now of the elements of an active international society. Amidst the tragedy of war one can glimpse also the promise of a broader outlook, of a much deeper understanding of the issues than in 1918. It is because the peoples are ready for action that they cannot wait. We have no means and no standing to work out some fine constitution and try to impose it in time upon the world. But we do have the standing and the means to prepare for immediate practical action. We do not know what will be the sentiments of the peoples of Europe and of other continents at the end of the war, but we do know what their needs will be. *Any* political scheme would start a disputation; *any* working arrangement would raise a hope and make for confidence and patience.

The functional way may seem a spiritless solution—and so it is, in the sense that it detaches from the spirit the things which are of the body. No advantage has accrued to anyone when economic and other social activities are wedded to fascist or communist or other political ideologies; their progeny has always been confusion and conflict. Let these things appear quite starkly for what they are, practical household tasks, and it will be more difficult to make them into the household idols of "national interest" and "national honor." The ideological movements of our time, because of their indiscriminate zeal, have sometimes been compared to religious movements. They may be, but at their core was not a promise of life hereafter. The things which are truly of the spirit—and therefore personal to the individual and to the nation—will not be less winged for being freed in their turn from that worldly ballast. Hence the argument that opposes democracy to totalitarianism does not call the real issue. It is much too simple. Society is everywhere in travail because it is everywhere in transition. Its problem after a century of laissez faire philosophy is to sift anew, in the light of new economic possibilities and of new social aspirations, what is private from what has to be public; and in the latter sphere what is local and national from what is wider. And for that task of broad social refinement a more discriminating instrument is needed than the old political sieve. In the words of a statement by the American National Policy Committee, "Part of the daring required is the daring to find new forms and to adopt them. We are lost if we dogmatically assume that the procedures of the past constitute the only true expression of democracy."

14 Political Community and the North Atlantic Area

KARL W. DEUTSCH ET AL.

In the 1950s, with memories of World War II still fresh and the Cold War threatening to burn hot, the issue of war and peace in Europe remained vital. European politicians were busy abolishing war between France and Germany by laying the foundation for a united Europe. Across the Atlantic, however, U.S. social scientists, many of them immigrants from the Continent, began systematically studying the European integration process to discover what propelled it and whether it would actually assure peace.

One of these academics, a 1938 Czech refugee named Karl W. Deutsch (1912–1992), helped revolutionize the study of international relations by introducing scientific and quantitative methods. While at the Massachusetts Institute of Technology (he later taught at Yale and Harvard), he and seven of his colleagues applied their new social scientific skills to "the study of possible ways in which men someday might abolish war." The result of this study was Political Community and the North Atlantic Area *(1957). The work did not focus on the new supranational institutions of Europe, but rather examined ten historical cases of integration to see if lessons could be applied to an area that included Western Europe, Canada, and the United States. After comparing these cases, they concluded that successful integration required a sense of community—a "we-feeling"—among the populations of the integrating territories, a core political area around which*

*this community could coalesce, and a rise in administrative capabili-
ties to meet the challenge of an enlarged domain. To meet these requirements for an "amalgamated security-community," Deutsch and
his colleagues argued that the integrating territories must share a common set of values and that the communication and transactions between them must expand in numerous ways. This was their key insight: integration was a learning process that took place over a long
period of extensive and sustained contact between people from the
politically relevant strata of society. They were skeptical of the functionalists' claim (see Chapter 13) that integrating government tasks one
step at a time would lead to more successful amalgamation, but they
did confirm that functionalism had succeeded in the past.*

*Deutsch's transactionalist approach to integration was largely
overshadowed by the rise of neofunctionalism (see Chapter 15) in the
late 1950s and early 1960s, but recently Deutsch has attracted attention from a new generation of scholars impressed by his prescient insights. His relevance seems to grow as the European Union enlarges
to the east and the question of who is a "European" increases in importance.*

■ THE PROBLEM

We undertook this inquiry as a contribution to the study of possible
ways in which men someday might abolish war. From the outset, we
realized the complexity of the problem. It is difficult to relate
"peace" clearly to other prime values such as "justice" and "freedom." There is little common agreement on acceptable alternatives
to war, and there is much ambiguity in the use of the terms "war"
and "peace." Yet we can start with the assumption that war is now
so dangerous that mankind must eliminate it, must put it beyond serious possibility. The attempt to do this may fail. But in a civilization
that wishes to survive, the central problem in the study of international organization is this: How can men learn to act together to
eliminate war as a social institution?

This is in one sense a smaller, and in another sense a larger, question than the one which occupies so many of the best minds today:
how can we either prevent or avoid losing "the next war"? It is
smaller because there will, of course, be no chance to solve the
long-run problem if we do not survive the short-run crisis. It is larger
because it concerns not only the confrontation of the nations of East
and West in the twentieth century, but the whole underlying question

of relations between political units at any time. We are not, therefore, trying to add to the many words that have been written directly concerning the East-West struggle of the 1940–1950's. Rather, we are seeking new light with which to look at the conditions and processes of long-range or permanent peace, applying our findings to one contemporary problem which, though not so difficult as the East-West problem, is by no means simple: peace within the North Atlantic area.

Whenever a difficult political problem arises, men turn to history for clues to its solution. They do this knowing they will not find the whole answer there. Every political problem is unique, of course, for history does not "repeat itself." But often the reflective mind will discover situations in the past that are essentially similar to the one being considered. Usually, with these rough parallels or suggestive analogies, the problem is not so much to find the facts as it is to decide what is essentially the same and what is essentially different between the historical facts and those of the present.

. . .

We are dealing here with political communities. These we regard as social groups with a process of political communication, some machinery for enforcement, and some popular habits of compliance. A political community is not necessarily able to prevent war within the area it covers: the United States was unable to do so at the time of the Civil War. Some political communities do, however, eliminate war and the expectation of war within their boundaries. It is these that call for intensive study. We have concentrated, therefore, upon the formation of "security-communities" in certain historical cases. The use of this term starts a chain of definitions, and we must break in here to introduce the other main links needed for a fuller understanding of our findings.

A SECURITY-COMMUNITY is a group of people which has become "integrated."

By INTEGRATION we mean the attainment, within a territory, of a "sense of community" and of institutions and practices strong enough and widespread enough to assure, for a "long" time, dependable expectations of "peaceful change" among its population.

By SENSE OF COMMUNITY we mean a belief on the part of individuals in a group that they have come to agreement on at least this one point: that common social problems must and can be resolved by processes of "peaceful change."

By PEACEFUL CHANGE we mean the resolution of social problems, normally by institutionalized procedures, without resort to large-scale physical force.

A security-community, therefore, is one in which there is real assurance that the members of that community will not fight each other physically, but will settle their disputes in some other way. If the entire world were integrated as a security-community, wars would be automatically eliminated. But there is apt to be confusion about the term "integration."

In our usage, the term "integration" does not necessarily mean only the merging of peoples or governmental units into a single unit. Rather, we divide security-communities into two types: "amalgamated" and "pluralistic."

By AMALGAMATION we mean the formal merger of two or more previously independent units into a single larger unit, with some type of common government after amalgamation. This common government may be unitary or federal. The United States today is an example of the amalgamated type. It became a single governmental unit by the formal merger of several formerly independent units. It has one supreme decision-making center.

The PLURALISTIC security-community, on the other hand, retains the legal independence of separate governments. The combined territory of the United States and Canada is an example of the pluralistic type. Its two separate governmental units form a security-community without being merged. It has two supreme decision-making centers. Where amalgamation occurs without integration, of course a security-community does not exist.

Since our study deals with the problem of ensuring peace, we shall say that any political community, be it amalgamated or pluralistic, was eventually SUCCESSFUL if it became a security-community—that is, if it achieved integration—and that it was UNSUCCESSFUL if it ended eventually in secession or civil war.

Perhaps we should point out here that both types of integration require, at the international level, some kind of organization, even though it may be very loose. We put no credence in the old aphorism that among friends a constitution is not necessary and among enemies it is of no avail. The area of practicability lies in between.

Integration is a matter of fact, not of time. If people on both sides do not fear war and do not prepare for it, it matters little how long it took them to reach this stage. But once integration has been reached, the length of time over which it persists may contribute to its consolidation.

It should be noted that integration and amalgamation overlap, but not completely. This means that there can be amalgamation without integration, and that there can be integration without amalgamation. When we use the term "integration or amalgamation" in this book, we are taking a short form to express an alternative between integration (by the route of either pluralism or amalgamation) and amalgamation short of integration. We have done this because unification movements in the past have often aimed at both of these goals, with some of the supporters of the movements preferring one or the other goal at different times. To encourage this profitable ambiguity, leaders of such movements have often used broader symbols such as "union," which would cover both possibilities and could be made to mean different things to different men.

.   .   .

■   **THE INTEGRATIVE PROCESS:
SOME GENERAL CHARACTERISTICS**

For purposes of exposition, we have divided our findings into two parts: first, general changes in our way of thinking about political integration; and second, specific findings about the background conditions and the dynamic characteristics of the integrative process. . . . [W]e we shall first discuss our general findings. Our more specific findings will follow in later sections. . . .

□   *Reexamining Some Popular Beliefs*

To begin with, our findings have tended to make us increasingly doubtful of several widespread beliefs about political integration. The first of these beliefs is that modern life, with rapid transportation, mass communications, and literacy, tends to be more international than life in past decades or centuries, and hence more conducive to the growth of international or supranational institutions. Neither the study of our cases, nor a survey of more limited data from a larger number of countries, has yielded any clear-cut evidence to support this view. Nor do these results suggest that there has been

inherent in modern economic and social development any unequivocal trend toward more internationalism and world community.

. . .

Another popular belief that our findings make more doubtful is that
the growth of a state, or the expansion of its territory, resembles a
snowballing process, or that it is characterized by some sort of band-
wagon effect, such that successful growth in the past would accelerate the rate of growth or expansion of the amalgamated political
community in the future. In this view, as villages in the past have
joined to make provinces, and provinces to make kingdoms, so contemporary states are expected to join into ever-larger states or federations. If this were true, ever larger political units would appear to be
the necessary result of historical and technological development. Our
findings do not support this view. While the successful unification of
England facilitated the later amalgamation of England and Wales,
and this in turn facilitated the subsequent amalgamation of England
and Wales with Scotland in the union of the two kingdoms, the
united kingdom of Britain did not succeed in carrying through a successful and lasting amalgamation with Ireland. Nor could it retain its
political amalgamation with the American colonies. These seceded
from the British Empire in 1776 to form the United States; and Ireland seceded in effect in the course of the Anglo-Irish civil war of
1918–1921. The unity of the Habsburg monarchy became increasingly strained in the course of the nineteenth century and was followed by disintegration in the twentieth; and so was the more limited
union of the crowns of Norway and Sweden.

. . .

Another popular notion is that a principal motive for the political integration of states has been the fear of anarchy, as well as of warfare
among them. According to this view, men not only came to look
upon war among the units concerned as unpromising and unattractive, but also as highly probable. For they came to fear it acutely
while believing it to be all but inevitable in the absence of any strong
superior power to restrain all participants. Consequently, according
to this theory, one of the first and most important features of a
newly-amalgamated security-community was the establishment of
strong federal or community-wide laws, courts, police forces, and
armies for their enforcement against potentially aggressive member
states and member populations. Beliefs of this kind parallel closely
the classic reasoning of Thomas Hobbes and John Locke; and some
writers on federalism, or on international organization, have implied

a stress on legal institutions and on the problem of coercing member states. Our findings suggest strong qualifications for these views. The questions of larger-community police forces and law enforcement, and of the coercion of member states, turned out to be of minor importance in the early stages of most of the amalgamated security-communities we studied.

.   .   .

This stress on the supposed importance of the early establishment of common laws, courts, and police forces is related to the suggestion that it is necessary to maintain a balance of power among the member states of a larger union or federation, in order to prevent any one state from becoming much stronger than the others. There is much to be said for this point of view: if a member state is far stronger than all the rest together, its political elite may well come to neglect or ignore the messages and needs of the population of the smaller member units, and the resulting loss of responsiveness may prevent integration or destroy it. The evidence from our cases suggests, however, that not merely amalgamation, but also responsiveness and integration can all be achieved and maintained successfully without any such balance of power among the participating states or political units. Neither England within the United Kingdom, nor Prussia in Germany after 1871, nor Piedmont in Italy for some time after 1860, was balanced in power by any other member or group of members, yet each of the larger political communities achieved integration.

.   .   .

□   *General Findings*

Among our positive general findings, the most important seems to us that both amalgamated security-communities and pluralistic security-communities are practicable pathways toward integration. In the course of our research, we found ourselves led by the evidence to attribute a greater potential significance to pluralistic security-communities than we had originally expected. Pluralistic security-communities turned out to be somewhat easier to attain and easier to preserve than their amalgamated counterparts. . . .

The strengths of pluralism. The somewhat smaller risk of breakdown in the case of pluralistic security-communities seems indicated by an examination of the relative numbers of successes and failures of each type of security-community. We can readily list a dozen instances of success for each type. . . .

On the other hand, we find a sharp contrast in the number of failures for each type. We have found only one case of a pluralistic security-community which failed in the sense that it was followed by actual warfare between the participants, and it is doubtful whether a pluralistic security-community existed even in that case: this was the relationship of Austria and Prussia within the framework of the German Confederation since 1815. . . .

On balance, therefore, we found pluralistic security-communities to be a more promising approach to the elimination of war over large areas than we had thought at the outset of our inquiry.

But this relative superiority of a pluralistic security-community as a more easily attainable form of integration has limited applications. It worked only in those situations in which the keeping of the peace among the participating units was the main political goal overshadowing all others. This goal has been the main focus of our study. In our historical cases, however, we found that men have often wanted more: they have wanted a political community that would not merely keep the peace among its members but that would also be capable of acting as a unit in other ways and for other purposes. In respect to this capacity to act—and in particular, to act quickly and effectively for positive goals—amalgamated security-communities have usually been far superior to their pluralistic counterparts. In many historical cases, men have preferred to accept the somewhat greater risk of civil war, or of war among the participating units, in order to insure this greater promise of joint capacity for action. It is only today, in the new age of nuclear weapons, that these risks and gains must be reevaluated. Now a pluralistic security-community may appear a somewhat safer device than amalgamation for dealing with man's new weapons.

The thresholds of integration. Our second general finding concerns the nature of integration. In our earliest analytical scheme, we had envisaged this as an all-or-none process, analogous to the crossing of a narrow threshold. On the one side of this threshold, populations and policy-makers considered warfare among the states or political units concerned as still a serious possibility, and prepared for it; on the other side of the threshold they were supposed to do so no longer. . . .

Somewhat contrary to our expectations, however, some of our cases taught us that integration may involve a fairly broad zone of transition rather than a narrow threshold; that states might cross and recross this threshold or zone of transition several times in their relations with each other; and that they might spend decades or generations wavering uncertainly within it.

Thus we found that states could maintain armed forces which were potentially available for warfare against each other, but which were not specifically committed to this purpose. The American state militias from 1776 to 1865 and the forces of the Swiss cantons from the thirteenth to the nineteenth centuries seem to have been available for such purposes if the political temper of their respective communities had warranted such employment, as it did on a few occasions. It would thus be extraordinarily difficult to say just in which year warfare between the Protestant and Catholic cantons ceased to be a practical political possibility after 1712, or when it again became temporarily a practical possibility between 1815 and 1847; or just when integration within the United States was lost in the period between 1820 and 1861, and warfare between North and South became a substantial possibility.

.   .   .

The threshold of integration thus turned out to be far broader, and far less easy to discern, in our historical cases than we had envisaged at the outset. Not only the approach toward integration, but the very act of crossing the integration threshold, have turned out to be much lengthier and more uncertain processes than had been expected.

Communication and the sense of community. Integration has proved to be a more continuous process than our earliest analytical scheme had suggested; but it continues to be characterized by important thresholds. Within this framework of our revised general concept of integration, we have arrived at a somewhat deeper understanding of the meaning of "sense of community." It appears to rest primarily on something other than verbal assent to some or many explicit propositions. The populations of different territories might easily profess verbal attachment to the same set of values without having a sense of community that leads to political integration. The kind of sense of community that is relevant for integration, and therefore for our study, turned out to be rather a matter of mutual sympathy and loyalties; of "we-feeling," trust, and mutual consideration; of partial identification in terms of self-images and interests; of mutually successful predictions of behavior, and of cooperative action in accordance with it—in short, a matter of a perpetual dynamic process of mutual attention, communication, perception of needs, and responsiveness in the process of decision-making. "Peaceful change" could not be assured without this kind of relationship.

.   .   .

Growth around core areas. As such a process of integrative behavior, sense of community requires some particular habits of political behavior on the part of individuals and some particular traditions and institutions on the part of social groups and of political units, such as provinces or states.

These habits, in turn, are acquired by processes of social learning. People learn them in the face of background conditions which change only slowly, so that they appear at any moment as something given—as political, economic, social, or psychological facts that must be taken for granted for the purposes of short-range politics. The speed and extent of this learning of habits of integrative political behavior are then influenced in each situation by these background conditions, as well as by the dynamics of the particular political process—the particular movement toward integration. Some of our more specific findings deal with the importance of certain background conditions in each area studied, while others deal with the successive stages of the integrative political process that occurred.

The outcome, then, of the integrative process among any particular group of countries depends on the interplay of the effects of background conditions with moving political events. One aspect of this interplay deserves to be singled out for particular attention. It is the matter of political, economic, and social capabilities of the participating political units for integrative behavior.

Generally, we found that such integrative capabilities were closely related to the general capabilities of a given political unit for action in the fields of politics, administration, economic life, and social and cultural development. Larger, stronger, more politically, administratively, economically, and educationally advanced political units were found to form the cores of strength around which in most cases the integrative process developed.

Political amalgamation, in particular, usually turned out to be a nuclear process. It often occurred around single cores, as in the case of England, Piedmont, Prussia, and Sweden. Each of these came to form the core of a larger amalgamated political community (even though the Norwegian-Swedish union turned out to be transitory). . . .

The need for rising capabilities. The extent of integrative capabilities which already existed in the individual political units at the beginning of a major drive toward amalgamation thus turned out to be very important for the future development of the process. But another step was no less important: the further increase of these capabilities in the course of the movement toward amalgamation. The presence or absence of growth in such capabilities played a major role in every integrative process we studied, and particularly in every case of an amalgamation movement.

Generally, amalgamation did not come to pass because the government of the participating units had become weaker or more inefficient; nor did it come to pass because men had been forced to turn away from these increasingly incapable organizations to the building of a larger and less decrepit common government. Rather, amalgamation occurred after a substantial increase in the capabilities of at least some of the participating units, or sometimes of all of them. Examples are the increase in the capabilities of the American colonies before 1789, and in the capabilities of Prussia before 1871. The increase in the capabilities of the political organizations or governments of the individual states, cantons, principalities, and the like, formed a major element in the dynamic political process leading to amalgamation in each instance.

Such capabilities relevant to integration were of two broad kinds. One was related to the capacity to act of a political unit—such as its size, power, economic strength, administrative efficiency, and the like. The other kind was related to the ability of a unit to control its own behavior and to redirect its own attention. More accurately, this means the ability of its political decision-makers and relevant political elites to redirect and control their own attention and behavior so as to enable rulers to receive communications from other political units which were to be their prospective partners in the integrative process. It means, further, the ability to give these messages from other political units adequate weight in the making of their own decisions, to perceive the needs of the populations and elites of these other units, and to respond to them quickly and adequately in terms of political or economic action. The first kind of capabilities—those related to the capacity to act and to overcome external obstacles—are closely linked to what we often call power; the second kind are linked to what we propose to call responsiveness.

.   .   .

The race between capabilities and loads. Another set of data we found to be of crucial importance pertained to the burdens thrown upon the tangible and intangible resources of political units by the requirements of establishing or maintaining either an amalgamated or a pluralistic security-community. Such loads or burdens, as we have called them, were of many kinds. They included military or financial burdens, drains on manpower or wealth; the burden of risk from political or military commitments; costs of social and economic readjustments, such as at the establishment of a customs union; and similar burdens of a material kind. But they also included intangible burdens upon government, which could be visualized as somewhat similar to traffic loads of vehicles at a road intersection or of messages at a telephone exchange. In the cases of crossroads or switchboards, the flow of vehicles or messages requires more than a certain volume of material facilities for its accommodation; it also requires a certain number of decisions which must be made in a limited amount of time by the traffic officer who controls traffic at the intersection, or by the persons or apparatus that control the flow of calls through the telephone exchange.

It is this burden, imposed by the traffic load of messages and signals upon the attention-giving and decision-making capabilities of the persons or organizations in control, that has close parallels in the burden of government upon rulers. It is a burden upon the attention-giving, information-processing, and decision-making capabilities of administrators, political elites, legislatures, or electoral majorities. Thus the failure of the British Parliament to respond quickly and adequately to the disastrous Irish famine of 1846 was not caused primarily by any lack of material or financial resources to provide relief. Rather, the failure was one of adequate attention, perception, and decision-making to meet the burdens of responsibility which the Parliament had taken upon itself under the terms of Anglo-Irish union. It was nonetheless a failure that was to have far-reaching effects upon the future of Anglo-Irish relations.

Political amalgamation in general tended to increase the load of demands upon the material resources and the decision-making capabilities of governments, since decisions for larger areas and populations had to be made by fewer central institutions. The success or failure of amalgamation, then, depended in considerable part upon the relationship of two rates of change: the growing rate of claims and burdens upon central governments as against the growing—in some instances, the insufficiently growing—level of capabilities of the governmental institutions of the amalgamated political community. The load of communications, demands, and claims upon the capabilities of government was also growing from independent causes—such as the increasing complexity of economic life, the increasing level of popular expectations in terms of living standards, social opportunities, and political rights, and the increasing political activity of previously passive groups and strata. Hence the outcome of the race between the growth of loads and capabilities sometimes remained precarious for a longer period, or it changed from one period to another.

.   .   .

■ THE IMPORTANCE OF BACKGROUND CONDITIONS

In general, our cases have left us impressed with the importance of certain background conditions for the success or failure of the integrative process. The influence of background conditions appears to be larger, and the opportunities for decisive action by political leaders or movements appear to be somewhat more limited, than we had thought at the beginning of our study.

To be sure, we found that the importance of a few background conditions had been somewhat overrated. Certain conditions which had often been considered as essential for the establishment of an amalgamated security-community turned out to be helpful to that end but not essential to it. Such helpful but nonessential conditions included previous administrative and/or dynastic union; ethnic or linguistic assimilation; strong economic ties; and foreign military threats. While all of these turned out to be helpful to integration, none of them appeared to be essential since each of them was absent in the successful establishment of at least one amalgamated security-community.

.   .   .

■ SOME ESSENTIAL REQUIREMENTS FOR THE ESTABLISHMENT OF AMALGAMATED SECURITY-COMMUNITIES

A number of conditions appear to be essential, so far as our evidence goes, for the success of amalgamated security-communities—that is, for their becoming integrated. None of these conditions, of course, seems to be by itself sufficient for success; and all of them together may not be sufficient either, for it is quite possible that we have overlooked some additional conditions that may also be essential. Nonetheless, it does seem plausible to us that any group of states or territories which fulfilled all the essential conditions for an amalgamated security-community which we have been able to identify should also be at least on a good part of the way to successful amalgamation.

□ *Values and Expectations*

The first group of essential conditions deals with motivations for political behavior, and in particular with the values and expectations held in the politically relevant strata of the political units concerned. In regard to values, we found in all our cases a compatibility of the main values held by the politically relevant strata of all participating units. Sometimes this was supplemented by a tacit agreement to deprive of political significance any incompatible values that might remain.

. . .

Values were most effective politically when they were not held merely in abstract terms, but when they were incorporated in political institutions and in habits of political behavior which permitted these values to be acted on in such a way as to strengthen people's attachment to them. This connection between values, institutions, and habits we call a "way of life," and it turned out to be crucial. In all our cases of successful amalgamation we found such a distinctive way of life—that is, a set of socially accepted values and of institutional means for their pursuit and attainment, and a set of established or emerging habits of behavior corresponding to them. To be distinctive, such a way of life has to include at least some major social or political values and institutions which are different from those which existed in the area during the recent past, or from those prevailing among important neighbors. In either case, such a way of life usually involved a significant measure of social innovation as against the recent past.

Putting the matter somewhat differently, we noted in our cases that the partial shift of political habits required in transferring political loyalties from the old, smaller political units, at least in part, to a new and larger political community has only occurred under conditions when also a great number of other political and social habits were in a state of change. Thus we find that the perception of an American people and an American political community, as distinct from the individual thirteen colonies, emerged between 1750 and 1790. This occurred at the same time as the emergence of a distinct American way of life clearly different from that of most of the people of Great Britain or French Canada. This way of life had been developing since the beginnings of colonial settlement in the seventeenth century, but had undergone accelerated change and development in the course of the American Revolution and its aftermath. . . .

In regard to expectations, we found that in all our cases amalgamation was preceded by widespread expectations of joint rewards for the participating units, through strong economic ties or gains envisaged for the future. By economic ties, we mean primarily close relations of trade permitting large-scale division of labor and almost always giving rise to vested interests. It was not necessary, however, for such strong economic ties to exist prior to amalgamation. . . . Only a part of such expectation had to be fulfilled. A "down payment" of tangible gains for a substantial part of the supporters of amalgamation soon after the event, if not earlier, seems almost necessary. . . .

Some noneconomic expectations also turned out to be essential. In all our cases of successful amalgamation we found widespread expectations of greater social or political equality, or of greater social or political rights or liberties, among important groups of the politically relevant strata—and often among parts of the underlying populations—in the political units concerned.

□ *Capabilities and Communication Processes*

Values and expectations not only motivate people to performance, but the results of this performance will in turn make the original values and expectations weaker or stronger. Accordingly, we found a number of essential conditions for amalgamation which were related to the capabilities of the participating units or to the processes of communication occurring among them. The most important of these conditions was an increase in the political and administrative capabilities of the main political units to be amalgamated. Thus the amalgamation of Germany was preceded by a marked increase in the political and administrative capabilities of Prussia from 1806 onward, and by a lesser but still significant increase in the corresponding capabilities of Bavaria and of other German states. . . .

Another essential condition for amalgamation, closely related to the increase in capabilities, is the presence of markedly superior economic growth, either as measured against the recent past of the territories to be amalgamated, or against neighboring areas. Such superior economic growth did not have to be present in all participating units prior to amalgamation, but it had to be present it least in the main partner or partners vis-à-vis the rest of the units to be included in the amalgamated security-community. . . .

Another essential requirement for successful amalgamation was the presence of unbroken links of social communication between the political units concerned, and between the politically relevant strata within them. By such unbroken links we mean social groups and institutions which provide effective channels of communication, both horizontally among the main units of the amalgamated security-community and vertically among the politically relevant strata within them. Such links thus involve always persons and organizations.

·   ·   ·

[A final] essential condition, related to the preceding one, is the broadening of the political, social, or economic elite, both in regard to its recruitment from broader social strata and to its continuing connections with them. An example of such a broadening of the elite was the emergence of a new type of political leader among the landowners of Virginia, such as George Washington, who retained the respect of his peers and at the same time also knew, well before the American Revolution, how to gain the votes of poorer farmers and frontiersmen at the county elections in Virginia. . . .

□ *Mobility of Persons*

Another condition present in all our cases of successful amalgamation was the mobility of persons among the main units, at least in the politically relevant strata. It is quite possible that this condition, too, may be essential for the success of amalgamation. In any event, our cases have persuaded us that the mobility of persons among the main political units of a prospective amalgamated security-community should be given far more serious consideration than has often been the case. Full-scale mobility of persons has followed every successful amalgamated security-community in modern times immediately upon its establishment. . . .

□ *Multiplicity and Balance of Transactions*

We also found that it was not enough for a high level of communications and transactions to exist only on one or two topics, or in one or two respects, among two or more political units if their amalgamation was to be successful. Rather it appeared that successfully amalgamated security-communities require a fairly wide range of different common functions and services, together with different institutions and organizations to carry them out. Further, they apparently require a multiplicity of ranges of common communications and transactions and their institutional counterparts. . . .

Two other conditions may well turn out to be essential for the success of amalgamation, but these will have to be investigated further. The first of them is concerned with the balance in the flow of communications and transactions between the political units that are to be amalgamated, and particularly with the balance of rewards between the different participating territories. It is also concerned with the balance of initiatives that originate in these territories or groups of population, and finally with the balance of respect—or of symbols standing for respect—between these partners. In the course of studying cases of successful amalgamation, we found that it was apparently important for each of the participating territories or populations to gain some valued services or opportunities. It also seemed important that each at least sometimes take the initiative in the process, or initiate some particular phase or contribution; and that some major symbol or representative of each territory or population should be accorded explicit respect by the others. . . .

The second condition follows from the preceding one. It was not essential that the flow of rewards, of initiatives, or of respect should balance at any one moment, but it seems essential that they should balance over some period of time. Sometimes this was accomplished by alternating flows or by an interchange of group roles. Territories which received particular prestige, or material benefits, at one time might become sources of benefits for their partners at another; or territories whose political elites found themselves ranged with a majority on one political issue might find themselves in a minority on another, without any one particular division between majorities and minorities becoming permanent. . . .

□ *Mutual Predictability of Behavior*

A final condition that may be essential for the success of amalgamation may be some minimum amount of mutual predictability of behavior. Members of an amalgamated security-community—and, to a lesser extent, of a pluralistic security-community—must be able to expect from one another some dependable interlocking, interchanging, or at least compatible behavior; and they must therefore be able, at least to that extent, to predict one another's actions. Such predictions may be based on mere familiarity. . . . While familiarity appears to have contributed successfully to the growth of mutual trust in some of our cases, such as that between Scottish Highlanders and Lowlanders, and later between Scots and Englishmen, or between German, French, and Swiss during much of the eighteenth century, we found in a number of our cases that mutual predictability of behavior was eventually established upon a firmer basis.

This firmer basis was the acquisition of a certain amount of common culture or of common group character or "national character." In this manner, an increasing number of Germans in the German states, of Italians in the Italian principalities, and of Americans in the American colonies, came to feel that they could understand their countrymen in the neighboring political units by expecting them, by and large, to behave much as they themselves would behave in similar situations; that is to say, they came to predict the behavior of their countrymen in neighboring political units on the basis of introspection: by looking into their own minds they could make a fairly good guess as to what their neighbors would do, so they could trust them or at least understand them, to some extent much as they would trust or understand themselves. The extent of mutual predictability of behavior, however, seems to have varied from case to case, and it also seems to have varied with the particular political elites or relevant strata concerned. That some mutual predictability of political behavior is an essential condition for an amalgamated security-community seems clear from our cases; but the extent of such predictability must remain a matter for further research.

□ *Summary*

Altogether we have found nine essential conditions for an amalgamated security-community: (1) mutual compatibility of main values; (2) a distinctive way of life; (3) expectations of stronger economic ties or gains; (4) a marked increase in political and administrative capabilities of at least some participating units; (5) superior economic growth on the part of at least some participating units; (6) unbroken links of social communication, both geographically between territories and sociologically between different social strata; (7) a broadening of the political elite; (8) mobility of persons, at least among the politically relevant strata; and, (9) a multiplicity of ranges of communication and transaction. And we have found indications that three other conditions may be essential: (10) a compensation of flows of communications and transactions; (11) a not too infrequent interchange of group roles; and, (12) considerable mutual predictability of behavior.

·   ·   ·

■ **BACKGROUND CONDITIONS CONDUCIVE TO DISINTEGRATION**

Several conditions were found present in all cases of disintegration of amalgamated political communities which we studied, and they appear likely to promote disintegration wherever they occur. This does not mean, however, that they are sufficient by themselves to produce disintegration. We have found these conditions also present in some cases where disintegration did not follow but where other factors favoring integration were present in particular strength. The establishment and preservation of amalgamated security-communities thus turned out to depend upon a balance of favorable and adverse conditions. Amalgamation does not seem likely to be established, or to persist, except in the presence of the nine essential conditions for amalgamation which we listed earlier in this chapter; but even in their presence, the disintegrative conditions which we shall discuss below could prevent, destroy, or at least endanger an amalgamated security-community.

In our earlier general discussion, we have described integration as a process depending upon a balance between political loads upon a government, and its capabilities for maintaining amalgamation, or its capabilities for maintaining integration within a pluralistic security-community. In accordance with this general view, we may group the disintegrative conditions in our cases under two headings: conditions that increased the burdens upon amalgamated governments, and conditions that reduced the capability of such governments to cope with the burdens put upon them.

One of the outstanding conditions that tended to destroy amalgamated security-communities by placing excessive burdens upon them was the effect of excessive military commitments. Common armies with light burdens and conspicuous gains in prestige or privileges, or short wars of similar character, were helpful, though not essential, to the deeper integration of a political community; but heavy military burdens with few conspicuous gains over the *status quo* tended to have the opposite effect.

.   .   .

Another condition which tended to increase greatly the load upon governments, and thus tended to disintegrate amalgamated security-communities, was a substantial increase in political participation on the part of populations, regions, or social strata which previously had been politically passive. Such a substantial increase in political participation meant in each case that the needs, wishes, and pressures of additional social strata or regions had to be accommodated within an old system of political decision-making that might be—and often was—ill-suited to respond to them adequately and in time. . . .

A further disintegrative condition related to this rise in political participation is the increase in ethnic or linguistic differentiation. Another aspect of the same condition is a rise in the political awareness of such differentiation as already may exist. Both of these are likely to be a consequence of the rise in political participation among groups that are already thus differentiated, in language and culture, from the predominant nationality or regional-cultural group within the political community in question. . . .

Another group of disintegrative conditions tends to weaken or destroy amalgamated security-communities by reducing the capabilities of their governments and political elites for adequate and timely action or response. One such condition in our cases appeared to be any prolonged economic decline or stagnation, leading to economic conditions comparing unfavorably with those in neighboring areas.

Another disintegrative condition of this kind was the relative closure of the established political elite. This tended to promote the rise of frustrated counter-elites, somewhat in Pareto's sense, among ethnic or cultural out-groups, or in outlying regions.

Another disintegrative condition, related to the foregoing, was the excessive delay in social, economic, or political reforms which had come to be expected by the population—reforms which sometimes had already been adopted in neighboring areas.

· · ·

■ SPECIAL FEATURES OF PLURALISTIC SECURITY-COMMUNITIES

In regard to the problem of a pluralistic security-community, we found that its attainment would be favored by any conditions favorable to the success of an amalgamated security-community, and that it was sometimes hindered by conditions or processes harmful to the latter. Pluralistic security-communities sometimes succeeded, however, under far less favorable conditions than the success of an amalgamated government would have required; and they sometimes survived unfavorable or disintegrative processes which would have destroyed an amalgamated political community.

· · ·

Of the twelve conditions that appeared to be essential for the success of an amalgamated security-community, or at least potentially so, only two or possibly three were found to be very important for a pluralistic security-community as well. The first of these was the compatibility of major values relevant to political decision-making. The second was the capacity of the participating political units or governments to respond to each other's needs, messages, and actions quickly, adequately, and without resort to violence. . . . A third essential condition for a pluralistic security-community may be mutual predictability of behavior; this appears closely related to the foregoing. But the member-states of a pluralistic security-community have to make joint decisions only about a more limited range of subject matters, and retain each a far wider range of problems for autonomous decision-making within their own borders. Consequently the range and extent of the mutual predictability of behavior required from members of a pluralistic security-community is considerably less than would be essential for the successful operation of an amalgamated one.

. . .

Altogether, our findings in the field of background conditions tend to bring out the great and potentially restrictive importance of these conditions for the establishment and preservation of amalgamated security-communities. Further, our findings tend to bring out the very considerable potentialities of pluralistic security-communities for overcoming even partially unfavorable background situations.

■   **POLITICAL INTEGRATION AS A DYNAMIC PROCESS**

The transition from background to process is fluid. The essential background conditions do not come into existence all at once; they are not established in any particular fixed sequence; nor do they all grow together like one organism from a seed. Rather, it appears to us from our cases that they may be assembled in almost any sequence, so long only as all of them come into being and take effect. Toward this end, almost any pathway will suffice. As each essential condition is fulfilled, it is added, one by one or a few at a time, as strands are added to a web, or as parts are put together on an assembly line.

So long as this assembling of conditions occurs very slowly, we may treat the status of each condition and the status of all of them together at any one time as a matter of stable, seemingly unchanging background. Indeed, in our historical cases they were so considered, as practically unchanged or slow-changing situations, by most of their contemporaries. But as the last of the conditions in each sequence are added to those whose attainment was assembled previously, the tempo of the process quickens. Background and process now become one. A multiplicity of ranges of social communication and transaction was a background condition for amalgamation, but the rapid adding of new ranges of such communications and transactions is a process. Moreover, it is a process that may become accelerated as a by-product of other processes of political and social change. A balance of flows of transactions between the different units eligible for amalgamation is another of the necessary background conditions for amalgamation. This is particularly true in regard to a balance of initiatives, of rewards, and of respect. But substantial progress toward the establishment of some such balance may be a matter of political process, or else a political process directed toward the attainment of amalgamation may produce a better balance of transaction flows as one of its by-products.

·   ·   ·

■ THE ISSUE OF FUNCTIONALISM AS A
PATHWAY TO AMALGAMATION

Our finding that the bringing together of the necessary background conditions for amalgamation in our cases resembled an assembly-line process suggests indirectly an answer to an old question: does merging of one or more governmental functions among two or more political units promote progress toward later over-all amalgamation of their governments? Or, on the contrary, does what we shall call functional amalgamation impede such over-all amalgamation by inadequate performance of the few already amalgamated functions? Does it take the wind from the sails of the movement for full-scale amalgamation by making the few already amalgamated functions serve adequately the main needs which had supplied most of the driving power for the over-all amalgamation movement?

Before we answer this question, we must say exactly what we mean by functionalism. As we are using the term here, it includes all cases of partial amalgamation, where some governmental functions are delegated by the participating units on a low or a high level of decision-making. Whether a particular function or institution is so important that its pooling with another government would have the effect of over-all amalgamation rather than partial—and thus take it out of the field of functionalism—depends on the importance of this particular function or institution in the domestic politics of the participating units.

·   ·   ·

How helpful, then, has functionalism been? We have found, first of all, that over-all amalgamation can be approached functionally and by steps, with successful over-all amalgamation at the end. This occurred in the cases of Germany with the Zollverein (of which, significantly, Austria was not a member); the United States with the common administration of Western lands under the Articles of Confederation; the Swiss cantons since the fourteenth century, and the common citizenship between Geneva, Bern, and Fribourg, and later other Swiss cantons from the sixteenth century onward; finally, between England and Wales and England and Scotland before the union of crowns preceding full amalgamation. In all these cases amalgamation eventually was successful. But functional amalgamation was also proposed and rejected among the Italian states in the 1840's, and eventually amalgamation was achieved without its aid. Moreover, functional amalgamation took place in at least three of our cases that were eventually unsuccessful: there was the union of crowns between Austria, Bohemia, and Hungary from 1526 onward; there was the union of crowns between Norway and Sweden in 1814; and there were various forms of partial amalgamation between England and Ireland before 1801.

These examples are taken from a sample collection of historical cases and situations in which instances of successful amalgamation outnumber the unsuccessful ones by more than two to one. From this it should be clear that the historical evidence in favor of functionalism is quite inconclusive.

It seems safest to conclude that the issue of functionalism has been greatly overrated. Functionalism, it appears, is a device that has been widely used both in successful and in unsuccessful movements toward amalgamation, somewhat as functional devolution and decentralization have been used in successful and in unsuccessful attempts at secession. The outcome in all such situations seems mostly to have been the result of other conditions and other processes—depending largely on whether functionalism mainly was associated with experiences of joint rewards or of joint deprivations—with functionalism in itself doing little to help or to harm. . . . Perhaps the most that can be said for functionalism as an approach to integration is that it seems less hazardous than any sudden attempt at over-all amalgamation.

.   .   .

15 The Uniting of Europe

ERNST B. HAAS

Ernst B. Haas (University of California–Berkeley), an immigrant born in Frankfurt, was among the U.S. social scientists applying behavioral methods to international relations in the 1950s. In 1958 he published a book entitled The Uniting of Europe: Political, Social, and Economic Forces, 1950–1957 *in which he used the European Coal and Steel Community as a case study in an attempt to dissect the "actual 'integration process'. . . to derive propositions about its nature." Haas recognized that functional integration was taking place in Europe, but that functionalism as a theory had failed to explain why decision-makers chose to integrate in some areas and not others. Functionalism needed a theory of politics, which Haas provided.*

Haas first defined political integration as "the process whereby political actors in several distinct national settings are persuaded to shift their loyalties, expectations and political activities toward a new center, whose institutions possess or demand jurisdiction over the pre-existing national states." Then he drew on democratic theory, systems theory, group theory, and a host of other approaches to produce a scientifically rigorous explanation for European political integration that he also believed held predictive power. This neofunctionalist approach (here introduced by Haas in the preface to The Uniting of Europe *and described in greater detail by Leon Lindberg in Chapter 16) views the integration process as group driven. Federal institutions are established because important political groups see tangible benefits from joint governance in specific areas. The integration process pushes forward when federal institutions affect the interests of groups that respond by organizing across national boundaries and pushing for more integration. Thus integration in one area spills over into another when groups perceive it in their interest.*

Haas wrote prolifically on integration in the 1960s and early 1970s as the acknowledged leader of the neofunctionalist school. Neofunctionalism, while no longer as dominant as it was in the 1960s, is still very influential. And Ernst Haas is still widely read.

"United Europe" is a phrase meaning many things to many men. To some it implies the creation of a full-fledged federation of the independent states of Western Europe, either the Six of "Schumania" or the Fifteen of the Council of Europe. To others the phrase means no more than the desirability of creating a loose concert or confederation. Some see in it the guarantee for future greatness, a political, economic and cultural renaissance for the Old Continent, about to be eclipsed by the United States, the Soviet world, and perhaps the Arab-Asians. But others identify it with the death of cherished patterns of national uniqueness. Even government policy, on both sides of the Atlantic, sometimes hesitates between endorsing the creation of a new center of economic and political power and fearing the evolution of a high-tariff region or of institutionalized "third force" sentiments. One must add the still lively controversy over whether economic or military unification, or both, is possible without prior or simultaneous political federation. The arguments over the merits and types of unification have continued since the end of World War II; they are unlikely to be exhausted soon.

But for the political scientist the unification of Europe has a peculiar attraction quite irrespective of merits and types. He may see in it, as I do, an instance of voluntary "integration" taking place before his eyes, as it were under laboratory conditions. He will wish to study it primarily because it is one of the very few current situations in which the decomposition of old nations can be systematically analyzed within the framework of the evolution of a larger polity—a polity destined, perhaps, to develop into a nation of its own. Hence, my purpose is not the evaluation of the virtues and drawbacks of a United Europe in terms of European, American, national, international, free-enterprise, or welfare-state values. Nor is it an analysis of the advantages of federation over intergovernmental cooperation, economic over military unity. My aim is merely the dissection of the actual "integration process" in order to derive propositions about its nature. Hence, I focused my analysis on selected groups, institutions and ideologies which have already been demonstrated to act as unifying agents in political systems clearly "integrated" by any applicable standard. Further, I confined the analysis to the impact of the one organization whose powers, functions and composition make it *a priori* capable of redirecting the loyalties and expectations of political actors: the European Coal and Steel Community. My study, then, attempts to advance generalizations about the processes by which political communities are formed among sovereign states, and my method is to select specific political groups and institutions, to study their reactions to a new species of "federal" government, and to analyze the impact of that government in terms of the reactions caused. On the assumption that "integration" is a two-way process in which the central institutions affect and are affected by the subject groups, the Coal and Steel Community is to serve as a case study illustrating the effects on the totality of interactions.

.   .   .

The essential conclusions may be briefly summarized. The initiation of a deliberate scheme of political unification, to be accepted by the key groups that make up a pluralistic society, does not require absolute majority support, nor need it rest on identical aims on the part of all participants. The European Coal and Steel Community was initially accepted because it offered a multitude of different advantages to different groups. Acceptance of a federal scheme is facilitated if the participating state units are already fragmented ideologically and socially. Moreover, the acceptance of such a scheme is considerably eased if among the participating industrial, political, or labor groups there is a tradition, however vague, of mutual consultation and of rudimentary value sharing. A helpful, but by no means indispensable, condition is the existence of an external threat, real or imagined.

Once established, the central institution will affect political integration meaningfully only if it is willing to follow policies giving rise to expectations and demands for more—or fewer—federal measures. In either case, the groups concerned will organize across national state boundaries in order to be able to influence policy. If the central institution, however, fails to assert itself in any way so as to cause strong positive or negative expectations, its impact on unity will be as small as the integrative role of such technically powerful international administrative unions as the Danube Commissions or the Universal Postal Union. As far as the industrial groups—business and labor—are concerned, they tend to unite beyond their former national confines in an effort to make common policy and obtain common benefits. Thus perhaps the chief finding is that group pressure will spill over into the federal sphere and thereby add to the integrative impulse. Only industries convinced that they have nothing to gain from integration will hold out against such pressures. But industrial sectors initially opposed to integration for a variety of motives do change their attitude and develop strong positive expectations if they feel that certain common problems can be more easily met by a federal authority. More commonly still, groups are likely to turn to the federal authority for help in the solution of purely national problems if the local government proves uncooperative. Groups with strong initial positive expectations do not necessarily turn against the principle of integration if their hopes are disappointed: they merely intensify their efforts to obtain the desired advantages on the federal level, thus integrating themselves into organizations less and less dependent on and identified with the national state. Political parties, if allowance is made for their varying ideologies and constituencies, tend to fall into the same pattern. National governments, operating in the nexus of all these forces, may on occasion attempt to sidestep, ignore, or sabotage the decisions of the federal authority. The study of the Coal and Steel Community shows, however, that governments also recognize a point beyond which such evasions are unprofitable, and that in the long run they tend to defer to federal decisions, lest the example of their recalcitrance set a precedent for other governments.

After five years of activity, the pattern of supranational pressure and counter-pressure has become apparent: groups, parties, and governments have reassessed and reformulated their aims in such a way that the drive for a United Europe has become the battle cry of the Left. The "sinistration" of federalism has been accomplished in the recognition of trade unions and Socialist parties that their version of the welfare state and of peace can rationally be achieved only in a federated Western Europe. Perhaps the most salient conclusion we can draw from the community-building experiment is the fact that major interest groups as well as politicians determine their support of, or opposition to, new central institutions and policies on the basis of a calculation of advantage. The "good Europeans" are not the main creators of the regional community that is growing up; the process of community formation is dominated by nationally constituted groups with specific interests and aims, willing and able to adjust their aspirations by turning to supranational means when this course appears profitable.

Our study thus substantiates the pluralistic thesis that a larger political community can be developed if the crucial expectations, ideologies, and behavior patterns of certain key groups can be successfully refocussed on a new set of central symbols and institutions. Yet this conclusion also begs the question of the generality of the process laid bare. Can larger political communities be created on this basis in all sections of the world, in all ages, irrespective of the specific powers initially given to the central authority? I suggest that the value of this case study is confined to the kind of setting which reproduces in essence the physical conditions, ideologies, class structure, group relations, and political traditions and institutions of contemporary Western Europe. In short, I maintain that these findings *are* sufficiently general in terms of the socio-political context to serve as propositions concerning the formation of political communities—*provided* we are dealing with (1) an industrialized economy deeply enmeshed in international trade and finance, (2) societies in which the masses are fully mobilized politically and tend to channel their aspirations through permanent interest groups and political parties, (3) societies in which these groups are habitually led by identifiable elites competing with one another for influence and in disagreement on many basic values, and (4) societies in which relations among these elites are governed by the traditions and assumptions of parliamentary (or presidential) democracy and constitutionalism. It may well be that the specific economic conditions under which the European coal and steel industries operate act as additional factors limiting the possibility of generalizing. Monopolistic competition and the prevalence of private ownership are such factors, though isolated pockets of nationalized industry exist in the total industrial complex. It may also be true that the impact of an overwhelmingly powerful external economic center acts as a limiting condition. Economic integration in Europe might have been much slower if the governments had been compelled to come to grips with investment, currency and trade questions—decisions which were in effect spared them by the direct and indirect role of United States economic policy. Hence, I would have little hesitation in applying the technique of analysis here used to the study of integration under NATO, the Scandinavian setting, the Organization for European Economic Co-operation, or Canadian-United States relations. I would hesitate to claim validity for it in the study of regional political integration in Latin America, the Middle East, or South-East Asia.

. . .

Political Integration: Definitions and Hypotheses

LEON N. LINDBERG

Leon Lindberg (University of Wisconsin–Madison), one of Haas's students at Berkeley, helped define and advance neofunctionalism with the publication of three books in the 1960s and early 1970s. In the first chapter of The Political Dynamics of European Economic Integration *(1963), Lindberg illustrates early neofunctionalism's systematic approach to explaining integration, as well as its enthusiasm for a European project that promised to "move beyond the nation-state as a basic framework for action." Lindberg first draws on Haas to define "political integration," then goes on to identify conditions for integration. The central roles played by political actors are key to Lindberg's view of the integration process. New central institutions, for instance, help "precipitate unity"; political groups "restructure their expectations and activities" in response to integration; and member states must possess "the will to proceed" if integration is to continue. Also important is the role of "spillover," which propels integration forward as cooperation in one area spills over into other areas. Lindberg does not argue that spillover is inevitable (and thus integration, once started, will proceed indefinitely), but he does display a faith in its power that is not yet tempered by Charles de Gaulle and the Luxembourg Compromise.*

Neofunctionalism proved fertile and flexible in the 1960s and early 1970s. Numerous scholars in international relations and comparative politics applied their considerable energies to dissecting the integration process. Several empirical and theoretical problems cropped up along the way, but creative thinkers modified neofunctionalism to settle most of the issues. By 1970, the theory was rigorously specified but very complex—hardly the elegant model of the early 1960s. Problems with the theory continued to mount in the early 1970s, and in 1975 Ernst Haas declared regional integration theory (read neofunctionalism) "obsolescent." Most neofunctionalists took Haas's hint and moved on to other theories of international political economy, such as interdependence theory and regime theory. But neofunctionalism did not die, as we shall see in Part 3.

The Europe that gave birth to the idea of the nation state appears to be well on the way to rejecting it in practice. The Treaty establishing the European Economic Community (EEC), signed in Rome on 25 March 1957, represents the latest in a series of steps designed to break down the bastions of European national separatism. Its six signatories, France, Germany, Italy, Belgium, the Netherlands, and Luxembourg, were already members of the European Coal and Steel Community (ECSC), whose foundation in 1952 had created a common market restricted to coal and steel. The experience with this first effort at sector integration led ultimately to the creation of the EEC as well as the European Atomic Energy Community (EURATOM):

> It soon became evident that integration by sectors could only yield limited results. Its restricted scope, unconnected with the other parts of the economic and financial system, ruled out any large-scale activities and made it impossible to achieve an overall equilibrium. To sweep away from Europe protectionism and economic nationalism with their resulting high production costs, high costs of living and economic stagnation, a different approach was required, a wide attack in more than one dimension as it were; it must have the depth of integration and the wide scope of a freeing of trade. This approach was provided first by the Beyen Plan and then by the Spaak Report, which marked the first step towards the Common Market.

The EEC has as its primary goal the creation of an area in which goods, people, services, and capital will be able to circulate freely. To achieve this, a customs union is created, but a customs union in which attention is devoted not only to barriers between states, but to economic, financial, and social reactions that may take place in the member states. The main purpose is the abolition of trade barriers, tariffs, and quotas, which is to be accomplished more or less automatically during a twelve- to fifteen-year transition period, divided into three four-year stages. A series of targets is assigned to each stage, and these relate not only to progress in removal of trade barriers, but also to parallel measures of economic and social alignment. This process is to be accompanied by the establishment of a common external tariff, within which an alignment of the several economies is to go on in order to adjust differences in price and working conditions, and in productive resources. Advancement from one stage to another is dependent upon achieving these respective targets. All this is to be supervised by institutions specially set up by the Treaty.

The economic and social significance of these developments is certainly far-reaching—one need only read the newspapers to confirm this. For the political scientist, too, they are of consuming interest, for here he can observe the actual processes whereby political actors move beyond the nation state as a basic framework for action, appearing finally to realize the oft-proclaimed "fact" of the international interdependence of nations. Forces are at work in Western Europe that may alter the nature of international relations, as well as offer promise of a fuller and more prosperous life for the inhabitants of the region.

The stated goal of the EEC is the creation of a customs union and ultimately the achievement of a significant measure of economic integration. The fundamental motivation is political. It is, in the words of the Treaty, to establish "an ever closer union among the European peoples." Our concern will be with the political *consequences* of economic integration. We shall try to measure the extent to which the creation of the EEC and the activities which take place in its framework give rise to the phenomenon of political integration. Whereas in terms of commercial policy the establishment of the EEC is "already the most important event of this century," its vast political significance is still only a potential.

■ POLITICAL INTEGRATION

What, then, do we mean by political integration? Some writers define it as a *condition,* and others as a *process.* In the works of Karl W. Deutsch, integration refers to the probability that conflicts will be resolved without violence. The central concept is that of a "security-community," which is "a group of people which has become integrated": that is, they have attained "within a territory . . . a 'sense of community' and . . . institutions and practices strong enough and widespread enough to assure, for a 'long' time, dependable expectations of 'peaceful change' among its population." Integration may come about through several types of security-communities, "amalgamated" or "pluralistic," implying respectively either the presence or the absence of any real central decision-making institutions or delegations of national autonomy. In either case, integration is achieved when the states concerned cease to prepare for war against each other.

Similarly, North, Koch, and Zinnes list six criteria in terms of which one can consider integration: the probability of violence given a conflict situation (same as Deutsch); the frequency of conflicts between any given number of organizations in a given span of time; the number of compatible policy conditions; the degree of interdependency between n given organizations; the number and significance of interlocking communications systems or structures; and the extent to which membership overlaps.

Such conceptualizations of political integration as a *condition* have been criticized on the grounds that they permit only a general discussion of the environmental factors influencing integration, and that they fail to provide us with the tools needed to make a clear distinction between the situation prior to integration and the situation prevailing during the process, thus obscuring the role of social change. For these reasons, Haas insists that we should look at political integration as a *process:* "Political integration is the process whereby political actors in several distinct national settings are persuaded to shift their loyalties, expectations and political activities toward a new center, whose institutions possess or demand jurisdiction over the preexisting national states. The end result of a process of political integration is a new political community, superimposed over the preexisting ones."

In Haas's work, this definition is rigorously tied to an ideal-type analysis in which the institutions of the ECSC are compared to those of an ideal federal-type system. This kind of heuristic device is certainly above reproach and did in fact yield extremely valuable results. My own investigations, however, have led me to adopt a more cautious conception of political integration, one limited to the development of devices and processes for arriving at collective decisions by means other than autonomous action by national governments. It seems to me that it is logically and empirically possible that collective decision-making procedures involving a significant amount of political integration can be achieved without moving toward a "political community" as defined by Haas. In fact, use of this type of ideal, or model, analysis may well direct the researcher to a different set of questions and a different interpretation of the data collected:

European integration is developing, and may continue so for a
long time, in the direction of different units. . . . We can only
speculate about the outcome, but a forecast of the emergence of
a pluralistic political structure, hitherto unknown, might not be
wholly erroneous. Such a structure might very well permit to a
great extent the participating nations to retain their identity
while yet joined in the organizations that transcend nationality.

For the purpose of this study, political integration will be defined
as a *process*, but without reference to an end point. In specific terms,
political integration is (1) the process whereby nations forgo the desire
and ability to conduct foreign and key domestic policies independently
of each other, seeking instead to make *joint decisions* or to *delegate* the
decision-making process to new central organs; and (2) the process
whereby political actors in several distinct settings are persuaded to
shift their expectations and political activities to a new center.

Although this dual definition lacks the analytical clarity and pre-
cision of model analysis, it is, I believe, appropriate to the problem at
hand. Not only does it provide us with a set of interrelated indicators
by means of which to judge the experience of the EEC, but it specifies
what I take to be the process of political integration. The first part of
the definition refers to two modes of decisionmaking which are, in my
opinion, intimately related, the existence of delegated decisionmaking
being a basic precondition for progress in shared decisionmaking. The
processes of *sharing* and of *delegating* decisionmaking are likely to affect the governmental structure in each state involved, creating new
internal problems of coordination and policy direction, especially between Ministries of Foreign Affairs and such specialized ministries as
Economic Affairs, Agriculture, and Labor that are accustomed to regarding their spheres as wholly or primarily of domestic concern.
States with traditions of representative and parliamentary government
are also faced with the problem created by the development of decision-making centers whose authority derives from an international,
rather than a national, consensus.

The second part of the definition refers to the patterns of behavior shown by high policy makers, civil servants, parliamentarians, interest-group leaders, and other elites. Here our attention is directed to
the perceptions and resulting behavior of the political actors in each
of the states involved. The relationship between this set of indicators
and those referring to governmental decisionmaking is very close. By
the nature of the process, government policy-makers and civil servants
are involved increasingly in the new system of decisionmaking: they
attend meetings of experts, draft plans, and participate in an over-all
joint decision-making pattern. Similarly, as the locus of decisionmak-

ing changes, so will the tactics of groups and individuals seeking to influence the decision-making process. They may oppose the change, but once made they will have to adjust to it by changing their tactics, or their organization, or both, to accommodate to the new situation. In Haas's words: "Conceived not as a condition but as a *process,* the conceptualization [of political integration] relies on the perception of interests . . . by the actors participating in the process. Integration takes place when these perceptions fall into a certain pattern and fails to take place when they do not." Moreover, "as the process of integration proceeds, it is assumed . . . that interests will be redefined in terms of regional rather than a purely national orientation."

So much for defining the concept of political integration. The problem now is to try to spell out how it can be made to occur in actual life. Since there have been numerous efforts at transnational organization and cooperation that have not had political results of this kind, political scientists have tried to identify constant background, or environmental, factors or conditions upon which political integration is contingent. Thus Deutsch isolates the following conditions as essential or helpful for a pluralistic or amalgamated security-community: initially compatible value systems, mutually responsive elites, adequate communications channels, a commitment to a "new way of life," and the existence of a "core area." Similarly, Haas calls for a pluralistic social structure, a high level of economic and industrial development, and a modicum of ideological homogeneity.

But the examination of background factors or conditions does not help us account completely for the *process* of political integration, nor does it permit differentiation between the situation prior to integration and the situation prevailing during the process. Accordingly, it is necessary to try to identify some additional variable factors to specify *how* political integration occurs. On the basis of Haas's researches and my own experiences in Western Europe, I suggest that the process of political integration requires the following conditions: (1) Central institutions and central policies must develop. (2) The tasks assigned to these institutions must be important enough and specific enough to activate socioeconomic processes to which conventional international organizations have no access. (3) These tasks must be inherently expansive. (4) The member states must continue to see their interests as consistent with the enterprise.

■ CENTRAL INSTITUTIONAL DEVELOPMENT

Central institutions are required in order to *represent* the common interests which have brought the member states together, and in order to *accommodate* such conflicts of interest as will inevitably arise. In discussing the institutions of the EEC, I prefer to avoid the concept of "supranationality" and to focus instead on the extent to which the Community institutions are enabled to deal directly with fields of activity, rather than merely influencing the actions of individual governments in respect of these fields. There are four main aspects to be considered:

1. North, Koch, and Zinnes seek to distinguish between compromise and "true integration," both seen as ways of dealing with conflict. Both depend upon *reducing the intensity* of the conflict by uncovering its sources, and by taking the demands of both sides and breaking them into their constituent parts. Each party to the conflict is forced to reexamine and reevaluate its own desires against those of the other party and against the implications of the total situation. True integration is achieved when a solution has been found in which "both desires have found a place," in which the interests of the parties "fit into each other." I suggest that the central institutions of the EEC, by isolating issues and identifying common interests, may play a crucial role here in "precipitating unity."

2. The integrative impact of the central institutions will depend in part upon the *competencies* and *roles* assigned to them. Much, however, depends upon whether or not the institutions make full use of their competencies and upon *how they define their role*. The literature on organizational decisionmaking suggests some relevant questions in this context. What formal and informal decisionmaking and relational patterns will develop? What patterns of commitment will be enforced by organizational imperatives, by the social character of the personnel, by "institutionalization," by the social and cultural environment, and by centers of interest generated in the course of action and decision? I suggest that the early years of the existence of these institutions will be significant in determining their long-range competence, that patterns of internal differentiation and conflicting values will develop, that organizational behavior will be conditioned by the necessity of adjusting to the environment, and that cooptation will be used as a tactic to head off opposition.

3. Central institutions lacking real competency to affect policymaking directly may develop a *consensus* that will influence those national or international decision makers who do determine policy.

4. Finally, the patterns of interaction engendered by the central institutions may affect *the overall system* in which they operate; in other words, these institutions may have latent effects that contribute to political integration. Participants in the activities of central institu-

tions may develop multiple perspectives, personal friendships, a camaraderie of expertise, all of which may reflect back upon the national governments and affect future national policymaking. Such latent effects, however, are significant only if the individuals concerned are influential at the national level, *and* if their activities in the central institutions involve significant policymaking.

■ ELITE ACTIVATION

Thanks to the efforts of the so-called "group theorists," political scientists today know that any analysis of the political process must give a central place to the phenomena of group conflict, to the beliefs, attitudes, and ideologies of groups participating in the process of policy formation. If political integration, as we have defined it, is going on, then we would expect to find a change in the behavior of the participants. Consequently we must identify the aims and motives of the relevant political groups, the conditions of their emergence, and the means by which they seek and attain access to centers of political power.

One of the main obstacles to political integration has been the fact that international organizations lack direct access to individuals and groups in the national communities involved. "Short of such access, the organization continues to be no more than a forum of intergovernmental consultation and cooperation."

Actors with political power in the national community will restructure their expectations and activities only if the tasks granted to the new institutions are of immediate concern to them, and only if they involve a significant change in the conditions of the actors' environment. Several patterns of reaction may be expected:

1. Individual firms may undertake measures of self-protection or adjustment in the form of cartels to limit competition, the conclusion of agreements, and so on.
2. Groups may change their political organization and tactics in order to gain access to, and to influence, such new central decision-making centers as may be developing.
3. These activities may act back upon the central institutions and the member states by creating situations that cannot be dealt with except by further central institutional development and new central policies. An example would be a developing need for antitrust legislation in response to an evolving network of agreements between firms in several countries.

4. Such activities may also have latent effects of the kind already described, operative under the same conditions.

■ INHERENTLY EXPANSIVE TASKS

Here is a problem of central importance because changes in the policy needs of the member states create definite phases in the life of international organizations. To remedy this, the task assigned to the institutions must be inherently expansive and thus capable of overcoming what Haas calls "the built-in autonomy of functional contexts."

> Lessons about integrative processes associated with one phase do not generally carry over into the next because the specific policy context . . . determines what is desired by governments and tolerated by them in terms of integrative accommodations. . . . There is no dependable, cumulative process of precedent formation leading to ever more community-oriented organizational behavior, unless the task assigned to the institutions is inherently expansive, thus capable of overcoming the built-in autonomy of functional contexts and of surviving changes in the policy aims of member states.

This is the principle involved in the concept of "spillover." In its most general formulation, "spillover" refers to a situation in which a given action, related to a specific goal, creates a situation in which the original goal can be assured only by taking further actions, which in turn create a further condition and a need for more action, and so forth. The concept has been used by Haas to show that integrating one sector of the economy—for example, coal and steel—will inevitably lead to the integration of other economic and political activities. We shall formulate it as follows: the initial task and grant of power to the central institutions creates a situation or series of situations that can be dealt with only by further expanding the task and the grant of power. Spillover implies that a situation has developed in which the ability of a member state to achieve a policy goal may depend upon the attainment by another member state of one of its policy goals. The situation may show various features:

1. The dynamics of spillover are dependent upon the fact that support for any given step in integration is the result of a convergence of goals and expectations. These often competing goals give rise to competing activities and demands, which may be the basis of further convergence leading to further integration.

2. Lack of agreement between governments may lead to an expanded role for the central institutions; in other words, member states may delegate difficult problems.
3. At the level of elite groupings, demands and expectations for further actions may be expressed as a result of partial actions taken by the central institutions.
4. The activities of the central institutions and nonofficial elites may *create situations* that cannot be dealt with except by further central institutional development and new central policies.
5. Far-reaching economic integration, involving all sectors of the economy, as in the EEC, may offer great scope for spillover *between* sectors. Conflicts over further integration in a given sector, involving disparate national interests, may be resolved by bargains between such sectors (e.g., agriculture and energy).
6. Participation in a customs union will probably elicit reactions from nonmember states, a situation which may create problems that can be resolved only by further integration or by expanding the role of the central institutions.

■ **CONTINUITY OF NATIONAL POLICY AIMS**

"Spillover" assumes the continued commitment of the member states to the undertaking. The Treaty of Rome was the result of a creative compromise, a convergence of national aspirations. Political and economic integration cannot be expected to succeed in the absence of a will to proceed on the part of the member states. Granted that it would be difficult for a state to withdraw from the EEC, it must be stressed that little could be done to move beyond minimal obligations if one or several states were to maintain a determined resistance. It seems likely, however, that with the operation of the other integrative factors, the alternatives open to any member state will gradually be limited so as to reduce dependence upon this factor. For the will to proceed need not have a positive content. Given only a general reluctance to be charged with obstruction, or to see the enterprise fail, the stimulus to action can be provided by the central institutions or by other member states.

The way in which decisions are made, in which conflicts of interest among the member states are resolved, will be of definitive importance for political integration, because the kind of accommodation that prevails will indicate the nature of the positive convergence of pro-integration aims, and of the extent to which the alternatives open to national decision makers may have been limited by participation in the enterprise. In this connection we may ask the question, under what conditions does conflict produce a stronger bond between the parties than that which existed before? Moreover, as already mentioned, the mode of accommodation is directly correlated to the developmental potential of the central institutions.

Conflicts between states may be resolved on the basis of "the minimum common denominator," by "splitting the difference," or by "upgrading common interests." The "minimum common denominator" type, characteristic of classical diplomatic negotiations, involves relatively equal bargainers who exchange equal concessions while never going beyond what the least cooperative among them is willing to concede. Accommodation by "splitting the difference" involves a similar exchange of concessions, but conflicts are ultimately resolved somewhere between the final bargaining positions, usually because of the mediatory role performed by a secretariat or expert study groups, or out of deference to third-party pressure such as might be institutionalized in "parliamentary diplomacy." This implies "the existence of a continuing organization with a broad frame of reference, public debate, rules of procedure governing the debate, and the statement of conclusions arrived at by some kind of majority vote." Although such mediating organs may not be able to define the terms of agreement, they do participate in setting limits within which the ultimate accommodation is reached. Accommodation on the basis of "upgrading common interests," whether deliberately or inadvertently, depends on the participation of institutions or individuals with an autonomous role that permits them to participate in actually defining the terms of the agreement. It implies greater progress toward political integration, for it shows that

> the parties succeeded in so redefining their conflict so as to work out a solution at a higher level, which almost invariably implies the expansion of the mandate or task of an international or national governmental agency. In terms of results, this mode of accommodation maximizes . . . the "spillover" effect of international decisions: policies made pursuant to an initial task and grant of power can be made real only if the task itself is expanded, as reflected in the compromises among the states interested in the task.

This last type comes closest to what North, Koch, and Zinnes call "true integration."

We now have a set of definitions, variable factors, indicators, and hypotheses with which to assess the extent to which the EEC is contributing to the process of political integration. We are concerned above all with determining the impact of the EEC on official and nonofficial decision-making patterns in the "Europe of the Six," and with analyzing the structure and content of such central decision-making as may develop.

.   .   .

17 Obstinate or Obsolete? The Fate of the Nation-State and the Case of Western Europe

STANLEY HOFFMANN

The early 1960s were optimistic years for students of integration. The European Economic Community was pressing integration forward at a rapid pace, and neofunctionalists seemed to have discovered the means by which advanced industrialized nations could dramatically reduce the possibility of war by pushing the international community beyond the sovereign state. But was this, in fact, the end of the nation-state? De Gaulle's precipitation of the "empty chair crisis" in 1965 indicated to many that the nation-state was alive and well. One of them was a European émigré, Stanley Hoffmann of Harvard University.

Hoffmann argued in this very long 1966 Daedalus *article (which bears close reading in its entirety) that the states of Europe were still self-interested entities with clear interests, despite their willingness to engage in closer cooperation in areas of "low politics," such as agriculture and trade. The members of the European Communities stubbornly hung on to the sovereignty that counts—control over foreign policy, national security, and the use of force ("high politics")—while only reluctantly bargaining away control over important aspects of their economies in exchange for clear material benefits. Thus functionalism as a method of integration reaches its limits very quickly, failing to take Europe "beyond the nation-state." On the*

"Obstinate or Obsolete?" reprinted with permission from *Daedalus*, Journal of the American Academy of Arts and Sciences, 95(3)(1966): 862–915. Notes omitted.

contrary, integration, according to Hoffmann, is "a vindication of the nation-state as the basic unit."

In his approach to international relations, Hoffmann is a realist. He sees the integration process as a series of bargains between sovereign states pursuing their national interests, a view often labeled "intergovernmentalism" by students of integration. Intergovernmentalism, with its emphasis on the strength of the nation-state, provides a theoretical counter to neofunctionalism with its accent on the erosion of sovereignty by supranational actors. Hoffmann, as one of the first intergovernmentalists to challenge the core assumptions of the neofunctionalists, laid the foundation for the great theoretical debate of the 1990s.

The critical issue for every student of world order is the fate of the nation-state. In the nuclear age, the fragmentation of the world into countless units, each of which has a claim to independence, is obviously dangerous for peace and illogical for welfare. The dynamism which animates those units, when they are not merely city-states of limited expanse or dynastic states manipulated by the Prince's calculations, but nation-states that pour into their foreign policy the collective pride, ambitions, fears, prejudices, and images of large masses of people, is particularly formidable. An abstract theorist could argue that any system of autonomous units follows the same basic rules, whatever the nature of those units. But in practice, that is, in history, their substance matters as much as their form; the story of world affairs since the French Revolution is not merely one more sequence in the ballet of sovereign states; it is the story of the fires and upheavals propagated by nationalism. A claim to sovereignty based on historical tradition and dynastic legitimacy alone has never had the fervor, the self-righteous assertiveness which a similar claim based on the idea and feelings of nationhood presents: in world politics, the dynastic function of nationalism is the constitution of nation-states by amalgamation or by splintering, and its emotional function is the supplying of a formidable good conscience to leaders who see their task as the achievement of nationhood, the defense of the nation, or the expansion of a national mission.

This is where the drama lies. The nation-state is at the same time a form of social organization and—in practice if not in every brand of theory—a factor of international non-integration; but those who argue in favor of a more integrated world, either under more centralized power or through various networks of regional or functional agencies, tend to forget Auguste Comte's old maxim that *on ne détruit que ce qu'on remplace*: the new "formula" will have to provide not only world order, but also the kind of social organization in which leaders, élites, and citizens feel at home. There is currently no agreement on what such a formula will be; as a result, nation-states—often inchoate, economically absurd, administratively ramshackle, and impotent yet dangerous in international politics—remain the basic units in spite of all the remonstrations and exhortations. They go on *faute de mieux* despite their alleged obsolescence; indeed, not only do they profit from man's incapacity to bring about a better order, but their very existence is a formidable obstacle to their replacement.

If there was one part of the world in which men of goodwill thought that the nation-state could be superseded, it was Western Europe. One of France's most subtle commentators on international politics has recently reminded us of E. H. Carr's bold prediction of 1945: "we shall not see again a Europe of twenty, and a world of more than sixty independent sovereign states." Statesmen have invented original schemes for moving Western Europe "beyond the nation-state," and political scientists have studied their efforts with a care from which emotional involvement was not missing. The conditions seemed ideal. On the one hand, nationalism seemed at its lowest ebb; on the other, an adequate formula and method for building a substitute had apparently been devised. Twenty years after the end of World War II—a period as long as the whole interwar era—observers have had to revise their judgments. The most optimistic put their hope in the chances the future may still harbor, rather than in the propelling power of the present; the less optimistic ones, like myself, try simply to understand what went wrong.

My own conclusion is sad and simple. The nation-state is still here, and the new Jerusalem has been postponed because the nations in Western Europe have not been able to stop time and to fragment space. Political unification could have succeeded if, on the one hand, these nations had not been caught in the whirlpool of different concerns, as a result both of profoundly different internal circumstances and of outside legacies, and if, on the other hand, they had been able or obliged to concentrate on "community-building" to the exclusion of all problems situated either outside their area or within each one of them. Domestic differences and different world views obviously mean diverging foreign policies; the involvement of the policy-makers in issues among which "community-building" is merely one has meant a deepening, not a decrease, of those divergencies. The reasons follow: the unification movement has been the victim, and the survival of nation-states the outcome, of three factors, one of which characterizes every international system, and the other two only the present system. Every international system owes its inner logic and its unfolding to the diversity of domestic determinants, geo-historical situations, and outside aims among its units; any international system based on fragmentation tends, through the dynamics of unevenness (so well understood, if applied only to economic unevenness, by Lenin) to reproduce diversity. However, there is no inherent reason that the model of the fragmented international system should rule out by itself two developments in which the critics of the nation-state have put their bets or their hopes. Why must it be a diversity of nations? Could it not be a diversity of regions, of "federating" blocs, superseding the nation-state just as the dynastic state had replaced the feudal puzzle? Or else, why does the very logic of conflagrations fed by hostility not lead to the kind of catastrophic unification of exhausted yet interdependent nations, sketched out by Kant? Let us remember that the unity movement in Europe was precisely an attempt at creating a regional entity, and that its origins and its springs resembled, on the reduced scale of a half-continent, the process dreamed up by Kant in his *Idea of Universal History*.

The answers are not entirely provided by the two factors that come to mind immediately. One is the legitimacy of national self-determination, the only principle which transcends all blocs and ideologies, since all pay lip service to it, and provides the foundation for the only "universal actor" of the international system: the United Nations. The other is the newness of many of the states, which have wrested their independence by a nationalist upsurge and are therefore unlikely to throw or give away what they have obtained only too recently. However, the legitimacy of the nation-state does not by itself guarantee the nation-state's survival in the international state of nature, and the appeal of nationalism as an emancipating passion does not assure that the nation-state must everywhere remain the basic form of social organization, in a world in which many nations are old and settled and the shortcomings of the nation-state are obvious. The real answers are provided by two unique features of the present international system. One, it is the first truly global international system: the regional subsystems have only a reduced autonomy; the "relationships of major tension" blanket the whole planet; the domestic polities are dominated not so much by the region's problems as by purely local and purely global ones, which conspire to divert the region's members from the internal affairs of their area, and indeed would make an isolated treatment of those affairs impossible. As a result, each nation, new or old, finds itself placed in an orbit of its own, from which it is quite difficult to move away: for the attraction of the regional forces is offset by the pull of all the other forces. Or, to change the metaphor, those nations that coexist in the same apparently separate "home" of a geographical region find themselves both exposed to the smells and noises that come from outside through all their windows and doors, and looking at the outlying houses from which the interference issues. Coming from diverse pasts, moved by diverse tempers, living in different parts of the house, inescapably yet differently subjected and attracted to the outside world, those cohabitants react unevenly to their exposure and calculate conflictingly how they could either reduce the disturbance or affect in turn all those who live elsewhere. The adjustment of their own relations within the house becomes subordinated to their divergences about the outside world; the "regional subsystem" becomes a stake in the rivalry of its members about the system as a whole.

However, the coziness of the common home could still prevail if the inhabitants were forced to come to terms, either by one of them, or by the fear of a threatening neighbor. This is precisely where the second unique feature of the present situation intervenes. What tends to perpetuate the nation-states decisively in a system whose universality seems to sharpen rather than shrink their diversity is the new set of conditions that govern and restrict the rule of force: Damocles' sword has become a boomerang, the ideological legitimacy of the nation-state is protected by the relative and forced tameness of the world jungle. Force in the nuclear age is still the "midwife of societies" insofar as revolutionary war either breeds new nations or shapes regimes in existing nations; but the use of force along traditional lines, for conquest and expansion—the very use that made the "permeable" feudal units not only obsolete but collapse and replaced them with modem states often built on "blood and iron"—has become too dangerous. The legitimacy of the feudal unit could be undermined in two ways: brutally, by the rule of force—the big fish swallowing small fish by national might; subtly or legitimately, so to speak, through self-undermining—the logic of dynastic weddings or acquisitions that consolidated larger units. A system based on national self-determination rules out the latter; a system in which nations, once established, find force a much blunted weapon rules out the former. Thus agglomeration by conquest or out of a fear of conquest fails to take place. The new conditions of violence tend even to pay to national borders the tribute of vice to virtue: violence which dons the cloak of revolution rather than of interstate wars, or persists in the form of such wars only when they accompany revolutions or conflicts in divided countries, perversely respects borders by infiltrating under them rather than by crossing them overtly. Thus all that is left for unification is what one might call "national self-abdication" or self-abnegation, the eventual willingness of nations to try something else; but precisely global involvement hinders rather than helps, and the atrophy of war removes the most pressing incentive. What a nation-state cannot provide alone—in economics, or defense—it can still provide through means far less drastic than hara-kiri.

These two features give its solidity to the principle of national self-determination, as well as its resilience to the U.N. They also give its present, and quite unique, shape to the "relationship of major tension": the conflict between East and West. This conflict is both muted and universal—and both aspects contribute to the survival of the nation-state. As the superpowers find that what makes their power overwhelming also makes it less usable, or rather usable only to deter one another and to deny each other gains, the lesser states discover under the umbrella of the nuclear stalemate that they are not condemned to death, and that indeed their nuisance power is impressive—especially when the kind of violence that prevails in present circumstances favors the porcupine over the elephant. The superpowers experience in their own camps the backlash of a rebellion against domination that enjoys broad impunity, and cannot easily coax or coerce third parties into agglomeration under their tutelage. Yet they retain the means to prevent other powers from agglomerating away from their clutches. Thus, as the superpowers compete, with filed nails, all over the globe, the nation-state becomes the universal point of salience, to use the new language of strategy—the lowest common denominator in the competition.

Other international systems were merely conservative of diversity; the present system is profoundly conservative of the diversity of nation-states, despite all its revolutionary features. The dream of Rousseau, concerned both about the prevalence of the general will—that is, the nation-state—and about peace, was the creation of communities insulated from one another. In history, where "the essence and drama of nationalism is not to be alone in the world," the clash of non-insulated states has tended to breed both nation-states and wars. Today, Rousseau's ideals come closer to reality, but in the most un-Rousseauean way: the nation-states prevail in peace, they remain unsuperseded because a fragile peace keeps the Kantian doctor away, they are unreplaced because their very involvement in the world, their very inability to insulate themselves from one another, preserves their separateness. The "new Europe" dreamed by the Europeans could not be established by force. Left to the wills and calculations of its members, the new formula has not jelled because they could not agree on its role in the world. The failure (so far) of an experiment tried in apparently ideal conditions tells us a great deal about contemporary world politics, and about the functional approach to unification. For it shows that the movement can fail not only when there is a surge of nationalism in one important part but also when there are differences in assessments of the national interest that rule out agreement on the shape and on the world role of the new, supranational whole.

. . .

Since it is the process of European integration that is its [Western Europe's] most original feature, we must examine it also. We have been witnessing a kind of race, between the logic of integration set up by Monnet and analyzed by Haas, and the logic of diversity, analyzed above. According to the former, the double pressure of necessity (the interdependence of the social fabric, which will oblige statesmen to integrate even sectors originally left uncoordinated) and of men (the action of the supranational agents) will gradually restrict the freedom of movement of the national governments by turning the national situations into one of total enmeshing. In such a milieu, nationalism will be a futile exercise in anachronism, and the national consciousness itself will, so to speak, be impregnated by an awareness of the higher interest in union. The logic of diversity, by contrast, sets limits to the degree to which the "spill-over process" can limit the freedom of action of the governments; it restricts the domain in which the logic of functional integration operates to the area of welfare; indeed, to the extent that discrepancies over the other areas begin to prevail over the laborious harmonization in welfare, even issues belonging to the latter sphere may become infected by the disharmony which reigns in those other areas. The logic of integration is that of a blender which crunches the most diverse products, overcomes their different tastes and perfumes, and replaces them with one, presumably delicious juice. One lets each item be ground because one expects a finer synthesis: that is, ambiguity helps rather than hinders because each "ingredient" can hope that its taste will prevail at the end. The logic of diversity is the opposite: it suggests that, in areas of key importance to the national interest, nations prefer the certainty, or the self-controlled uncertainty, of national self-reliance, to the uncontrolled uncertainty of the untested blender; ambiguity carries one only a part of the way. The logic of integration assumes that it is possible to fool each one of the associates some of the time because his over-all gain will still exceed his occasional losses, even if his calculations turn out wrong here or there. The logic of diversity implies that, on a vital issue, losses are not compensated by gains on other (and especially not on other less vital) issues: nobody wants to be fooled. The logic of integration deems the uncertainties of the supranational function process creative; the logic of diversity sees them as destructive past a certain threshold; Russian roulette is fine only as long as the gun is filled with blanks. Ambiguity lures and lulls the national consciousness into integration as long as the benefits are high, the costs low, the expectations considerable. Ambiguity may arouse and stiffen national consciousness into nationalism if the benefits are slow, the losses high, the hopes dashed or deferred. Functional integration's gamble could be won only if the method had sufficient potency to promise a permanent excess of gains over losses, and of hopes over frustrations. Theoretically, this may be true of economic integration. It is not true of political integration (in the sense of "high politics").

The success of the approach symbolized by Jean Monnet depended, and depends still, on his winning a triple gamble: on goals, on methods, on results. As for goals, it is a gamble on the possibility of substituting motion as an end in itself, for agreement on ends. It is a fact that the transnational integrationist élites did not agree on whether the object of the community-building enterprise ought to be the construction of a new super-state—that is, a federal potential nation, à la U.S.A., more able because of its size and resources to play the traditional game of power than the dwarfed nations of Western Europe—or whether the object was to demonstrate that power politics could be overcome through cooperation and compromise, to build the first example of a radically new kind of unit, to achieve a change in the nature and not merely in the scale of the game. Monnet himself has been ambiguous on this score; Hallstein has been leaning in the first direction, many of Monnet's public relations men in the second. Nor did the integrationists agree on whether the main goal was the creation of a regional "security-community," that is, the pacification of a former hotbed of wars, or whether the main goal was the creation of an entity whose position and might could decisively affect the course of the cold war in particular, of international relations in general. Now, it is perfectly possible for a movement to feed on its harboring continental nationalists as well as anti-power idealists, inward-looking politicians and outward-looking politicians—but only as long as there is no need to make a choice. Decisions on tariffs did not require such choices. Decisions on agriculture already raise basic problems of orientation. Decisions on foreign policy and membership and defense cannot be reached unless the goals are clarified. One cannot be all things to all people all of the time.

As for methods, there was a gamble on the irresistible rise of supranational functionalism. It assumed, first, that national sovereignty, already devalued by events, could be chewed up leaf by leaf like an artichoke. It assumed, second, that the dilemma of governments having to choose between pursuing an integration that ties their hands and stopping a movement that benefits their people could be exploited in favor of integration by men representing the common good, endowed with the advantages of superior expertise, initiating proposals, propped against a set of deadlines, and using for their cause the technique of package deals. Finally, it was assumed that this approach would both take into account the interests of the greater powers and prevent the crushing of the smaller ones. The troubles with this gamble have been numerous. One, even an artichoke has a heart, which remains intact after the leaves have been eaten. It is of course true that a successful economic and social integration would considerably limit the freedom governments would still enjoy in theory for their diplomacy and strategy; but why should one assume that they would not be aware of it? As the artichoke's heart gets more and more denuded, the governments' vigilance gets more and more alerted. To be sure, the second assumption implies that the logic of the movement would prevent them from doing anything about it: they would be powerless to save the heart. But, two, this would be true only if governments never put what they consider essential interests of the nation above the particular interests of certain categories of national, if superior expertise were always either the Commission's monopoly or the solution of the issue at hand, if package deals were effective in every argument, and, above all, if the governments' representatives were always determined to behave as a "community organ" rather than as the agents of states that are not willing to accept a community under any conditions. Finally, functional integration may indeed give lasting satisfaction to the smaller powers, precisely because it is for them that the ratio of "welfare politics" to high politics is highest, and that the chance of gaining benefits through intergovernmental methods that reflect rather than correct the power differential between the big and the small is poorest; but this is also why the method is not likely *à la longue* to satisfy the bigger powers as much: facing them, the supranational civil servants, for all their skill and legal powers, are a bit like Jonases trying to turn whales into jellyfish. Of course, the idea—ultimately—is to move from an essentially administrative procedure in which supranational civil servants enter a dialogue with national ministers, to a truly federal one in which a federal cabinet is responsible to a federal parliament; but what is thus presented as linear progress may turn out to be a vicious circle, since the ministers hold the key to the transformation, and may refuse it unless the goals are defined and the results already achieved are satisfactory.

There was a gamble about results as well. The experience of integration would entail net benefits for all, and bring about clear progress toward community formation. Such progress could be measured by the following yardsticks: in the realm of interstate relations, an increasing transfer of power to the new common agencies, and the prevalence of solutions "upgrading the common interest" over other kinds of compromises; in the realm of transnational society, an increasing flow of communications; in the area of national consciousness—which is important both for interstate relations, because (as seen above) it may set limits to the statesmen's discretion, and for transnational society, because it affects the scope and meaning of communication flows—progress would be measured by increasing compatibility of views about external issues. The results achieved so far are mixed: negative on the last count (see below), limited on the second, and marked on the first by features that the enthusiasts of integration did not expect. On the one hand, there has been some strengthening of authority of the Commission, and in various areas there has been some "upgrading of common interests." On the other hand, the Commission's unfortunate attempt to consolidate those gains at de Gaulle's expense, in the spring of 1965, has brought about a startling setback for the whole enterprise; moreover, in their negotiations, the members have conspicuously failed to find a common interest in some vital areas (energy, England's entry), and sometimes succeed in reaching apparently "integrating" decisions only after the most ungainly, traditional kinds of bargaining, in such uncommunity-like methods as threats, ultimatums and retaliatory moves, were used. In other words, either the ideal was not reached, or it was reached in a way that was both the opposite of the ideal and ultimately its destroyer. If we look at the institutions of the Common Market as an incipient political system in Europe, we find that its authority remains limited, its structure weak, its popular base restricted and distant.

.   .   .

There are two important general lessons one can draw from a study of the process of integration. The first concerns the limits of the functional method: its very (if relative) success in the relatively painless area in which it works relatively well lifts the participants to the level of issues to which it does not apply well anymore—like swimmers whose skills at moving quickly away from the shore suddenly brings them to the point where the waters are stormiest and deepest, at a time when fatigue is setting in, and none of the questions about the ultimate goal, direction, and length of swim has been answered. The functional process was used in order to "make Europe"; once Europe began being made, the process collided with the question: "making Europe, what for?" The process is like a grinding machine that can work only if someone keeps giving it something to grind. When the users start quarreling and stop providing, the machine stops. For a while, the machine worked because the governments poured into it a common determination to integrate their economies in order to maximize wealth; but with their wealth increasing, the question of what to do with it was going to arise: a technique capable of supplying means does not *ipso facto* provide the ends, and it is about those ends that quarrels have broken out. They might have been avoided if the situation had been more compelling—if the Six had been so cooped up that each one's horizon would have been nothing other than his five partners. But this has never been their outlook, nor is it any more their necessity. Each one is willing to live with the others, but not on terms too different from his own; and the Six are not in the position of the three miserable prisoners of *No Exit*. Transforming a dependent "subsystem" proved to be one thing; defining its relations to all other subsystems and to the international system in general has turned out to be quite another—indeed, so formidable a matter as to keep the transformation of the subsystem in abeyance until those relations can be defined.

The model of functional integration, a substitute for the kind of instant federation which governments had not been prepared to accept, shows its origins in important respects. One, it is essentially an administrative model, which relies on bureaucratic expertise for the promotion of a policy defined by the policy authorities, and for the definition of a policy that political decision-makers are technically incapable of shaping—something like French planning under the Fourth Republic. The hope was that in the interstices of political bickering the administrators could build up a consensus; but the mistake was to believe that a formula that works well within certain limits is a panacea—and that even within the limits of "welfare politics" administrative skill can always overcome the disastrous effects of political paralysis or mismanagement (cf. the impact of inflation, or balance of payment troubles, on planning). Two, the model assumes that the basic political decisions, to be prepared and pursued by the civil servants but formally made by the governments, would be reached through the process of short-term bargaining, by politicians whose mode of operation is empirical muddling through, of the kind that puts immediate advantages above long-term pursuits: this model corresponds well to the nature of parliamentary politics with a weak Executive, for example, the politics of the Fourth Republic, but the mistake was to believe that all political regimes would conform to this rather sorry image, and also to ignore the disastrous results which the original example produced whenever conflicts over values and fundamental choices made mere empirical groping useless or worse than useless (cf. decolonization).

The second lesson is even more discouraging for the advocates of functionalism. To revert to the analogy of the grinder, what has happened is that the machine, piqued by the slowing down of supply, suddenly suggested to its users that in the future the supplying of grinding material be taken out of their hands and left to the machine. The institutional machinery tends to become an actor with a stake in its own survival and expansion. But here we deal not with one but with six political systems, and the reason for the ineffectiveness of the Council of Ministers of the Six may be the excessive toughness, not the weakness, of the national political systems involved. In other words, by trying to be a force, the bureaucracy here, inevitably, makes itself even more of a stake that the nations try to control or at least to affect. A new complication is thus added to all the substantive issues that divide the participants.

.   .   .

What are the prospects in Western Europe? What generalizations can one draw from the whole experience?

.   .   .

It has become possible for scholars to argue both that integration is proceeding and that the nation-state is more than ever the basic unit, without contradicting each other, for recent definitions of integration "beyond the nation-state" point not toward the emergence of a new kind of political community, but merely toward "an obscur[ing of] the boundaries between the system of international organizations and the environment provided by member states." There are two important implications.

The first one is, not so paradoxically, a vindication of the nation-state as the basic unit. So far, anything that is "beyond" is "less": that is, there are cooperative arrangements with a varying degree of autonomy, power, and legitimacy, but there has been no transfer of allegiance toward their institutions, and their authority remains limited, conditional, dependent, and reversible. There is more than a kernel of truth in the Federalist critique of functional integration: functionalism tends to become, at best, like a spiral that coils *ad infinitum*. So far, the "transferring [of] exclusive expectations of benefits from the nation-state to some larger entity" leaves the nation-state both as the main focus of expectations, and as the initiator, pace-setter, supervisor, and often destroyer of the larger entity: for in the international arena the state is still the highest possessor of power, and while not every state is a political community there is as yet no political community more inclusive than the state. To be sure, the military function of the nation-state is in crisis; but, insofar as the whole world is "permeable" to nuclear weapons, any new type of unit would face the same horror, and, insofar as the prospect of such horror makes war more subdued and conquest less likely, the decline of the state's capacity to defend its citizens is neither total nor sufficient to force the nation-state itself into decline. The resistance of the nation-state is proven not only by the frustrations of functionalism but also by both the promise and the failure of Federalism. On the one hand, Federalism offers a way of going "beyond the nation-state," but it consists in building a new and larger nation-state. The scale is new, not the story, the gauge not the game. Indeed, the Federalist model applies to the "making of Europe" the Rousseauistic scheme for the creation of a nation: it aims at establishing a unit marked by central power and based on the general will of a European people. The Federalists are right in insisting that Western Europe's best chance of being an effective entity would be not to go "beyond the nation-state," but to become a larger nation-state in the process of formation and in the business of world politics: that is, to become a sovereign political community in the formal sense at least. The success of Federalism would be a tribute to the durability of the nation-state; its failure so far is due to the irrelevance of the model. Not only is there no general will of a European people because there is as of now no European people, but the institutions that could gradually (and theoretically) shape the separate nations into one people are not the most likely to do so. For the domestic problems of Europe are matters for technical decisions by civil servants and minsters rather than for general wills and assemblies (a general will to prosperity is not very operational). The external problems of Europe are matters for executives and diplomats. As for the common organs set up by the national governments, when they try to act as a European executive and parliament, they are both condemned to operate in the fog maintained around them by the governments and slapped down if they try to dispel the fog and reach the people themselves. In other words, Europe cannot be what some nations have been: a people that creates its state; nor can it be what some of the oldest states are and many of the new ones aspire to be: a people created by the state. It has to wait until the separate states decide that their peoples are close enough to justify a European state whose task will be the welding of the many into one; and we have just examined why such a joint decision has been missing. The very obstacles which make the Federalist model irrelevant to nations too diverse and divided also make all forms of union short of Federalism precarious. Functionalism is too unstable for the task of complete political unification. It may integrate economies, but either the nations will then proceed to a full political merger (which economic integration does not guarantee)—in that case the federal model will be vindicated at the end, the new unit will be a state forging its own people by consent and through the abdication of the previous separate states, but the conditions for success described above will have to be met—or else the national situations will remain too divergent, and functionalism will be merely a way of tying together the preexisting nations in areas deemed of common interest. Between the cooperation of existing nations and the breaking in of a new one there is no stable middle ground. A federation that succeeds becomes a nation; one that fails leads to secession; half-way attempts like supranational functionalism must either snowball or roll back.

But the nation-state, preserved as the basic unit, survives transformed. Among the men who see in "national sovereignty" the Nemesis of mankind, those who put their hopes in the development of regional superstates are illogical, those who put their hopes in the establishment of a world state are utopian, those who put their hopes in the growth of functional political communities more inclusive than the nation-state are too optimistic. What has to be understood and studied now—far more than has been done, and certainly far more than this essay was able to do—is, rather than the creation of rival communities, the transformation of "national sovereignty": it has not been superseded, but to a large extent it has been emptied of its former sting; there is no supershrew, and yet the shrew has been somewhat tamed. The model of the nation-state derived from the international law and relations of the past, when there was a limited number of players on a stage that was less crowded and in which violence was less risky, applies only fitfully to the situation of today. The basic unit, having proliferated, has also become much more heterogeneous; the stage has shrunk, and is occupied by players whose very number forces each one to strut, but its combustibility nevertheless scares them from pushing their luck too hard. The nation-state today is a new wine in old bottles, or in bottles that are sometimes only a mediocre imitation of the old; it is not the same old wine. What must be examined is not just the legal capacity of the sovereign state, but the *de facto* capacity at its disposal; granted the scope of its authority, how much of it can be used, and with what results? There

The Theory of Economic Integration: An Introduction

BELA BALASSA

Federalists, functionalists, and neofunctionalists in the postwar pe-
riod were largely concerned with the political results of integration,
even if some of them (i.e., most federalists and functionalists) paid lit-
tle attention to the political dimension of the integration process.
They were, after all, chiefly interested in the peaceful resolution of in-
ternational conflict. Postwar economists were also interested in the
integration process in Europe but for different reasons. They were en-
gaged in describing the process of economic integration and its im-
pact on welfare. As war among West European nations became un-
thinkable in the years immediately following World War II, the
economic gains of integration became the chief motive for continu-
ing the process. Thus, the work of the economists took on added im-
portance.

Bela Balassa (1928–1991), a professor of political economy at
The Johns Hopkins University, was one of the most productive stu-
dents of economic integration. Drawing on the work of Jacob Viner
and others, Balassa made a major contribution to our understanding
of the effects of integration on trade and other economic activities in
the 1960s and 1970s. In this introductory chapter to his important
work, The Theory of Economic Integration *(1961), Balassa defines*
economic integration, identifies its stages, discusses political and ide-
ological aspects of the integration process, and specifies what he
means by "economic welfare." Finally, Balassa argues that functional

integration, while, perhaps, politically expedient, is not as economically defensible as "the simultaneous integration of all sectors."

■ **THE CONCEPT AND FORMS OF INTEGRATION**

In everyday usage the word "integration" denotes the bringing together of parts into a whole. In the economic literature the term "economic integration" does not have such a clear-cut meaning. Some authors include social integration in the concept, others subsume different forms of international cooperation under this heading, and the argument has also been advanced that the mere existence of trade relations between independent national economies is a sign of integration. We propose to define economic integration as a process and as a state of affairs. Regarded as a process, it encompasses measures designed to abolish discrimination between economic units belonging to different national states; viewed as a state of affairs, it can be represented by the absence of various forms of discrimination between national economies.

In interpreting our definition, distinction should be made between integration and cooperation. The difference is qualitative as well as quantitative. Whereas cooperation includes actions aimed at lessening discrimination, the process of economic integration comprises measures that entail the suppression of some forms of discrimination. For example international agreements on trade policies belong to the area of international cooperation, while the removal of trade barriers is an act of economic integration. Distinguishing between cooperation and integration, we put the main characteristics of the latter—the abolition of discrimination within an area—into clearer focus and give the concept definite meaning without unnecessarily diluting it by the inclusion of diverse actions in the field of international cooperation.

Economic integration, as defined here, can take several forms that represent varying degrees of integration. These are a free-trade area, a customs union, a common market, an economic union, and complete economic integration. In a free-trade area, tariffs (and quantitative restrictions) between the participating countries are abolished, but each country retains its own tariffs against nonmembers. Establishing a customs union involves, besides the suppression of discrimination in the field of commodity movements within the union, the equalization of tariffs in trade with nonmember countries. A higher form of economic integration is attained in a common market, where not only trade restrictions but also restrictions on factor movements are abolished. An economic union, as distinct from a common market, combines the suppression of restrictions on commodity and factor policies, in order to remove discrimination that was due to disparities in these policies. Finally, total economic integration presupposes the unification of monetary, fiscal, social, and countercyclical policies and requires the setting-up of a supra-national authority whose decisions are binding for the member states.

Adopting the definition given above, the theory of economic integration will be concerned with the economic effects of integration in its various forms and with problems that arise from divergences in national monetary, fiscal, and other policies. The theory of economic integration can be regarded as a part of international economics, but it also enlarges the field of international trade theory by exploring the impact of a fusion of national markets on growth and examining the need for the coordination of economic policies in a union. Finally, the theory of economic integration should incorporate elements of location theory, too. The integration of adjacent countries amounts to the removal of artificial barriers that obstruct continuous economic activity through national frontiers, and the ensuing relocation of production and regional agglomerative and deglomerative tendencies cannot be adequately discussed without making use of the tools of locational analysis.

■   **THE RECENT INTEREST IN ECONOMIC INTEGRATION**

In the twentieth century no significant customs unions were formed until the end of the Second World War, although several attempts had been made to integrate the economies of various European countries. Without going into a detailed analysis, political obstacles can be singled out as the main causes for the failure of these projects to materialize. A certain degree of integration was achieved during the Second World War via a different route, when—as part of the German *Grossraum* policy—the Hitlerites endeavored to integrate economically the satellite countries and the occupied territories with Germany. In the latter case, economic integration appeared as a form of imperialist expansion.

The post–Second World War period has seen an enormous increase in the interest in problems of economic integration. In Europe the customs union and later the economic union of the Benelux countries, the European Coal and Steel Community, the European Economic Community (Common Market), and the European Free Trade Association (the "Outer Seven") are manifestations of this movement. Plans have also been made for the establishment of a free-trade area encompassing the countries of the Common Market and the Outer Seven, but negotiations in the years 1957–60 did not meet with success. However, concessions offered in early 1961 by the United Kingdom with regard to the harmonization of tariffs on non-agricultural commodities give promise for the future enlargement of the Common Market in some modified form.

·   ·   ·

The interwar period has witnessed a considerable degree of disintegration of the European and the world economy. On the European scene the mounting trade-and-payments restrictions since 1913 deserve attention. Ingvar Svennilson has shown that, as a result of the increase in trade impediments, the import trade of the advanced industrial countries of Europe shifted from the developed to the less developed economies of this area, which did not specialize in manufactured products. This shift implies a decline in competition between the industrial products of the more advanced economies and a decrease in specialization among these countries. But lessening of specialization was characteristic not only among the more advanced European economies but also of the European economy as a whole. This development can be demonstrated by trade and production figures for the period of 1913–38. While the volume of commodity production in Europe increased by 32 per cent during those years, intra-European trade increased by 10 per cent. The formation of a European union can be regarded, then, as a possible solution for the reintegration of European economies.

Another factor responsible for the disintegration of the European economy has been the stepping-up of state intervention in economic affairs in order to counteract cyclical fluctuations, sustain full employment, correct income distribution, and influence growth. Plans for economic integration are designed partly to counteract the element of discrimination inherent in the increased scope of state intervention.

A related argument regards the establishment of customs unions as desirable for mitigating cyclical fluctuations transmitted through foreign-trade relations. The foreign-trade dependence of the European Common Market countries decreases, for example, by about 35 per cent if trade among the six countries is regarded as internal trade. The memory of the depression in the 1930s gives added weight to this argument. Note, however, that for this proposition to be valid, there is need for some degree of coordination in counter-cyclical policies among the participating countries.

Last but not least, it is expected that integration will foster the growth of the European economies. This outcome is assumed to be the result of various dynamic factors, such as large-scale economies on a wider market, lessening of uncertainty in intra-area trade, and a faster rate of technological change. In this regard, the increased interest in economic growth has further contributed to the attention given to possibilities of economic integration.

.   .   .

To summarize, economic integration in Europe serves to avoid discrimination caused by trade-and-payments restrictions and increased state intervention, and it is designed to mitigate cyclical fluctuations and to increase the growth of national income.

.   .   .

■   **INTEGRATION AND POLITICS**

In examining the recent interest in economic integration, we have yet to comment on the role of political factors. There is no doubt that— especially in the case of Europe—political objectives are of great consequence. The avoidance of future wars between France and Germany, the creation of a third force in world politics, and the re-establishment of Western Europe as a world power are frequently mentioned as political goals that would be served by economic integration. Many regard these as primary objectives and relegate economic considerations to second place. No attempt will be made here to evaluate the relative importance of political economic considerations. This position is taken, partly because this relationship is not quantifiable, partly because a considerable degree of interdependence exists between these factors. Political motives may prompt the first step in economic integration, but economic integration also reacts on the political sphere; similarly, if the initial motives are economic, the need for political unity can arise at a later stage.

From the economic point of view, the basic question is not whether economic or political considerations gave the first impetus to the integration movement, but what the economic effects of integration are likely to be. In some political circles the economic aspects are deliberately minimized and the plan for economic integration is regarded merely as a pawn in the play of political forces. Such a view unduly neglects the economic expediency of the proposal. Even if political motives did have primary importance, this would not mean that the economist could not examine the relevant economic problems without investigating elusive political issues. By way of comparison, although the formation of the United States was primarily the result of political considerations, nobody would deny the economic importance of its establishment.

We shall not disregard the political factors, however. Political *ends* will not be considered, but at certain points of the argument we shall examine various economic problems the solution of which is connected with political *means* and political processes. We shall explore, for example, how the objective of exploiting the potential benefits of economic integration affects the decision-making process. Changes in the decision-making process, on the other hand, become a political problem. Nevertheless, we shall go no further than to state the need for coordinated action in certain fields and will leave it for the political scientist to determine the political implications of such developments.

■ THE "LIBERALIST" AND THE "DIRIGIST" IDEAL OF ECONOMIC INTEGRATION

The recent interest in economic integration has prompted various proposals concerning the means and objectives of integration. Two extreme views—an all-out liberalist and a dirigist solution—will be contrasted here. The champions of economic liberalism regard regional integration as a return to the free-trade ideals of the pre–First World War period within the area in question and anticipate the relegation of national economic policy to its pre-1914 dimensions. If this approach is followed, integration simply means the abolition of impediments to commodity movements. At the other extreme, integration could also be achieved through state trading and through the coordination of national economic plans without the lifting of trade barriers. This alternative discards the use of market methods and relies solely on administrative, nonmarket means. It can be found in the integration projects of Soviet-type economies; the operation of the Council of Mutual Economic Assistance, comprising the Soviet Union and her European satellites, is based on the coordination of long-range plans and bilateral trade agreements. A similar method, but one which put more reliance on market means, was used by Germany during the last war. In this study we shall examine problems of economic integration in market economies and shall not deal with Nazi Germany and Soviet-type economies. Nevertheless, we shall see that dirigistic tendencies appear in the writings of some Western authors, too.

Among the proponents of the liberalist solution, Allais, Röpke, and Heilperin may be cited. They regard economic integration as identical with trade (and payments) liberalization. Allais asserts that "practically, the only mutually acceptable rule for close economic cooperation between democratic societies is the rule of the free market." Röpke is of the opinion that European economic integration is nothing else than an attempt to remedy the disintegration of the post-1914 period that destroyed the previous integration of national economies. A less extreme position is taken by Heilperin, who rejects the consideration of regional development plans and subsidies to industries for reconversion purposes but accepts state responsibility for investment decisions in certain areas. To the majority of observers, however, the liberalist ideal of integration is a relic from the past, and its application to present-day economic life appears rather anachronistic. As Jean Weiller put it, "It would be a great error to believe that the decision to create a regional union would re-establish the conditions of an economic liberalism, extirpating with one stroke all so-called dirigistic policies."

It can rightly be said that considerations such as the avoidance of depressions, the maintenance of full employment, the problems of regional development, the regulation of cartels and monopolies, and so forth, require state intervention in economic life, and any attempts to integrate national economies would necessarily lead to harmonization in various policy areas. This idea is not new. The need for the coordination of fiscal, monetary, social, and countercyclical policies was stressed in the League of Nations study on customs unions published immediately after the end of the Second World War. In fact, the question is not whether government intervention is needed or not in an integrated area, but whether economic integration results in a more intensive participation of the state in economic affairs or in a more intensive reliance on market methods.

Some authors advocate an intensification of state intervention in economic affairs. The need for economic planning in a union is emphasized, for example, by André Philip and by other French Socialists. In Philip's opinion, "there is no alternative to a directed economy," since "the market can be extended not by liberalizing but by organizing." Although not an advocate of centralized planning, the stepping-up of state intervention is also recommended by Maurice Bye, who contrasts his "integration theory" with Heilperin's "market theory." Considering the pronouncements of French economists and industrialists, it can be said that, by and large, the French view of economic integration contains more dirigistic elements than, for example, that of most German economists and entrepreneurs.

The defenders of dirigistic tendencies fail to consider, however, the lessening of planning and government intervention—and the beneficial effects thereof—in Europe since the end of the Second World War. Although this change does not indicate a return to the pre-1914 situation, it brought about an increased use of the market mechanism and contributed to the spectacular growth of the European economy during the 1950's. It appears, then, that a reintroduction of dirigistic methods would slow down, rather than accelerate, future growth. State intervention may be stepped up in some areas, such as regional development planning, and will also be required to deal with transitional problems, but it is expected that an enlargement of the economic area will intensify competition and lead to less interference with productive activities at the firm level. Therefore, those who regard the European Common Market as a *marché institué* err in the opposite direction from the holders of old-fashioned liberalist views.

·   ·   ·

■ ECONOMIC INTEGRATION AND WELFARE

It can be said that the ultimate objective of economic activity is an increase in welfare. Thus, in order to assess the desirability of integration, its contribution to welfare needs to be considered. But the concept of welfare is fraught with much obscurity. First, the noneconomic aspects present some ambiguity; second, even restricting the meaning of the concept to "economic welfare" in the Pigovian tradition, we are confronted with the well-known difficulties of interpersonal comparisons if we try to say anything over and above the Pareto condition: an increase in one man's welfare leads to an increase in social welfare only if there is no reduction in the welfare of any other members of the group. In the case of integration, economic welfare will be affected by (a) a change in the quantity of commodities produced, (b) a change in the degree of discrimination between domestic and foreign goods, (c) a redistribution of income between the nationals of different countries, and (d) income redistribution within individual countries. Accordingly, distinction is made between a real-income component and a distributional component of economic welfare. The former denotes a change in potential welfare (efficiency); the latter refers to the welfare effects of income redistribution (equity).

With regard to potential welfare, separate treatment is allotted to changes in the quantity of goods produced and changes in their distribution. First, there is an increase (decrease) in potential welfare if—owing to the reallocation of resources consequent upon integration—the quantity of goods and services produced with given inputs increases (decreases) or, alternatively, if the production of the same quantity of goods and services requires a smaller (larger) quantity of inputs. If we regard inputs as negative outputs, we may say that a rise in net output leads to an increase in potential welfare. A higher net output entails an increase in potential welfare in the sense that a larger quantity of goods and services can now be distributed among individuals so as to make some people better off without making others worse off. Second, potential welfare is also affected through the impact of economic integration on consumers' choice. Restrictions on commodity movements imply discrimination between domestic and foreign commodities; a tariff causes consumers to buy more of lower-valued domestic and less of higher-valued foreign goods. The removal of intra-union tariffs will do away with discrimination between the commodities of the member countries but will discriminate against foreign goods in favor of the commodities of partner countries. In short, economic efficiency means efficiency in production and efficiency in exchange, and an improvement in one or both constitutes an increase in potential welfare.

Given a change in potential welfare (the real-income component), we also have to consider the distributional component in order to determine changes in economic welfare. It can easily be seen that an evaluation of changes in income distribution would require interpersonal comparisons of welfare. The new welfare economics, however, does not admit the possibility of making interpersonal comparisons. As a possible solution, it has then been suggested that changes in welfare could be determined in terms of potential welfare; that is, the *possibility* of making everybody better off (or, at least, no one worse off) would be taken as equivalent to an increase in economic welfare. This proposition can be criticized primarily on the grounds that the hypothetical situation *after* compensation is irrelevant if compensation actually does not take place. Nevertheless, changes in the real-income component give a good approximation of changes in welfare *within a country,* since compensation is politically feasible, and in case of integration this would actually be carried out to some degree in the form of assistance to relocating workers or reconverting firms. In addition, a nation can be regarded as an entity, where a redistribution of income accompanying an increase in real income can be accepted—provided that the redistribution does not run counter to generally accepted ideals of equity.

The distribution component cannot be neglected if economic integration redistributes income between countries, especially between the member states of a union, on the one hand, and the non-participating economies, on the other. It is not possible to claim an increase in world welfare in every case when the increase in real income in the participating countries will be greater than the loss to third countries. This proposition would hold true only if international comparisons of welfare could be made or if we disregarded differences in the marginal utility of income between countries. The first possibility was ruled out above, and the equality of the marginal utility of income is no less implausible. According to some, the marginal utility of income in an underdeveloped economy might be two or three times as high as in the rest of the world. If such a view were accepted, a union of developed economies which would register gains in the real-income component might still reduce world welfare by redistributing income from "poor" to "rich" countries.

In the preceding discussion we have followed the customary exposition of welfare economics in using the concept of potential welfare in a static sense. Thus an increase in potential welfare was taken as equivalent to an improvement in the allocation of resources at a point of time. Static efficiency, however, is only one of the possible success criteria that can be used to appraise the effects of economic integration. Instead of limiting our investigation to a discussion of efficiency in resource allocation under static assumptions, greater attention should be paid to the impact of integration on dynamic efficiency. I have elsewhere defined dynamic efficiency as the hypothetical growth rate of national income achievable with given resource use and saving ratio. In technical terms, whereas static efficiency would require that the economy operate on its production-possibility frontier, dynamic efficiency can be represented by the movement of this frontier in the northeast direction. The concept of dynamic efficiency can be used in intercountry comparisons to indicate which economy is capable of faster growth under identical conditions with regard to resources and saving, or, alternatively, it can be applied for comparing the growth potentialities of an economy at different points of time. In the present context, we wish to compare the hypothetical growth rate attainable *before* and *after* integration, under the assumption of given initial resources and saving ratio.

Given the static efficiency of an economy, the main factors affecting its dynamic efficiency are technological progress, the allocation of investment, dynamic interindustry relationships in production and investment, and uncertainty and inconsistency in economic decisions. In addition to these factors, the actual growth of national income would also be affected by an increase in the proportion of national income saved and/or by interference with the individual's choice between work and leisure. Changes in the latter variables will be disregarded here, partly because we assume that they are but rarely affected by economic integration, partly because their effects cannot be evaluated in welfare terms, given the disutility of increased saving and/or work. Under these assumptions an increase in the rate of growth can be considered as equivalent to an improvement in dynamic efficiency and represents a rise in potential welfare.

In evaluating the effects of economic integration, we shall use dynamic efficiency as the primary success indicator, taking into account both changes in the efficiency of resource allocation in the static sense and the dynamic effects of integration. In addition, attention will be paid to the impact of integration on income distribution, on the regional pattern of production and income, and on the stability of the participating economies.

· · ·

■ THE SECTORAL APPROACH TO INTEGRATION

In this chapter, distinction has been made between various forms of economic integration. All these forms require concerted action in the entire field of economic activity, be it the abolition of customs barriers or the coordination of fiscal policies. Another approach to economic integration would be to move from sector to sector, integrating various industries successively. The application of this method had already been commended in the interwar period, and it found many champions in the period following the Second World War. Proposals were made to integrate various sectors such as the iron and steel industry, transportation, and agriculture. The Stikker Plan advocated the integration of national economies by removing barriers, industry by industry. Supporters of this view contended that national governments were more inclined to make limited commitments with reasonably clear implications than to integrate all sectors at the same time. The flexibility of this method was also extolled, and it was hoped that integration in one sector would encourage integration on a larger scale.

From the theoretical point of view, various objections can be raised against the sectoral approach. Whereas the simultaneous integration of all sectors allows for compensating changes, integration in one sector will lead to readjustment in this sector alone, the reallocation of resources in other sectors being impeded by the continued existence of tariffs and other trade barriers—hence the losses suffered by countries whose productive activity in the newly integrated sector contracts will not be compensated for until the next phase. More generally, under the sectoral approach every step in integration results in a new and temporary equilibrium of prices, costs, and resource allocation, and this "equilibrium" is disturbed at every further step. Production decisions will then be made on the basis of prices that are relevant only in a certain phase of integration, and shifts in resource allocation will take place which may later prove to be inappropriate. On the other hand, the adjustment of relative prices and the reallocation of resources proceed more smoothly if all sectors are integrated at the same time, since some industries are expanding, others contracting, and unnecessary resource shifts do not take place.

Integration sector by sector puts an additional burden on the external balance also. At various steps, pressures will be imposed on the balance of payments of countries where the newly integrated sector is a high-cost producer. In the absence of exchange-rate flexibility, this process unnecessarily burdens exchange reserves in some, and inflates reserves in other, participating countries. If, on the other hand, exchange rates are left to fluctuate freely, temporary variations in rates of exchange will bring about transitional and unnecessary changes in the international division of labor.

In addition, lack of coordination in monetary, fiscal, and other policies is likely to cause difficulties under the sectoral approach, since differences in economic policies can lead to perverse movements of commodities and factors. For example, if inflationary policies are followed in one country while deflationary policies are pursued in another, an overadjustment will take place in the integrated sector (or sectors), while trade barriers restrict adjustments in other industries. Finally, any joint decisions made with respect to the integrated sector will affect all other branches of the participating economies.

A noneconomic objection of considerable importance should also be mentioned here. The sectoral approach is bound to bring about a conflict between producer and user interests in individual countries. In countries with relatively high production costs, for example, users will welcome integration because of its price-reducing effect; high-cost producers, however, will object to it. Experience suggests that producer interests have greater influence on governmental decisionmaking; hence these pressures are likely to have a restrictive effect on integration if the sectoral approach is followed. The interests of exporting and importing countries being opposed, there can be no "give and take"—the necessary pre-condition for intercountry agreements in most practical instances.

These theoretical objections suggest the inadvisability of integration sector by sector. This conclusion does not mean, however, that integration in one sector may not be beneficial if political obstacles hinder integration in all areas. The European Coal and Steel Community is a case in point. At the time of its inception, the realization of a European Common Market was not yet possible, but the governments of the participating countries were prepared to accept a limited measure of integration. The establishment of the Coal and Steel Community has been conducive to the expansion of production and trade in the partaking industries, and the Community demonstrated the possibility of integration in Europe, thereby contributing to the establishment of the Common Market.

It has also been argued that the difficulties of adjustment in production and trade in the Coal and Steel Community have been less than expected because the considerable increase in the national incomes of every participating country has made adjustment easier. This does not, however, rule out the possibility of maladjustments in other industries which will not be corrected until trade barriers are removed in all sectors. In addition, the Coal and Steel Community has encountered serious difficulties with respect to transportation policies, fiscal and social problems, etc., which have been due—to a great degree—to the fact that integration extends over only one sector.

PART 3

Current Debates in Integration Theory

19

European Community and Nation-State: A Case for a Neofederalism?

JOHN PINDER

The apparent stagnation of the European Community (EC) in the 1970s and early 1980s and the consequent abandonment of neofunctionalism after 1975 had a chilling effect on integration theory. Most scholars (at least in the United States) migrated to other areas; those who remained interested in the EC (primarily Europeans) focused on how the Community actually worked, steering far clear of grand theory. Studies of EC decisionmaking in specific policy areas proliferated. These studies often relied on the theoretical concepts developed during the halcyon days of neofunctionalism and quietly laid the groundwork for later theoretical advances.

Overshadowed by this scientific examination of the inner workings of the EC were the European federalists, the idealistic "true believers" in a United States of Europe. They still believed that the most democratic and just way to prevent war and promote prosperity in Europe was to create a European super-state with full federal powers. Most maintained that functional integration had failed to dent national sovereignty. They continued to argue quietly for a great leap to federalism.

John Pinder, a British senior fellow at the Policy Studies Institute in London and a professor at the College of Europe in Bruges, Belgium, has been an outspoken federalist for several decades. He believes in federal institutions for Europe, but he is critical of the feder-

Reprinted with permission from *International Affairs* (London), 62, 1 (winter 1985–1986):41–54. Notes omitted.

alists for failing to think practically about how to achieve their goal. Federalism, in his view, needs to "refer both to a federalizing process and to a federal end." The EC has engaged in "incremental federalism," but no one has examined the exact circumstances under which federalist advances take place. Pinder suggests that the background conditions outlined by Deutsch (Chapter 14) have all been met in Europe, but political leadership is missing. With leadership from the member states, Pinder asserts (writing in 1986) that prospects are good for "taking further steps in a federal direction, whether in the form of a system of majority voting to complete the internal market, developing the EMS [European Monetary System] in the direction of monetary union, an increase in the powers of the European Parliament, or a package of such reforms that could deserve to be called European Union." Sounds like the Maastricht treaty. It also sounds like some version of functionalism. Could neofederalism, despite Pinder's protestations, be neofunctionalism with a clear goal?

Pinder's call to think theoretically and practically about how to achieve a European Union was an early indication that integration theory was making a comeback.

. . .

Thinking other than that of the federalists has had relevance to the Community experience. But the "realist" and the "regime" and "system" schools have been too reductionist about the possibilities of movement in the direction of federal institutions with substantial competences. The neofunctionalists took, on the contrary, too facile a view of such possibilities, without clarity about the conditions under which integrative steps would be possible and without appreciating the strength of the nation-state. Federalists are less inclined to err in either of these directions. But, although they have acted in support of the Community's step-by-step development, they have not thought deeply enough about "the intermediary stage between normal interstate relations and normal intrastate relations" or about the concept of constitution-building as not just a single act, but also "an evolutionary development." If it is to help us assess the prospects for development of the Community, federalist theory needs to refer both to a federalizing process and to a federal end which implies substantial transfers of sovereignty. Its scope needs to incorporate steps in the development of European institutions and in their assumption of functions and competences; the resistance of member states to this process and the pressures that may induce them to accept it; and the perspective of possible "qualitative breaks" involving a "constitutional redistribution of powers." Existing theories do not seem to deal adequately with these things.

The neofunctionalists appeared strangely uninterested in evaluating how far any particular functions needed to be performed by supranational institutions. The assumption that such institutions would come to assume all important functions begged the critical question of the circumstances in which states would establish institutions with federal characteristics, or transfer competences to them, as they did when they launched the ECSC [European Coal and Steel Community], the Treaties of Rome and, to some extent, the EMS [European Monetary System]. . . . Nor did the neofunctionalists seem much concerned about the form of democratic control by European institutions that can be seen as a corollary of the more far-reaching transfers of competence. The classic federalists were clearer about this, proposing democratic federal institutions to accompany the transfer of the more basic competences such as money, taxation or armed forces. But because they did not consider any process of establishing federations other than through a single act transferring to them coercive and security powers, their thinking was not directly applicable to the transfer of less fundamental competences. Thus the political problem of transferring particular competences or instruments from the member states to the Community has been neglected by the various schools of thought, and much the same can be said of the political problem of securing the Community's institutional development, from the original addition of the Parliament, Court and Council to the High Authority mentioned in the Schuman declaration, through the establishment of the European Council, the European Parliament's budgetary powers and the direct elections, to the point where the Draft Treaty had only to propose majority voting and legislative codecision to convert the Community institutions into a federal form. A useful contribution to evaluating the prospects for the main elements in European Union proposals would be greater understanding of the circumstances which have enabled such increments of federal institutions or competences to be decided in the Community up to now.

One circumstance which stood in the way of such increments in the 1960s was . . . de Gaulle's leadership of France. He was doubtless unusual in the consistency with which his "supreme value" remained the nation-state. On the other hand, the British have been quite variable, from their loss of confidence in the nation-state in the late 1930s through the reassertion of confidence after the war to the rearguard action in its defense by contemporary "pragmatists." While the smaller member states harbor few illusions about the reality of national independence, the middle powers are still pulled in one direction by their attachment to the nation-state and in the other by their worries about the technological challenge from America and Japan, the power of the dollar, and security in the period of superpower tensions and the American Strategic Defense Initiative.

The background conditions which favor steps towards community or integration have been fairly extensively studied. Prominent among them are the degree of similarity or difference in certain attributes among members of the group. Economic and political systems and culture are usually regarded as sufficiently similar among West European countries to facilitate a substantial degree of integration. . . . In politics, it has been observed that like-mindedness between Adenauer, de Gasperi and Schuman facilitated the establishment of the ECSC, whereas different orientations among the political leaders of member countries can impede integration.

The intensity of interdependence and communication among the member countries is also held to condition the prospects for integration. There has, however, been surprisingly little effort to link measures of economic interdependence with constraints on national policies and with readiness for policy integration, in view of their potential significance for European integration. The MacDougall report showed that between 40 and 80 percent of regional gross domestic product was traded across the boundaries of each British region and of Brittany, compared with about 50 percent for Belgium and the Netherlands. Thus Belgium and the Netherlands appear to be as trade-dependent as at least a number of British and French regions. The larger EC [European Community] countries are about half as trade-dependent as Belgium and the Netherlands; and the trade-dependence of the great economies of the United States, Japan and the EC as a whole is about half that again. Thus the smaller countries' lack of illusions regarding national independence finds some statistical confirmation, and the larger EC member states, although their trade-dependence has greatly increased since the 1960s, may still feel themselves to be at a half-way house. But gross trade-dependence is only one measure of constraint on national policies; the influence of international capital markets and, hence, of American interest rates may, for example, be more important.

The conclusion of a study of various transnational links between the (then) six member countries in the late 1960s was that "if . . . India is seen as a nation, then Europe may well be described as an emergent nation." Some writers have tried to encapsulate the conditions that make federal institutions feasible in the formula that there must first be a single "people" or "nation." Yet this remains too vague an assertion unless the concept of a "people" or "nation" is defined and related to the characteristics of the population of the countries in question. It has indeed been observed that, in the field of theory, "no positive definition of the nation exists," and that national behavior is linked with "the situation of power, and probably depends on it." Is the assertion that a European nation is a precondition of a "fully democratic European Union" perhaps either tautological (a European nation being defined as a population which can uphold a European federal system), or merely another way of saying that we need to study the similarities, links, differences and divergences between member states in order to judge how far they can move towards federation?

One empirical way to judge the capacity of European peoples to sustain common institutions is observation of their behavior in relation to the institutions they already sustain together. The existence of prior association has long been seen as a condition that favors federalism. The experience of working the EC institutions, with their various federal attributes, may help us to judge whether member countries could support such reforms as codecision and a considerable expansion of the scope for majority votes. However favorable the conditions may be for steps towards federal institutions and competences, such steps are not likely to be taken without adequate political leadership. The neofunctionalists were too little concerned about the political efforts required to secure such steps; and they were justifiably criticized for concentrating on the Commission as the political motor for integration. The European Parliament has the electoral base that the Commission lacks; but the political leadership which the Parliament has shown with its Draft Treaty could hardly secure major reforms, as distinct from public support for such reforms, without corresponding leadership from among the member states. The roles of Monnet and of Schuman, Adenauer and de Gasperi in relation to the ECSC have been noted . . . ; Monnet and Spaak were outstanding among the promoters of the Rome Treaties; understanding between Heath and Pompidou was crucial to the first enlargement of the EC and that between Giscard and Schmidt to the creation of the European Monetary System. The American federalists and Washington only come first to mind among a number of historical examples. Theories which understate the need for political efforts and leadership will, like neofunctionalism, separate themselves to that extent from reality.

The argument of this article suggests that the British, in order to play a more constructive and successful role in future discussions and negotiations on European Union, will need to take more seriously the possibility of developing the Community's institutions, as well as its competences, thus continuing a process which, thanks mainly to the initiatives of the founder members, is already fairly far advanced in the form of the Community as it exists today. The tendency to identify federalism with a great leap to a federation with military and coercive power inhibits practical thought about the prospects for taking further steps in a federal direction, whether in the form of a system of majority voting to complete the internal market, developing the EMS in the direction of monetary union, an increase in the powers of the European Parliament, or a package of such reforms that could deserve to be called European Union. Such thought would be helped by systematic study of the specific steps that could be taken and of the conditions that favor or impede them. If the term "neofederalism" would help the British to come to terms with the process of incremental federalism, the neologism would be a small price to pay for a major advance in our capacity to play our proper part in contemporary European and international politics.

20

1992: Recasting the European Bargain

WAYNE SANDHOLTZ AND JOHN ZYSMAN

The adoption of the 1992 Program (1985) and the passage of the Single European Act (1986) revitalized the European Community and marked a new stage in the integration process. The new enthusiasm *in the Community awoke grand integration theory from a long slumber as scholars—some new, some veterans of former debates—attempted once again to explain what was happening in Europe. They initially focused their attention on the decision to create a single market and to revise the Treaty of Rome to expedite the process. Ultimately, they were trying to explain why, after years of stagnation, the integration process was suddenly moving forward again. These schol-* *ars drew on neofunctionalism and a number of other approaches derived from international relations and EC decisionmaking to provide answers to their theoretical questions.*

Wayne Sandholtz (University of California–Irvine) and John Zysman (University of California–Berkeley) opened the theoretical debate in 1989 with an attempt to explain the "1992 process" by focusing on supranational institutions. They argued first that changes in the international structure—specifically the decline of the United States and the rise of Japan—"triggered the 1992 process." They then coupled this idea with neofunctionalist and domestic politics notions to explain the timing and specific nature of recent integrative behavior. From neofunctionalism, they drew out the importance of supranational institutions (primarily the Commission) and European interest groups (organized European industrialists); from theories of

Reprinted with permission from *World Politics*, 41(1)(1989):95–128. Copyright 1989 by The Johns Hopkins University Press. Notes omitted.

domestic politics, they emphasized the effect of the domestic politi-
cal context on the receptiveness of national governmental elites to
initiatives from the Commission and European business. Thus in their
view, recent integration was best viewed as a bargain between elites
in EC institutions, European industry, and member governments, with
the Commission supplying most of the policy leadership.

The focus for Sandholtz and Zysman was primarily, although
not exclusively, on the actors working in the realm above the mem-
ber states. For this reason, other scholars have often labeled their
view supranationalist.

Under the banner of "1992," the European Communities are
putting in place a series of political and business bargains that will
recast, if not unify, the European market. This initiative is a disjunc-
tion, a dramatic new start, rather than the fulfillment of the original
effort to construct Europe. It is not merely the culmination of the integration begun in the 1950s, the "completion" of the internal market. The removal of all barriers to the movement of persons, capital,
and goods among the twelve member states (the formal goal of the
1992 process) is expected to increase economies of scale and decrease
transaction costs. But these one-time economic benefits do not capture the full range of purposes and consequences of 1992. Dynamic
effects will emerge in the form of restructured competition and
changed expectations. Nineteen ninety-two is a vision as much as a
program—a vision of Europe's place in the world. The vision is already producing a new awareness of European strengths and a seemingly sudden assertion of the will to exploit these strengths in competition with the United States and Japan. It is affecting companies as
well as governments. A senior executive of Fiat recently declared,
"The final goal of the European 'dream' is to transform Europe into
an integrated economic continent with its specific role, weight and
ability on the international scenario vis-à-vis the U.S. and Japan."

But why has this process begun, or begun again, now? In this
article, we propose that changes in the international structure triggered the 1992 process. More precisely, the trigger has been a real
shift in the distribution of economic power resources (crudely put,
relative American decline and Japanese ascent). What is just as important is that European elites perceive that the changes in the international setting require that they rethink their roles and interests in
the world. The United States is no longer the unique source of forefront technologies; in crucial electronics sectors, for example, Japanese firms lead the world. Moreover, Japanese innovations in organiz-

tially, therefore, experts in the supranational organization apply technical solutions to (primarily) economic problems. Integration proceeds through the "expansive logic" of spillovers. Spillovers occur when experience gained by one integrative step reveals the need for integration in functionally related areas. That is, in order to accomplish the original objectives, participants realize that they must take further integrative steps. Creating a common market, for example, might reveal the need for a regional fund to manage short-term current accounts imbalances among the members. That would constitute a spillover. In the long term, according to the formulations of Ernst Haas, as more technical functions shift to the integrated institutions, the loyalties and expectations of the populations transfer from the historical nation states to the larger supranational entity.

Haas and other scholars later modified these initial neofunctionalist conceptions. Nye noted that integration could progress by means of deliberate linkages that created "package deals." He also argued that functional links among tasks did not always lead to spillovers, but could have a negative impact on integration. Others further refined the kinds of internal dynamics of integration to include "spill-back," "spill-around," and "forward linkage." Haas recognized that spillovers could be limited by the "autonomy of functional contexts" and that integration turned out not to be the steady, incremental process originally envisioned.

For a number of reasons, we do not believe that integration theories are well suited for analyzing the 1992 movement. The major weaknesses were recognized by the integration theorists themselves; two of their criticisms are most relevant to the concerns of this paper. (1) The internal logic of integration cannot account for the stop-go nature of the European project. One possibility is that the Community attained many of its objectives, which led to "the disappearance of many of the original incentives to integrate." The question then becomes, why did the renewed drive for the single internal market emerge in the mid-1980s and why did it rapidly acquire broad support among governments and business elites? (2) Even where the Community did not meet expectations or where integration in one area pointed out problems in functionally related areas, national leaders could frequently opt for national means rather than more integration. That is, even in issue areas where the pressure for spillovers should have been strong, national means appeared sufficient and were preferred. In the 1960s, efforts to establish a common transport policy fell flat because national policies appeared adequate to interested parties. During the 1970s, the Commission's efforts on behalf of broad Community science and technology planning (the

Spinelli and Dahrendorf plans) got nowhere because governments perceived science and technology as areas in which national policies could and should be pursued. The national option always stands against the EC option and frequently wins.

An explanation rooted in the domestic politics of the various European countries is a second possible approach to explaining 1992. Certainly the shift of the socialist governments in France and Spain toward market-oriented economic policies (including privatization and deregulation) was essential for acceptance of the 1992 movement. The Thatcher government in the U.K. could also support measures that dealt primarily with reducing regulations and freeing markets. Thus, the favorable domestic political context was one of the necessary conditions that produced 1992.

But domestic politics cannot carry the full analytical burden, for three main reasons. (1) An argument based on domestic politics cannot answer the question, why now? Such an argument would have to account for the simultaneity of domestic developments that would induce states to act jointly. Attention to changes in the international context solves the problem. International changes posed challenges and choices to all the EC countries at the same time. (2) The political actors that figure in analyses of European domestic politics have not yet been mobilized in the 1992 project, though perhaps that is now beginning. Although the political parties and the trade unions now talk about 1992, they were not involved in the discussions and bargains that started the process. Governments (specifically, the national executives) and business elites initiated and defined 1992 and have moved it along. (3) An argument based on domestic politics cannot explain why domestic political change produced the 1992 movement. The project did not bubble up spontaneously from the various national political contexts. On the contrary: leadership for 1992 came from outside the national settings; it came from the Commission.

The third approach to analyzing 1992 is the one we advance in this paper. It focuses on elite bargains formed in response to changes in the international structure and in the domestic political context. The postwar order of security and economic systems founded upon American leadership is beginning to evolve after a period of relative U.S. decline and Japanese ascent. These developments have led Europeans to reconsider their relations with the United States and within the European Communities. The international and domestic situations provided a setting in which the Commission could exercise policy entrepreneurship, mobilizing a transnational coalition in favor of the unified internal market.

The 1992 movement (as well as the integration of the 1950s) can be fruitfully analyzed as a hierarchy of bargains. Political elites reach agreement on fundamental bargains embodying basic objectives; subsidiary bargains are required to implement these objectives. The fundamental bargains agreed upon for 1992 are embodied in the Single European Act and in the Commission's White Paper which outlined specific steps toward the unified internal market. The Single European Act extended majority voting in the Council and cleared the way politically for progress toward unifying the internal market. Endorsement of the Commission's proposals in the White Paper represents agreement on the fundamental objective of eliminating barriers to the movement of persons, goods, and capital. The specific measures proposed by the Commission (some 300 of them) can be thought of as implementing bargains.

. . .

The original European movement can be seen in terms of this framework. The integration movement was triggered by the wrenching structural changes brought about by World War II; after the war, Europe was no longer the center of the international system, but rather a frontier and cushion between the two new superpowers. Political entrepreneurship came initially from the group surrounding Robert Schuman and Jean Monnet. The early advocates of integration succeeded in mobilizing a transnational coalition supportive of integration; the core of that coalition eventually included the Christian Democratic parties of the original Six, plus many of the Socialist parties.

The fundamental objectives of the bargains underlying the European Coal and Steel Community (ECSC) and the expanded European Communities were primarily two: (1) the binding of German industry to the rest of Europe so as to make another war impossible, and (2) the restarting of economic growth in the region. These objectives may have been largely implicit, but they were carried out by means of a number of implementing bargains that were agreed upon over the years. The chief implementing bargains after the ECSC included the Common Market, the Common Agricultural Program, the regional development funds, and, most recently, the European Monetary System (EMS).

The fundamental external bargain made in establishing the Community was with the United States; it called for (certainly as remembered now in the U.S.) national treatment for the subsidiaries of foreign firms in the Common Market. That is, foreign (principally American) firms that set up in the Community could operate as if they were European. American policy makers saw themselves as willing to tolerate the discrimination and potential trade diversion of a united Europe because the internal bargain of the EEC would contribute to foreign policy objectives. Not only was part of Germany tied to the West, but sustained economic growth promised political stability. All of this was framed by the security ties seen as necessary on both sides of the Atlantic to counter the Soviet Union.

The European bargains—internal and external—were made at the moment of American political and economic domination. A bipolar security world and an American-directed Western economy set the context in which the European bargain appeared necessary. Many expected the original Community to generate ever more extensive integration. But the pressures for spillover were not that great. Economics could not drive political integration. The building of nation states remains a matter of political projects. Padoa-Schioppa has put it simply and well: "The cement of a political community is provided by indivisible public goods such as 'defence and security'. The cement of an economic community inevitably lies in the economic benefits it confers upon its members." The basic political objectives sought by the original internal bargain had been achieved: the threat of Germany was diminished and growth had been ignited. When problems arose from the initial integrative steps, the instruments of national policy sufficed to deal with them. Indeed, the Community could accommodate quite distinct national social, regulatory, and tax policies. National strategies for growth, development, and employment sufficed.

Several fundamental attributes of the economic community that emerged merit emphasis, as they prove important in the reignition of the European project in the mid-1980s. First, the initial effort was the product of governmental action, of intergovernmental bargains. Second, there was the partial creation of an internal market; that is a reduction, but not an elimination, of the barriers to internal exchange. The success of this initiative was suggested by the substantial increase in intra-European trade. Third, and equally important, there was toleration of national intervention; in fact, in the case of France such intervention was an element of the construction. There was an acceptance of national strategies for development and political management. Fourth, the European projects were in fact quite limited, restricted for the most part to managing retrenchment in declining industries and easing dislocations in the rural sector (and consequently managing the politics of agriculture) through the Common Agricultural Policy. There were several significant exceptions, including the European Monetary System that emerged as a Franco-German deal to cope with exchange-rate fluctuations that might threaten trade relations; however, the basic principle of national initiative persisted. Fifth, trade remained the crucial link between countries. Joint ventures and other forms of foreign direct investment to penetrate markets continued to be limited. Sixth, American multinationals were accepted, if not welcomed, in each country.

When the global context changed, the European bargains had to be adjusted for new realities. Wallace and Wessels have argued that "even if neither the EC nor EFTA had been invented long before, by the mid-eighties some form of intra-European management would have had to be found to oversee the necessary economic and industrial adjustments."

■ **THE POLITICAL MEANING OF
  CHANGING ECONOMIC STRUCTURES**

Changing international economic structures altered the choices and constraints facing European elites. Europe's options shifted with the changes in relative economic power resources. The relative position of the United States declined, prior to 1970, as its trade partners reconstructed themselves and developed. Gaps closed in technology, wealth, and productivity. The U.S. now has difficulty controlling its own economic environment, let alone structuring the system for others. The changed international setting is equally a story of the emergence of Japan, which has grown into the second-largest economy of the world, overtaking all of the individual European nations and even the Soviet Union. The significance of Japan's rise is frequently hidden rather than revealed by data about its growing share of world gross domestic product and its booming exports. The substantial consequences of the international changes are qualitative as well as quantitative. They alter the political as well as the economic choices for Europe. It is not a matter of trade quantities or economic well-being, though it may eventually be viewed in that way. For now, the problem is one of control and influence.

· · ·

The choices for European elites in technology, money, and trade have changed. Previously, the options had centered on the United States. If Europe could not lead in technology, at least it could acquire it relatively easily from the U.S. If Europe could not structure financial rules to its liking, at least it could accommodate to American positions. If Europe was not first, it was second, and a series of individual bargains by governments and companies could suffice. However, it would be quite another matter to be third. To be dependent on Japan in monetary and technology matters, without the integrated defense and trade ties that link the Atlantic partners, was a different problem. The new international structure required new bargains.

The structural changes we have been depicting do not "cause" responses. Structural changes pose challenges and opportunities. They present choices to decision makers. Three broad options, individually or in combination, were open to the countries of the EC. First, each nation could seek its own accommodation through purely national strategies; but, for reasons we explore below, going it alone appeared increasingly unpalatable. Second, Europe could adjust to Japanese power and shift ties from the U.S. to Japan. But the Japanese option had significant counts against it: (1) there were no common security interests with Japan to undergird the sorts of relations Europe has had with the United States; and (2) Japan has so far been unwilling to exercise a vigorous leadership role in the international system. The third option was that Europe could attempt to restructure its own position to act more coherently in a changing world. The international changes did not produce 1992; they provoked a rethinking. The 1992 Project emerged because the domestic context was propitious and policy entrepreneurs fashioned an elite coalition in favor of it.

■ **POLITICAL ENTREPRENEURSHIP: UNDERSTANDING THE CHANGING BARGAINS**

The surprisingly sudden movement by governments and companies toward a joint response does not have a clear and simple explanation. Uncertainty abounds. In a situation so open, so undefined, political science must rediscover the art of politics. The 1992 movement cannot be understood as the logical response to the situation in which actors and groups found themselves, and cannot therefore be understood through such formal tools as theories of games or collective action. Neither the payoff from nor preferences for any strategy were or are yet clear. European choices have been contingent on leadership, perception, and timing; they ought to be examined as an instance of elites constructing coalitions and institutions in support of new objectives.

This is not a story of mass movements, of pressure groups, or of legislatures. In the 1950s, the European project became a matter of party and group politics. In the 1980s, the EC institutions were not the object of debate; they were a political actor. Indeed, the Commission exercised leadership in proposing technical measures for the internal market that grabbed the attention of business and government elites, but were (in the initial stages at least) of little interest to the organs of mass politics. The governments and business elites had already been challenged by the international changes in ways that the parties and unions had not been. Some business and government leaders involved in 1992 are, in fact, trying to sidestep normal coalition politics in order to bring about domestic changes.

Consequently, any explanation of the choice of Europe and its evolution must focus on the actors—the leadership in the institutions of the European Community, in segments of the executive branch of the national governments, and in the business community (principally the heads of the largest companies)—and what they have achieved. These are the people who confronted the changes in the international environment and initiated the 1992 process. Each of these actors was indispensable, and each was involved with the actions of the others. The Community remains a bargain among governments. National governments—particularly the French—have begun to approach old problems in new ways and to make choices that are often unexpected. The Commission itself is an entrenched, self-interested advocate of further integration, so its position is no surprise. The multinationals are faced with sharply changed market conditions, and their concerns and reactions are not unexpected. The initiatives came from the EC, but they caught hold because the nature of the domestic political context had shifted. The interconnections and interactions among them will almost certainly defy an effort to assign primacy, weight, or relative influence.

In this section, we first address the domestic political context that prepared the ground for the Commission's plans. We then look at the Commission's initiatives, and finally at the role of the business elite in supporting the 1992 project.

The question is why national government policies and perspectives have altered. Why, in the decade between the mid-1970s and the mid-1980s, did European governments become open to European-level, market-oriented solutions? The answer has two parts: the failure of national strategies for economic growth and the transformation of the left in European politics. First, the traditional models of growth and economic management broke down. The old political strategies for the economy seemed to have run out. After the growth of the 1960s, the world economy entered a period of stagflation in the 1970s. As extensive industrialization reached its limits, the existing formulas for national economic development and the political bargains underpinning them had to be revised. Social critics and analysts in fact defined the crisis as the failure of established formulas to provide even plausible guides for action. It was not simply that the price of commodities rose, but that the dynamics of growth and trade changed.

Growth had been based on the shift of resources out of agriculture into industry; industrial development had been based on borrowing from abroad the most advanced technologies that could be obtained and absorbed. Suddenly, many old industrial sectors had to be closed, as in the case of shipbuilding. Others had to be transformed and reorganized, factories continuously upgraded, new machines designed and introduced, and work reorganized. The arguments that eventually emerged held that the old corporate strategies based on mass production were being forced to give way to strategies of flexibility and adaptability. Despite rising unemployment, the steady pace of improvement in productivity, coupled with the maintenance and sometimes reestablishment of a strong position in production equipment in vital sectors, suggested that Europe's often distinctive and innovative approaches to production were working. However, that was only to come toward the end of the decade. In short, during the 1970s, national executive and administrative elites found themselves facing new economic problems without adequate models for addressing them.

The 1970s were therefore the era of Europessimism. Europe seemed unable to adjust to the changed circumstances of international growth and competition after the oil shock. At first, the advanced countries stumbled, but then the United States and Japan seemed to pick themselves back up and to proceed. Japan's growth, which had originally been sustained by expansion within domestic markets, was bolstered by the competitive export orientation of major firms in consumer durables. New approaches to manufacturing created substantial advantages. In the United States, flexibility of the labor market—meaning the ability to fire workers and reduce real wages—seemed to assure jobs, albeit in services and often at lower wages, despite a deteriorating industrial position in global markets. Japan experienced productivity growth; the United States created jobs. Europe seemed to be doing neither and feared being left behind by the U.S.-Japanese competition in high technology.

For Europe, the critical domestic political issue was jobs, and the problem was said to be labor market rigidity. In some sense that was true, but the rigidities did not lie exclusively or even primarily with the workers' attitudes. They were embedded in government policy and industrial practice. In most of Western Europe, the basic postwar political bargain involved governmental responsibility for full employment and a welfare net. Consequently, many European companies had neither the flexibility of their American counterparts to fire workers or reduce wages, nor, broadly across Europe, the flexibility Japan displayed in redeploying its labor force. As unemployment rose, the old growth model built on a political settlement in each country was challenged—initially from the left by strategies of nationalization with state investment, and then from the right by strategies of deregulation with privatization. The political basis, in attitude and party coalition, for a more market-oriented approach was being put in place.

For a decade beginning with the oil shocks, the external environment for Europe was unstable, or turbulent, but its basic structure remained unchanged. While the United States was unwilling or unable to assure a system of fixed exchange rates, it remained the center of the financial system even as it changed the rules. The European Monetary System was an effort to create a zone of currency stability so that the expansion of trade inside Europe could continue. In the 1960s and 1970s, a long debate on technology gaps and the radical extension of American multinational power had not provoked joint European responses. During the 1970s, the mandate for the European Community was not altered; it was stretched to preserve its original objectives in the original context. The international economic turbulence and fears of a relative decline in competitive position did not provoke a full-blown European response. The extent of the shifts in relative economic power was not yet apparent. National strategies in many arenas had not yet failed, or at least were not yet perceived as having failed. In other arenas, the challenges could be dealt with by accommodations within the realm of domestic politics.

The question remains: Why did national policy change, why did the perceptions of choice evolve, the range of options shift? Policy failure must be interpreted; it can be assigned many meanings. National perceptions of position are filtered through parties and bureaucracies, shaped and flavored by factions, interests, and lobbies. In 1983, the French Socialist party was divided between those led by Laurent Fabius, who concluded that pressure on the franc was a reason to reverse policy direction and to stay within the European Community, and those like Chevènement, who felt the proper choice was to withdraw from the EMS, even if that resulted in an effective weakening of the Community. The choice, to stay in the EMS, was by no means a foregone matter. The French response to the currency crisis was a political choice made in the end by the president.

Thus, the second aspect of the changed domestic political context was the shift in government coalitions in a number of EC member states. Certainly the weakening of the left in some countries and a shift from the communist to the market-socialist left in others helped to make possible a debate about market solutions (including unified European markets) to Europe's dilemma. In Latin Europe, the communist parties weakened as the era of Eurocommunism waned. Spain saw the triumph of Gonzalez's socialists, and their unexpected emergence as advocates of market-led development and entry into the Common Market. Italy experienced a weakening of the position of the communists in the complex mosaic of party positioning. In France, Mitterrand's victory displaced the communists from their primacy on the left. The first two years of the French socialist government proved crucial in turning France away from the quest for economic autonomy. After 1983, Mitterrand embraced a more market-oriented approach and became a vigorous advocate of increased European cooperation. This had the unexpected consequence of engendering independence for the state-named managers of nationalized companies. When the conservative government of Jacques Chirac adopted deregulation as a central policy approach, a second blow was dealt to the authority of the French state in industry. In Britain and Germany, the Labour and Social Democratic parties lost power as well as influence on the national debate.

Throughout Europe the corporatist temptation waned; that is, management of the macroeconomy by direct negotiations among social groups and the government no longer seemed to work. In many union and left circles an understanding grew that adaptation to market processes would be required. (As the 1992 movement progressed, unions in most countries became wary that the European "competitive imperative" might be used to justify policies that would restrict their influence and unwind their positions and gains. As a counterpoint on the right, Thatcher began to fear a bureaucratized and socialized Europe.)

In an era when deregulation—the freeing of the market—became the fad, it made intuitive sense to extend the European internal market as a response to all ailments. Moreover, some governments, or some elites within nations, can achieve purely domestic goals by using European agreements to limit or constrain national policy choices. The EMS is not only a means of stabilizing exchange rates to facilitate trade, but also a constraint on domestic politics that pushes toward more restrictive macroeconomic policies than would otherwise have been adopted. There is little doubt that the course of the social experiment in 1981 would have been different if France had not been a member of the EMS, which required formal withdrawal from commitments if a country wanted to pursue independent expansionary policies. In a different vein, some Italians use the threat of competitive pressures as a reason to reform the administration. As one Italian commentator put it, "Europe for us will be providential. ... The French and Germans love 1992 because each thinks it can be the key country in Europe. The most we can hope for is that 1992 straightens us out."

In any case, in Europe we are watching the creation of like-minded elites and alliances that at first blush appear improbable—such as Mitterrand and Thatcher committed to some sort of European strategy. These elites are similar in political function (though not in political basis) to the cross-national Christian Democratic alliance that emerged in support of the original Community after World War II in Germany, France, and elsewhere. European-level, market-oriented solutions have become acceptable.

This was the domestic political soil into which the Commission's initiatives fell. Traditional models of economic growth appeared to have played themselves out, and the left had been transformed in such a way that socialist parties began to seek market-oriented solutions to economic ills. In this setting, the European Community provided more than the mechanisms of intergovernmental negotiation. The Eurocracy was a standing constituency and a permanent advocate of European solutions and greater unity. Proposals from the European Commission transformed this new orientation into policy, and, more importantly, into a policy perspective and direction. The Commission perceived the international structural changes and the failure of existing national strategies, and seized the initiative.

To understand how the Commission's initiatives led governments to step beyond failed national policy, let us examine the case of telematics, the economically crucial sector combining microelectronics, computers, and telecommunications. By 1980, European policy makers were beginning to realize that the national champion strategies of the past decade or so had failed to reverse the steady international decline of European telematics industries. Throughout the 1970s, each national government in Europe had sought to build up domestic firms capable of competing with the American giants. The state encouraged or engineered mergers and provided research-and-development subsidies; state procurement heavily favored the domestic firms. By 1980, none of these approaches had paid off. Europe's champions were losing market shares both in Europe and worldwide, and most of them were operating in the red. Even Europe's traditional electronics stronghold, telecommunications equipment, was showing signs of weakness: the telecommunications trade surplus was declining annually while U.S. and Japanese imports were accounting for ever larger shares of the most technologically advanced market segments.

In telematics, European collaboration emerged when the Commission, under the leadership of Etienne Davignon, struck an alliance with the twelve major electronics companies in the EC. Because of the mounting costs and complexity of R&D, rapid technological and market changes, and the convergence of hitherto separate technologies (e.g., computing and telecommunications), these twelve companies were motivated to seek interfirm partnerships. Although such partnerships were common with American firms, the possibilities within Europe had not been explored. The twelve firms designed the European Strategic Programme for Research and Development in Information Technology (ESPRIT) and then sold it to their governments. The RACE program (Research in Advanced Communications for Europe) emerged via a similar process. In short, the Community's high-technology programs of the early 1980s took shape in a setting in which previous national policies had been discredited, the Commission advanced concrete proposals, and industry lent essential support. In a sense, the telematics cases prefigure the 1992 movement and display the same configuration of political actors: the Commission, certain political leaders and specific agencies within the national governments, and senior business leaders.

The Commission again took the initiative with the publication of its "White Paper" in June 1985. The initiative should be seen as a response to the stagnation of the Community enterprise as a result of, among other things, the budget stalemates. When Jacques Delors took office as president of the European Commission in 1985, he consciously sought an undertaking, a vision, that would reignite the European idea. The notion of a single market by 1992 caught the imagination because the need for a broader Europe was perceived outside the Commission. Helen Wallace and Wolfgang Wessels suggest that if the EEC and the European Free Trade Association (EFTA) had not existed by the late 1980s, they would have had to be invented. Or, as was the case, reinvented.

The White Paper set out a program and a timetable for the completion of the fully unified internal market. The now famous set of three hundred legislative proposals to eliminate obstacles to the free functioning of the market, as well as the analyses that led up to and followed it, expressed a clear perception of Europe's position. European decline or the necessities of international competitiveness (choose your own phrasing) require—in this view—the creation of a continental market.

The White Paper's program had the political advantage of setting forth concrete steps and a deadline. The difficult political questions could be obscured by focusing on the mission and by reducing
the issues to a series of apparently technical steps. Advocates of market unification could emphasize highly specific, concrete, seemingly
innocuous, and long overdue objectives rather than their consequences. In a sense, the tactic is to move above and below the level of
controversy. The broad mission is agreed to; the technical steps are
unobjectionable. Of course, there is a middle ground where the questions of the precise form of Europe, the allocation of gain and pain in
the process, become evident. A small change in, say, health and safety
rules may appear unimportant, but may prove to be the shelter behind which a national firm is hiding from European and global com-
petitors. Here we find the disputes about outcomes, both in terms of
market results and of social values. Obscuring the issues and interests
was crucial in developing Europe the first time, one might note, and
has been instrumental once again.

Implementation of the White Paper required a separate initiative: the limitation, expressed in the Single European Act, of national
vetoes over Community decisions. At its core, the Community has always been a mechanism for governments to bargain. It has certainly
not been a nation state, and only a peculiar kind of federalism. Real
decisions have been made in the Council by representatives of national governments. The Commissioners, the department heads, are
drawn from a pool nominated by the governments. Broader representative institutions have played only a fictive (or, more generously,
a secondary) role. Moreover, decisions taken by the Council on major issues had to be unanimous, providing each government with a
veto. For this reason, it has been painfully difficult to extend the
Community's authority, to change the rules of finance, or to proceed
with the creation of a unified market and change the rules of business
in Europe. The most reluctant state prevailed. Furthermore, domestic
groups could block Community action by persuading their government to exercise their veto.

Many see the Single European Act as the most important
amendment to the Treaty of Rome since the latter was adopted in
1957. This act has replaced the Luxembourg Compromise (which required decisions to be taken by unanimity) with a qualified majority
requirement in the case of certain measures that have as their object
the establishment and functioning of the internal market. The national veto still exists in other domains, but most of the three hundred directives for 1992 can be adopted by qualified majority. As a
result, disgruntled domestic interest groups have lost a source of

leverage on their governments; the national veto no longer carries the clout it once did. Perhaps equally important, the Single European Act embodies a new strategy toward national standards that were an obstacle to trade within the Community. Previously, the EEC pinned its hopes on "harmonization," a process by which national governments would adopt "Euronorms" prepared by the Commission. The Single European Act instead adopts the principle affirmed in the famous Cassis de Dijon case. That principle holds that standards (for foodstuffs, safety, health, and so on) that prevail in one country must be recognized by the others as sufficient.

The third actor in the story, besides the governments and the Commission, is the leadership of the European multinational corporations. In a number of ways, they have experienced most directly some of the consequences of the international economic changes. They have acted both politically and in the market. The White Paper and the Single European Act gave the appearance that changes in the EC market were irreversible and politically unstoppable. Businesses have been acting on that belief. Politically, they have taken up the banner of 1992, collaborating with the Commission and exerting substantial influence on their governments. The significance of the role of business, and of its collaboration with the Commission, must not be underestimated. European business and the Commission may be said to have together bypassed national governmental processes and shaped an agenda that compelled attention and action.

Substantial support for the Commission's initiatives has come from the Roundtable of European Industrialists, an association of some of Europe's largest and most influential corporations, including Philips, Siemens, Olivetti, GEC, Daimler Benz, Volvo, Fiat, Bosch, ASEA and Ciba-Geigy. Indeed, when Jacques Delors, prior to assuming the presidency of the Commission in 1985, began campaigning for the unified internal market, European industrialists were ahead of him. Wisse Dekker of Philips and Jacques Solvay of Belgium's Solvay chemical company in particular were vigorously arguing for unification of the EC's fragmented markets. In the early 1980s, a booklet published by Philips proposed urgent action on the internal market. "There is really no choice," it argued, "and the only option left for the Community is to achieve the goals laid down in the Treaty of Rome. Only in this way can industry compete globally, by exploiting economies of scale, for what will then be the biggest home market in the world today: *the European Community home market.*"

It is hard, though, to judge whether the business community influenced Europe to pursue an internal market strategy or was itself constituted as a political interest group by Community action. Business began to organize in 1983, when the Roundtable of European Industrialists was formed under the chairmanship of Pehr Gyllenhammer, of Volvo. Many of the original business discussions included senior Community bureaucrats; in fact, Etienne Davignon reportedly recruited most of the members of the original group. The executives constituting the Roundtable (numbering 29 by mid-1987) were among the most powerful industrialists in Europe, including the non-EEC countries. The group initially published three reports: one on the need for development of a Europe-wide traffic infrastructure, one containing proposals for Europe's unemployment crisis, and one, *Changing Scales,* describing the economies of scale that would benefit European businesses in a truly unified market.

The European Roundtable became a powerful lobby vis-à-vis the national governments. One member of the Delors cabinet in Brussels has declared, "These men are very powerful and dynamic . . . when necessary they can ring up their own prime ministers and make their case." Delors himself has said, "We count on business leaders for support." Local and regional chambers of commerce have helped to establish about fifty European Information Centers to handle queries and publicize 1992. In short, the 1992 process is repeating the pattern established by ESPRIT: major businesses have allied with the Commission to persuade governments, which were already seeking to adapt to the changed international structure.

At the same time that the business community has supported the political initiatives behind the 1992 movement, it has been acting in the market place. A series of business deals, ventures, and mergers form a critical part of the 1992 movement. Even if nothing more happens in the 1992 process, the face of business competition in Europe is being changed. The structure of competition is being altered.

There has been a huge surge in joint ventures, share-swapping, and mergers in Europe. Many are justified on the grounds of preparing for a unified market, some for reasons of production and marketing strategies, and some as a means of defense against takeovers. But much of the movement is a response to business problems that would exist in any case. Still, the process has taken on a life of its own. The mergers provoke responses in the form of other business alliances; the responding alliances appear more urgent because of the political rhetoric. As the Europeans join together, American and Japanese firms scurry to put their own alliances in place and to rearrange their activities.

The meaning of the process is far from evident. Are we watching the creation of European competition, or the cartelization of industry at a European level? In some sectors, such as textiles and apparel, there already is an effective European market. In others, such as telecommunications, the terms of competition—whatever the corporate reshufflings—will turn on government regulation and choice. Since U.S. firms are already entrenched, the real newcomers are the Japanese. A surge of Japanese investment is taking place in Europe.

.   .   .

■ CONCLUSION

Europe is throwing the dice. It is confronted with a change in the structure of the international economy, with emerging Japanese and dwindling American power and position. It feels the shift in Asian competitive pressure in industry and finance. The problems are no longer those of American production in Europe, but of Japanese imports and production displacing European production. More importantly perhaps, Europe also feels the shift in rising Japanese influence in the monetary and technology domains. The industrial and governmental presumptions and deals with which Europe has operated are changing or will change. Indeed, Europeans may have to construct a coherent political presence on the global stage in order to achieve the most attractive accommodation to the new order.

We hypothesize that change in the international economic structure was necessary for the revival of the European project. A full-fledged test of this proposition will require detailed analysis of the perceptions and beliefs of those who participated in launching the 1992 movement. We have mentioned other analytical approaches—based on integration theory and domestic politics—that appear logically unsuited to explaining 1992. Of course, these approaches are not really alternatives. There are functional links among some of the bargains being struck, and domestic factors clearly shaped governmental responses to the international changes. But tests of alternative explanations often create a false sense of scientism by setting individually weak explanations against each other and finding "confirmation" by denying the worst of them. Competing explanations often represent different types of explanation, different levels of analysis. In the end, it is not a matter of which one is better, but of whether the right questions are being asked. This article is an effort to frame the proper questions and propose analytical links among them.

We argue that structural situations create the context of choice and cast up problems to be resolved, but they do not dictate the decisions and strategies. In other words, the global setting can be understood in neorealist terms, but the political processes triggered by changes in the system must be analyzed in other than structural terms. The choices result from political processes and have political explanations. In this case, the process is one of bargains among nations and elites within the region. The political process for implementing these bargains is labeled "Europe 1992," a complex web of intergovernmental bargains and accommodations among the various national business elites.

In this essay, we showed why 1992 has so far been a project of elites. The commitment of the governments to the process, the fundamental bargain, is expressed by the end of the single-nation veto system, which changed the logic of Community decisionmaking. Europe's states have thrown themselves into the drive for a unified market, unleashing business processes that in themselves are recasting the terms of competition within Europe. The terms of the final bargains are open.

The effort to reshape the European Communities has so far been guided by three groups: Community institutions, industrial elites, and governments. The Commission proposes and persuades. Important business coalitions exercise indispensable influence on governments. Governments are receptive because of changes in the world economy and shifts in the domestic political context. The domestic context has changed in two key ways: (1) with the failure of traditional models of growth and purely national strategies for economic management; and (2) with the defeat of the left in some countries, and with its transformation because of the weakening of communist parties in others. These changes opened the way for an unlikely set of elite alliances. In this context, EC initiatives began to demonstrate that there were joint European alternatives to failed national strategies. The telematics programs were one precursor. Delors built on the budding sense of optimism and gave energy and leadership to the notion of a genuine single market. Whether a broader range of political groups will become involved is an open issue, one that may determine both whether the process continues and what form it takes.

The outcomes are quite unknowable, dependent on the timing and dynamics of a long series of contingent decisions. But the story, and consequently the analysis, concerns political leadership in creating a common European interest and then constructing a set of bargains that embody that understanding. Many of the choices are simply calculated risks, or perhaps explorations that will be entrenched if they work and refashioned if they don't. Even if we could predict the outcomes of any single choice with a high degree of confidence, the sequencing of diverse decisions and their cumulative effects would be impossible to foresee. It would be ironic if 1992 succeeded formally but economic rejuvenation did not follow. In any case, Europe's choices—particularly the possibility of a coherent Western Europe emerging as an actor on the global stage—will powerfully influence the world economic system, and perhaps the security system as well.

21

Negotiating the Single European Act: National Interests and Conventional Statecraft in the European Community

ANDREW MORAVCSIK

Wayne Sandholtz and John Zysman (Chapter 20) argued that supranational actors played a major role in relaunching Europe. Neofunctionalism was suddenly back in style in the 1990s among many students of the European Community who saw spillover everywhere. As in the 1960s, neofunctionalism briefly held the field until challenged by the intergovernmentalists who insisted that member states still controlled the integration process. Leading the intergovernmentalist charge was a former student of Stanley Hoffmann's, Andrew Moravcsik (Harvard University).

Moravcsik, in a widely read 1991 article, offered a "liberal intergovernmentalist" challenge to Sandholtz and Zysman's explanation of the 1992 process. He argued that the "supranational institutionalism" of Sandholtz and Zysman could not, in fact, account for the "negotiating history" of the Single European Act (SEA). EC institutions, transnational business groups, and international political leaders simply were not as important to the passage of the SEA as the supranationalists claimed. Moravcsik argued instead that the SEA was

Reprinted from *International Organization* 45(1)(1991):651–688 by permission of The MIT Press. Copyright 1991 by the World Peace Foundation and the Massachusetts Institute of Technology. Notes omitted.

the result of bargaining among the heads of government of the three most powerful EC countries: Britain, France, and Germany; that these bargains represented the lowest common denominator; and that each leader jealously protected national sovereignty. Understanding the positions taken by the important states in the negotiations, according to Moravcsik, requires an investigation of the domestic sources of EC policy. He outlines several possible avenues of investigation, but does not come to a definitive conclusion as to which explanation of domestic policies works best.

Moravcsik has continued to critique supranational notions of integration while further refining his liberal intergovernmentalist approach. As we shall see in the following chapters, he has dramatically influenced the contemporary theoretical debate.

The European Community (EC) is experiencing its most important period of reform since the completion of the Common Market in 1968. This new impulse toward European integration—the "relaunching" of Europe, the French call it—was unexpected. The late 1970s and early 1980s were periods of "Europessimism" and "Eurosclerosis," when politicians and academics alike lost faith in European institutions. The current period is one of optimism and institutional momentum. The source of this transformation was the Single European Act (SEA), a document approved by European heads of government in 1986.

The SEA links liberalization of the European market with procedural reform. The first half of this reform package, incorporating 279 proposals contained in the 1985 EC Commission White Paper, aims to create "an area without internal frontiers in which the free movement of goods, persons, services, and capital is ensured." To realize this goal, European leaders committed themselves to addressing issues never successfully tackled in a multinational forum, such as the comprehensive liberalization of trade in services and the removal of domestic regulations that act as nontariff barriers. Previous attempts to set detailed and uniform European standards for domestic regulations ("harmonization") had proven time-consuming and fruitless. With this in mind, the White Paper called for a "new approach" based on "mutual recognition"—a less invasive form of liberalization whereby only minimal standards would be harmonized.

The second half of the SEA reform package consists of procedural reforms designed to streamline decisionmaking in the governing body of the EC, the Council of Ministers. Since January 1966, qualified majority voting had been limited in practice by the "Luxembourg compromise," in which France unilaterally asserted the right to veto a proposal in the Council of Ministers by declaring that a "vital" or "very important" interest was at stake. The SEA expands the use of qualified majority voting in the Council of Ministers, although only on matters pertaining to the internal market.

What accounts for the timing and the content of the reform package that relaunched Europe? Why did this reform succeed when so many previous efforts had failed?

The findings [of this paper] challenge the prominent view that institutional reform resulted from an elite alliance between EC officials and pan-European business interest groups. The negotiating history is more consistent with the alternative explanation that EC reform rested on interstate bargains between Britain, France, and Germany. An essential precondition for reform was the convergence of the economic policy prescriptions of ruling party coalitions in these countries following the election of the British Conservative party in 1979 and the reversal of French Socialist party policy in 1983. Also essential was the negotiating leverage that France and Germany gained by exploiting the threat of creating a "two-track" Europe and excluding Britain from it. This "intergovernmental institutionalist" explanation is more consistent with what Robert Keohane calls the "modified structural realist" view of regime change, a view that stresses traditional conceptions of national interests and power, than it is with supranational variants of neofunctionalist integration theory. For the source of state interests, however, scholars must turn away from structural theories and toward domestic politics, where the existence of several competing explanations invite further research.

■ EXPLANATIONS FOR THE SUCCESS OF THE SEA

Journalistic reportage, academic analysis, and interviews with European officials reveal a bewilderingly wide range of explanations, some contradictory, for the timing, content, and process of adopting the White Paper and the SEA. One French official I interviewed in Brussels quipped, "When the little boy turns out well, everyone claims paternity!" The various accounts cluster around two stylized explanations, the first stressing the independent activism of international or transnational actors and the second emphasizing bargaining between leaders of the most powerful states of Europe.

□   *Supranational Institutionalism*

Three supranational factors consistently recur in accounts of EC reform: pressure from EC institutions, particularly the Parliament and
Court; lobbying by transnational business interest groups; and the
political entrepreneurship of the Commission, led by President
Jacques Delors and Internal Market Commissioner Lord Arthur
Cockfield. Together these supranational factors offer an account of
reform guided by actors and institutions acting "above" the nation
state.

European institutions. Between 1980 and 1985, pressure for reform
grew within the EC institutions. In the European Parliament, resolutions and reports supported the programs of two groups, one "maximalist" and the other "minimalist" in approach. The first group,
which included many Italians and quite a number of Germans, advocated European federalism and a broad expansion in the scope of EC
activities, backed by procedural reforms focusing particularly on increasing the power of the Parliament. Following the Europarliamen-
tary penchant for animal names, these activists called themselves the
"Crocodile Group," after the Strasbourg restaurant where they first
met. Led by the venerable Altiero Spinelli, a founding father of the
EC, their efforts culminated in the European Parliament resolution of
February 1984 proposing a "Draft Treaty Establishing the European
Union"—a new, more ambitious document to replace the Treaty of
Rome.

The second group, founded in 1981 and consisting of Parliament members who were skeptical of federalism and parliamentary
reform, focused on working with national leaders to liberalize the
internal market. These activists called themselves the "Kangaroo
Group," based on the Australian marsupial's ability to "hop over
borders." Their efforts were funded by sympathetic business interests (primarily British and Dutch), and they counted Basil de Fer-
ranti, a leading British industrialist and Tory parliamentarian,
among their leaders. The Kangaroos encouraged parliamentary
studies on economic topics and in 1983 launched a public campaign
in favor of a detailed EC timetable for abolishing administrative,
technical, and fiscal barriers, a reference to which was included in
the draft treaty.

Transnational business interest groups. According to Wisse Dekker,
chief executive officer of Philips, European integration in the 1950s

was initiated by politicians, while in its current "industrial" phase it is initiated by business leaders. The evidence presented to date by partisans of this view stresses the actions of pan-European business interest groups. The Commission has long sought to encourage the development of a sort of pan-European corporatist network by granting these groups privileged access to the policy process, though this effort has met with little success.

In the mid-1980s, business interest groups, at times working together with EC officials, hoped to bolster the competitiveness of European firms by calling for a more liberal EC market. Viscount Etienne Davignon, the internal market commissioner from 1976 through 1984, brought together a group of large European information technology firms in 1981 to form the Thorn-Davignon Commission, which developed proposals for technology programs and European technical norms and reportedly also discussed market liberalization. In 1983, Pehr Gyllenhammer, the chief executive officer of Volvo, and Wisse Dekker helped found the Roundtable of European Industrialists, made up of the heads of a number of Europe's largest multinational corporations, some of whom were selected on Davignon's suggestion. Once the SEA was adopted, the Roundtable formed a "watchdog" committee to press for its implementation. In February 1984, the Union des Confederations de l'Industrie et des Employeurs d'Europe (UNICE), the leading EC industrial interest group, called for majority voting, and it has been active since then in promoting market liberalization.

In a series of speeches delivered in the autumn of 1984 and early 1985, Dekker proposed what became the best-known business plan for market liberalization, the "Europa 1990" plan. Its focus on internal market liberalization, its division of the task into categories (reform of fiscal, commercial, technical, and government procurement policies), its ideology of economies of scale, its recognition of the link between commercial liberalization and tax harmonization, its identification of the ultimate goal with a certain date, and many of its other details were echoed in Delors' proposal to the European Parliament a few months later and in the White Paper of June 1985. Transnational business pres-sure, some have argued, was "indispensable" to the passage of the SEA.

International political leaders. The Commission has traditionally been viewed as the agenda-setting arm of the EC. When Delors was nominated for the presidency of the Commission, he immediately sought a major initiative to rejuvenate the EC. When he assumed the office in January 1985, he visited government, business, and labor leaders in each of the European capitals to discuss possible reforms. According to his account, he considered reform in three areas—the EC decisionmaking institutions, European monetary policy, and political and defense collaboration—before deciding to "return to the origins" of the EC, the construction of a single internal market. Like Jean Monnet two decades before, Delors identified the goal with a date. He aimed to render the achievement of the program irreversible by 1988 and to complete it by 1992, coeval with the duration of two four-year terms of commissioners. It is commonly argued that Delors used the institutional power of the presidency as a platform from which to forge the link between the procedural improvements proposed by Parliament and the internal market liberalization advocated by Brussels-based business groups. According to this view, he encouraged Cockfield to elaborate the internal market agenda in the White Paper and then exaggerated the sense of economic decline to secure the approval of European heads of government.

☐   *Supranational Institutionalism and Neofunctionalism*

An elite alliance between transnationally organized big business groups and EC officials, led by Delors, constitutes the core of the supranational institutionalist explanation for the 1992 initiative. The explanation is theoretically coherent in that each of its elements emphasizes the autonomy and influence enjoyed by international institutions and transnational groups acting "above the state." Two leading scholars [Sandholtz and Zysman, see Chapter 20] have recently argued that the key role played by supranational actors decisively distinguishes the politics of the SEA from those of the Treaty of Rome three decades earlier: "Leadership for 1992 came from outside the national settings; it came from the Commission."

   This explanation is consistent with a certain variant of neofunctionalist theory. In *The Uniting of Europe,* Ernst Haas distinguishes between processes of integration that take place at what he called the "supranational" and "national" levels. Three key elements of the supranational process are the ability of a central institution (the EC) "to assert itself in such a way as to cause strong positive or negative expectations," the tendency of "business and labor . . . to unite beyond their former national confines in an effort to make common policy," and the "demonstration by a resourceful supranational executive that ends already agreed to cannot be attained without further united steps." An examination of the role of supranational actors in initiating the SEA tests this particular variant of neo-functionalism, though not, of course, the entire model.

☐ *Intergovernmental Institutionalism*

An alternative approach to explaining the success of the 1992 initiative focuses on interstate bargains between heads of government in the three largest member states of the EC. This approach, which can be called "intergovernmental institutionalism," stresses the central importance of power and interests, with the latter not simply dictated by position in the international system. Intergovernmental institutionalism is based on three principles: intergovernmentalism, lowest-common-denominator bargaining, and strict limits on future transfers of sovereignty.

Intergovernmentalism. From its inception, the EC has been based on interstate bargains between its leading member states. Heads of government, backed by a small group of ministers and advisers, initiate and negotiate major initiatives in the Council of Ministers or the European Council. Each government views the EC through the lens of its own policy preferences; EC politics is the continuation of domestic policies by other means. Even when societal interests are transnational, the principal form of their political expression remains national.

Lowest-common-denominator bargaining. Without a "European hegemon" capable of providing universal incentives or threats to promote regime formation and without the widespread use of linkages and logrolling, the bargains struck in the EC reflect the relative power positions of the member states. Small states can be bought off with side-payments, but larger states exercise a *de facto* veto over fundamental changes in the scope or rules of the core element of the EC, which remains economic liberalization. Thus, bargaining tends to converge toward the lowest common denominator of large state interests. The bargains initially consisted of bilateral agreements between France and Germany; now they consist of trilateral agreements including Britain.

The only tool that can impel a state to accept an outcome on a major issue that it does not prefer to the status quo is the threat of exclusion. Once an international institution has been created, exclusion can be expensive both because the nonmember forfeits input into further decisionmaking and because it forgoes whatever benefits result. If two major states can isolate the third and credibly threaten it with ex-

clusion and if such exclusion undermines the substantive interests of
the excluded state, the coercive threat may bring about an agreement
at a level of integration above the lowest common denominator.

Protection of sovereignty. The decision to join a regime involves
some sacrifice of national sovereignty in exchange for certain advantages. Policymakers safeguard their countries against the future
erosion of sovereignty by demanding the unanimous consent of
regime members to sovereignty-related reforms. They also avoid
granting open-ended authority to central institutions that might infringe on their sovereignty, preferring instead to work through intergovernmental institutions such as the Council of Ministers,
rather than through supranational bodies such as the Commission
and Parliament.

□ *Intergovernmental Institutionalism
   and Modified Structural Realism*

Convergent national interests, interstate bargains, and constraints
on further reform constitute the intergovernmental institutionalist
explanation for the SEA. This explanation is theoretically coherent
in that it stresses the autonomy and influence of national leaders
vis-à-vis international institutions as well as the importance of
power resources in determining the outcomes of intergovernmental
bargains.

Intergovernmental institutionalism affirms the realist foundations of what Keohane calls the "modified structural realist" explanation of regime formation and maintenance. States are the principal
actors in the international system. Interstate bargains reflect national
interests and relative power. International regimes shape interstate
politics by providing a common framework that reduces the uncertainty and transaction costs of interstate interactions. In the postwar
system, Keohane argues, regimes have preserved established patterns
of cooperation after the relative decline of the United States. Similarly, the EC regime, though neither created nor maintained by a
hegemon, fixes interstate bargains until the major European powers
choose to negotiate changes.

The emphasis of intergovernmental institutionalism differs decisively from that of modified structural realism, however, in that it
locates the sources of regime reform not only in the changing power
distribution but also in the changing interests of states. States are not
"black boxes"; they are entities entrusted to governments, which

themselves are responsible to domestic constituencies. State interests change over time, often in ways which are decisive for the integration process but which cannot be traced to shifts in the relative power of states.

■ NATIONAL INTERESTS AND 1992

The intergovernmental approach suggests that an analysis of the 1992 initiative must begin by examining the underlying preferences of Germany, France, and Britain. As indicated above, Delors identified four issue-areas that might have served as the vehicle for major EC reform: monetary coordination, political and defense cooperation, institutional reform, and internal market liberalization. A glance at the national preferences for monetary coordination and for political and defense cooperation suggests that there was little possibility of a formal agreement, since in both cases France was opposed by Britain and Germany. Procedural reform in the EC decisionmaking institutions and liberalization of the internal market offered more promise and later became the two components of the 1992 initiative.

□ *Germany: Consistent Support*

Among the three largest member states of the EC, Germany has enjoyed since the late 1950s the least partisan opposition to further European integration. As Europe's leading exporter, dependent on the EC for nearly half its exports, Germany profits directly from economic integration. German Foreign Minister Hans-Dietrich Genscher, leader of the Free Democrats, has also been a strong supporter of European political cooperation, which he views as a vital complement to *Ostpolitik*. Moreover, a greater role for the European Parliament is widely viewed as a desirable step toward political union. On the other hand, in the mid-1980s, Germany was suspicious of proposals for a European defense organization, was ambivalent about altering the agricultural policy so it would pay more or receive less, and was opposed to further monetary integration, at least until capital flows were liberalized.

□ *France: The Road to Damascus*

Although traditionally pro-European, the French Socialist party all but ignored the EC during the first few years of the Mitterrand presidency. France did call for more qualified majority voting and, to the surprise of many, supported a majority vote to override the threatened British veto of the cereal price package in May 1982. But substantive disagreements undermined Franco-German cooperation for EC reform. The most important French initiatives of this period, one in October 1981 on *un espace social européen* and another in the autumn of 1983 on *un espace industriel européen,* did not amount to much. The first initiative, which was an antiunemployment program of fiscal stimulation billed as the initial step toward a "socialist Europe," found few friends in either Bonn or London and was never discussed at the Council. The second offered support for technology policies already in the process of adoption by the EC.

France's role as a European outsider during this period reflected its unorthodox domestic economic policies, which ran counter to the more conservative policies of Germany and Britain. Until 1983, French economic policy was conceived by the more radical wing of the Socialist party, led by politicians such as Jean-Pierre Chevènement and Pierre Bérégovoy. Nationalization, direct intervention to increase employment, and increases in social welfare spending undermined international business and financial confidence in the French economy. By March 1983, the French government had already negotiated two devaluations of the franc within the European Monetary System (EMS) and was rapidly heading for a third. The governments of other European states, particularly Germany, made it clear that a continuation of expansive policies was incompatible with continued membership in the EMS.

Many Socialists urged Mitterrand to move toward autarky— import protection, capital controls, and repudiation of the EMS—to protect expansionist domestic policies. Others in the moderate wing of the Socialist party, represented by politicians Michel Rocard and Jacques Delors and backed nearly unanimously by the French economic technocracy, advocated continued EMS membership, external free trade, and an austerity policy consisting of wage restraint and cuts in public expenditures. Some moderates also realized that the economic fundamentals underlying traditional French support for the Common Agricultural Policy (CAP) were shifting. Although domestic politics dictated that the government not move too quickly against agricultural interests, France was no longer a large net beneficiary from the EC budget, and its prospects after the entry of Spain and Portugal were even bleaker.

Mitterrand's decision to remain in the EMS, announced on 21 March 1983, marked a turning point not only in French domestic politics but also in French policy toward the EC. While the EMS decision may have been influenced in part by an independent desire to remain "European," other factors included the failure of the autarkic policies, which would ultimately have compelled the French government to impose as much austerity as the policy they chose, and the decline of the Communist party, which allowed Mitterrand to align himself with moderate Socialists. French economic decisionmaking was thus vested in the hands of Rocard, Delors, and other politicians convinced of the virtues of conservative economic policies and firm in their belief that France must work within Europe to achieve its economic goals.

With the advent in January 1984 of the French presidency in the Council of Ministers and with elections to the European Parliament just two months away, Mitterrand—true to the European idealism he had espoused since the 1940s but undoubtedly also conscious of the political advantage to be gained by making a virtue out of necessity—announced a major diplomatic initiative for a relaunching of Europe. From that point on, Mitterrand played a decisive role in settling European disputes. French leadership and concessions helped resolve British agricultural and budget complaints. French negotiators began to support internal market liberalization and collaborative research and development. Mitterrand began to adopt the rhetoric of European federalism. He spoke of reconsidering the Luxembourg compromise and supporting procedural reform, as long as it was limited to the Council and the Commission and did not imply a radical democratization of EC politics. Although committed to using the EC to combat economic decline, the French government remained uncertain whether monetary policy, internal market liberalization, or cooperative research and development should be the heart of the new initiative. Thus, Mitterrand, without being entirely sure where the initiative was leading, became the primary spokesman for relaunching Europe. One senior French diplomat observed dryly, "Monsieur Mitterrand's term as president of the European Council has become his road to Damascus."

□   *Britain: The Road to Milan*

With France converted to the European cause, Britain remained the major obstacle to an initiative linking internal market liberalization and procedural reform. Britain's entry into the EC in 1973 had expanded the Community without strengthening it. Insofar as Thatcher was pro-European, it was largely because she saw the EC almost exclusively as an organization for promoting economic liberalism in the industrial and service sectors. By British standards, however, this represented a considerable commitment, since the opposition Labour party was against market liberalization and against European integration. Having abolished exchange controls in 1979, having begun liberalization of telecommunications services in 1981, having publicly promised to lower European air fares, and, last but not least, being fully aware that the city of London contained highly competitive banking and insurance sectors, Thatcher began to call for pan-European deregulation of services. The British government also favored strengthening European political cooperation, although without creating an independent bureaucracy.

In the early 1980s, the most important British objection to EC policy stemmed from the heavy British deficit under the CAP. With its small, efficient agricultural sector concentrated in areas not generously subsidized by the CAP (for example, in sheep husbandry), Britain gained little from the agricultural programs that comprise 70 percent of the EC budget. At the same time, Britain was by far the largest per capita net contributor to the budget. Thatcher campaigned to get "her money back" from the EC, and her frugality bolstered British opposition to the budgetary policy. When she was elected to office, she insisted that two-thirds of the British deficit over the past few years be rebated and that permanent adjustments be made to limit agricultural spending and to prevent future budgetary disequilibria.

More was at stake in the British objections than temporary budgetary imbalances. In 1973, Britain had been forced to accept the agricultural and budgetary policies as part of the *acquis communautaire,* the corpus of existing EC institutions. For those who had worked for decades in the Community and who saw the CAP as part of the initial Franco-German bargain at the heart of the EC, the British demand called into question the very foundation of European cooperation. French Foreign Minister Claude Cheysson declared in 1982 that "the United Kingdom [seeks] *juste retour,* which is not a Community idea. We and the British are not speaking of the same community."

The Thatcher government, even more than previous British governments, was wary of attempts to strengthen the Commission and Parliament and to expand EC competence into areas not directly connected with trade, such as indirect taxation and social legislation. Thatcher also firmly opposed format changes in Council procedures, in part because of a suspicion of written constitutions, a suspicion shared by most British conservatives. Although she was opposed to any treaty changes that undermined the sovereign prerogatives recognized by the Luxembourg compromise, she recognized the need for some movement away from unanimous decisionmaking and thus favored informal means of encouraging majority voting.

. . .

■ INTERPRETING THE NEGOTIATIONS

□ *Assessing Supranational Institutionalism*

The historical record does not confirm the importance of international and transnational factors. Let us consider each element in turn.

European institutions. The supranational model stresses the role of EC institutions, particularly the Parliament. Yet after Fontainebleau, government representatives, abetted by the Commission, deliberately excluded representatives of the Parliament from decisive forums. One of the Dooge Committee's first actions was to reject the Parliament's "Draft Treaty Establishing European Union" and begin negotiations with a French government draft instead. From that moment on, key decision makers ignored the maximalist agenda. National governments viewed the Parliament's proposals as too open-ended ("real reform . . . requires a treaty encompassing all Community policies and the institutions needed to implement them"), too democratic (the powers of the Parliament should be "extended to new spheres of activity"), and too automatic (the draft treaty would have gone into effect without unanimous Council approval). The Parliament members' continuous protests against the emasculation of the draft treaty and their exclusion from the "real participation" in the discussions were ignored. The fact that the member states parried parliamentary pressure with ease certainly casts doubt on the argument that the SEA was necessary to co-opt rising demands for even more thoroughgoing institutional reform. In the end, the Parliament overwhelmingly passed a resolution protesting that the SEA "in no way represent[s] the real reform of the Community that our peoples need," but it had little alternative but to accept the *fait accompli.*

Transnational business interest groups. The internal market program, like the EC itself thirty years before, appears to have been launched independently of pressure from transnationally organized business interest groups. The Kangaroo Group in Parliament, which had close contacts with business interests, remained relatively small until after the 1992 initiative was launched and established no formal links with the Council until 1986. The activities of the Roundtable of European Industrialists focused primarily on the concerns of its non-EC European membership. Before 1985, its chief involvement was in European infrastructure projects such as the Channel tunnel. The Roundtable was based in Geneva and did not move to Brussels until 1988, when Dekker assumed its presidency.

Most transnational business lobbies got involved late. By the time Dekker delivered his oft-quoted speeches, nearly a year had passed since the beginning of the path-breaking French presidency and the discussions of the Dooge Committee were well under way. But a few business groups, such as UNICE, had been pushing vainly for liberalization for a long time. Given their persistence, what needs to be explained is why governments finally listened.

International political leaders. Cockfield's boldness and Delors' extraordinary political skill are not in question. Cockfield and Delors acted on the margins to broaden the White Paper and the SEA, and they may have contributed to the remarkable speed of decisionmaking at the intergovernmental conference. Nevertheless, the broader outlines of both documents were proposed, negotiated, and approved, often in advance of Commission initiatives, by the heads of government themselves. Indeed, the breakthrough in the relaunching of the EC had already occurred before Delors became president of the Commission. The causality of the supranational explanation is thus reversed: the selection of a prestigious politician for the presidency was merely a symptom of mounting trilateral pressure for reform. In this regard, ironically enough, Delors' actions as Finance Minister of France may have contributed more to the SEA than those as president of the Commission.

It is worth dwelling for a moment longer on the intergovernmental conference, for this is the point at which the supranational institutionalist hypotheses about Commission influence might appear most plausible. Four specific arguments can be advanced, but none suggests that supranational actors influenced the substance of the SEA. First, the remarkable speed of the conference might be attributed, at least in part, to the role of Delors and the Commission in proposing and revising the specific wording of treaty amendments. While logistical support from the Commission may indeed have hastened a final agreement, there is little evidence that it altered its substance. Second, the Commission might be credited with having quietly slipped some new EC functions, such as environmental and research and development programs, into the revised treaty. But these were functions that the EC had been handling under indirect authorization for a number of years, and there was little opposition from member states to extending a concrete mandate to cover them. Third, in late September and early October 1985, Delors dropped strong advocacy of monetary and social reform and chose to stress instead the links between internal market reform, majority voting, and the increases in structural funds needed to gain support from Ireland and the Southern countries. Delors' conciliatory move, particularly the proposal for structural funding, may have facilitated a political compromise, but his position on these issues was nonetheless closely circumscribed by the views of the major states. This is particularly true in regard to monetary policy, where Delors' elimination of monetary reform from the package resulted from the direct pressure of domestic officials. Fourth and finally, Cockfield's White Paper might be seen as a key act of agenda setting. But the White Paper was a response to a mandate from the member states expressed both in the Council, which commissioned the paper, and in the interim report of the Dooge Committee. In previous years, the Commission had proposed many of the nearly three hundred items as part of various reform proposals, but governments had simply rejected them.

Delors' most important contributions to the process resulted not from his role as an initiator of unforeseen policies but instead from his keen awareness of the extreme constraints under which he was acting. A reexamination of his memoirs reveals that his arguments (as distinct from his tone) stress intergovernmental constraints rather than personal influence. Procedural reform without a substantive program, he reasoned, would get bogged down in ideological battles over sovereignty; a plan for European monetary union would encounter the opposition of the governors of the central banks, who, led by the Germans, had just rejected an expansion of the EMS; and European defense cooperation was neither within the current competence of the EC nor widely supported among member states. The sole remaining option was internal market reform. In this regard, Delors' most statesmanlike judgments concerned the proper moment to compromise—as he did in September and October 1985.

□ *Supranational Institutionalism and Neofunctionalism*

None of the three supranational variables—European institutional momentum, transnational business interest group activity, and international political leadership—seems to account for the timing, content, and process of negotiating the SEA. Moreover, governments did not bargain by "upgrading" the common interest or by linking issues but, rather, by accepting the lowest common denominator, backed by the threat of exclusion. The resulting bargain places major obstacles in the path of attempts to extend the reform to new issues, such as monetary policy.

In this regard, one striking aspect of the negotiations for the SEA is their parallel to the negotiations for the ECSC and EC in the 1950s. Even regional integration theorists are inclined to accept that the founding of the ECSC was an extraordinary act of political state-craft, but they contend that once it occurred it sparked a qualitatively different and potentially self-sustaining process of spillover. The negotiating history of the SEA, however, suggests that three decades later the factors encouraging a greater commitment to European unity are essentially the same: the convergence of national interests, the pro-European idealism of heads of government, and the decisive role of the large member states.

The importance of interstate bargains in the SEA negotiations is consistent with the broader experience of the EC since the mid-1960s. European integration did not proceed steadily and incrementally; it proceeded in fits and starts. Moreover, since the Luxembourg compromise in 1966, the EC has moved toward intergovernmental ("state-to-state") decisionmaking centered in the Council and summit meetings, rather than toward increasing authority for international bodies such as the Commission and Parliament. One detailed study concluded that the systems change in the EC has in fact proved to be more political and less technical than Haas predicted. While spillover and forward linkages may in some cases suffice to prompt the intensification of international decisionmaking under a specific mandate within a given sector, they play a minimal role in the processes of opening new issues, reforming decisionmaking procedures, and ratifying the accession of new members. Movement in these areas requires active intervention by heads of state and a considerable amount of nontechnocratic interstate bargaining.

The SEA negotiations suggest, furthermore, that in the 1980s, just as in the 1950s, pan-European business groups were relatively ineffective at influencing policy. Business, at least on the supranational level, was mobilized by the emerging interstate consensus for reform, rather than the reverse. This casts doubt on at least one mechanism underlying the long-term historical prediction of neofunctionalism—namely, that over time, growth in the autonomy and responsibility of supranational actors and organizations will facilitate further integration.

□   *Assessing Intergovernmental Institutionalism*

The historical record confirms the importance of the three elements of intergovernmental institutionalism. Again, these elements can be considered in turn.

Intergovernmentalism. Heads of government and their direct representatives carried out the negotiations. The result represents the convergence of domestic policy preferences in the largest member states. The dominance of the three largest states is revealed most clearly by the lack of cases (with the possible exception of the Danish stand on workers' rights) in which a smaller nation either initiated or vetoed a central initiative. The Southern nations and Ireland were appeased *en masse* with the promise of a sidepayment in the form of increased structural funds; the Benelux countries had been prepared in any case to go further than the others. The election of a Conservative government in Britain and, more important, the shift in French economic policy preferences in 1983 were the key turning points on the road to 1992.

Lowest-common-denominator bargaining. The only major exception to lowest-common-denominator bargaining concerned whether to amend the Treaty of Rome to promote majority voting on internal market matters. On this point, the British yielded to Franco-German pressure to convene an intergovernmental conference, at least in part because the Franco-German position was backed by the threat of exclusion. As Paul Taylor has observed, "British diplomacy . . . had to balance two objectives: that of satisfying specific interests, and that of staying in the game. A measure of compromise in the former [became] necessary to achieve the latter." Nonetheless, given the lowest-common-denominator bargaining characteristic of systems change in the EC, it is not surprising that the British were most satisfied with the final outcome. Thatcher's success in negotiating a fundamental revision of the rules for calculating the net obligations to the EC budget can be viewed as the end of extended negotiations over the terms of British accession. While the agricultural *acquis communautaire* represented a Franco-German deal, the new agreement reflected more closely the new trilateral balance of power within the EC. The British also succeeded in limiting institutional reform to internal market issues.

Protection of sovereignty. The steady narrowing of the institutional reform to a "minimalist" position in which majority voting is re-

stricted to internal market policy, the power of the Parliament is limited, and the future spillover to areas such as monetary policy is
blocked confirms the enduring preoccupation of all three major
states with maintaining sovereignty and control over future changes
in the scope of EC activities.

□   *International Institutionalism and Domestic Politics*

While the intergovernmental approach, based on the relative power
of member states and the convergence of their national policy preferences, offers a satisfactory account of the SEA negotiations, it raises a
second, equally important question: Why did underlying national
policy preferences converge at this point in time? As indicated earlier,
part of the answer can be found in the domestic politics of France,
Germany, and Britain. Four paradigmatic explanations can also be
identified: autonomous action by political leaders, pressure from
state bureaucracies, support from centrist coalitions, and pressure to
replace failed economic policies. Each offers a promising starting
point for analyzing the domestic roots of European integration, but
none is entirely satisfactory.

Statism: The autonomy of political leaders. The convergence of policy preferences in the mid-1980s may have reflected the views, either
pro-European or neoliberal, of the three major European leaders of
the time—Mitterrand, Kohl, and Thatcher—and their close associates. The history of the SEA suggests that heads of government in the
three largest member states possessed considerable autonomy from
domestic bureaucracies, political parties, and interest groups, at least
in the short run.

In 1984, Mitterrand's personal advocacy, against the opposition of the Quai d'Orsay and the left wing of his own party, gave a
decisive impetus to reform efforts. Delors himself stressed the importance of Mitterrand's shuttle diplomacy, recalling that Mitterrand
met six times each with Kohl and Thatcher during his 1984 Council
presidency alone. The key decisions in France were made in meetings
à quatre with Mitterrand, Dumas, Delors, and the French Minister of
European Affairs.

Like Adenauer and de Gaulle before them, Kohl and Mitterrand viewed economic integration as part of a geopolitical grand
strategy. In this sense, French support for the EC could not be separated from French initiatives in areas such as armaments coproduc-
tion, coordinated conventional defense, and nuclear strategy. Simi-

larly, Kohl followed Genscher in viewing German support for the EC as an indispensable precondition for German unification within a pan-European framework.

Thatcher's role in the reform effort was as important as Mitterrand's role, though somewhat more ambivalent. Obstacles to reform stemmed from Thatcher's personal crusade to constrain European bureaucracy, particularly in the social and monetary areas, despite the more pro-European sentiments of her closest civil service advisers and a majority of her own party. On the other hand, her extreme neoliberalism lent the SEA much of its substance.

In the case of Mitterrand and Thatcher, current views toward European unification reflect positions held for decades. In the case of Cockfield, Rocard, Delors, and others, support may also reflect positive experiences working with and within EC institutions.

Bureaucratic politics: The role of technocracy. The importance of bureaucracies is suggested by the long-term evolution of European policymaking. Since 1966, when the Luxembourg compromise was accepted, the EC has institutionalized an intergovernmental style of internal decisionmaking, centered in the Council. Committees consisting of national bureaucrats, members of permanent delegations (COREPER), or ministers (the Council of Ministers) have met regularly in Brussels and interacted through an increasingly cooperative and specialized mode of decisionmaking. By the early 1980s, a clear trend had emerged away from the traditional practice of consulting foreign ministries in each European state and toward specialization of functions in the Council. While the foreign ministries tended to be suspicious of transferring or pooling sovereignty through mechanisms such as majority voting, the bureaucratic specialists have often been strong supporters of European economic integration. Thus, increased specialization may have encouraged a steady increase in majority voting, with ten decisions based on qualified majority voting between 1966 and 1974, thirty-five between 1974 and 1979, and more than ninety between 1979 and 1984. In this sense, as Helen Wallace points out, the SEA represents "a return on investments made over many previous years" in developing a set of common norms for Council negotiating.

According to the bureaucratic politics view, this evolution in EC negotiating may also have had an effect at home. That is, as technocrats have internalized norms of cooperation, the national leaders have increasingly supported European integration. At a number of points in the negotiating history of the SEA, for example, domestic bureaucracies appear to have intervened to change the views of heads of government, most notably when British officials helped convince Thatcher to join the intergovernmental conference.

Like the statist explanation, the bureaucratic politics explanation has several weaknesses. First, both overlook the evidence that changes in domestic political support facilitated or frustrated the efforts of national leaders to implement policies favoring further European integration. Neither national leaders nor bureaucracies enjoy complete autonomy. Second, both of the explanations fail to offer a plausible account of the stop-and-go process of European integration over the past twenty years. Technocratic explanations overlook evidence of the splits between bureaucracies and the strong opposition among top officials to the dilution of national sovereignty through majority voting. But despite the weaknesses of these explanations, autonomous decisionmaking by heads of state or bureaucrats should be retained as a null hypothesis in future research on the domestic roots of policy initiation in the EC.

Partisan support: The role of centrist coalitions. A more promising explanation for the convergence of national policies stresses the role of political parties. While heads of government have some autonomy in European affairs, they are constrained, in this view, by the party coalitions that support their rule. Since Europe is a low-priority issue for the voters of the three largest member states, it is implausible to posit a mechanism by which politicians launch policy initiatives to seek direct electoral advantage, except perhaps immediately before European elections. European integration thus remains an elite affair. Nonetheless, the evolution of conceptions of national interest over time and the key role of partisan splits over European policy, as demonstrated by the decisive French turnaround in 1983 and the importance of British Tory support for neoliberal policies, suggest that the autonomy of heads of government in pursuing a European policy may be constrained by elites within their domestic partisan base.

Over the years, centrist parties, particularly those of the center-right, have tended to support EC reforms, while the strongest opposition to further integration has been located on the extremes of the ideological spectrum. At the founding of the EC, Christian Democratic parties provided the core of partisan support for European integration. Over the years, Germany's center-weighted party system, which pivots on alliances with the pro-European Free Democrats, generated constant support for European integration. Since the completion of the Common Market in 1968 and Britain's accession in 1973, however, a reform package of internal market liberalization and majority voting was blocked by the presence of an anti-EC party in at least one ruling coalition. In the 1970s and early 1980s, the far left (the British Labour party, the West German Greens, the French Communist party, and the more radical French Socialists) remained suspicious of economic liberalization, while the far right (the Thatcherite wing of the British Conservative party, the Gaullists and the party of Jean-Marie Le Pen in France, and the German Republicans) opposed the dilution of national sovereignty. The SEA thus had to navigate a narrow passage between the Scylla of far left opposition to economic liberalization and the Charybdis of conservative opposition to institutional reform.

In the mid-1980s, the dominance of centrists in ruling coalitions created a rare opening for reform. The election of Thatcher and the shift to the moderate wing of the French Socialist party in early 1983 dramatically altered the political landscape. For the first time in over a decade, ruling coalitions in each of the three major states of Europe were ideologically committed to relatively liberal domestic economic policies and were also committed, in varying degrees and for diverse reasons, to liberalization of the European market. If the Labour party had held power in Britain or if either the Gaullists or the Communists had held power in France, reform would have encountered bitter opposition. The SEA still had to satisfy British complaints about agricultural policy and surmount Thatcherite opposition to institutional reform. The first obstacle was overcome by the carrot of budget reform and the second by the stick of threatened exclusion. The partisan support explanation thus accounts for the high level of international conflict over budget and institutional reform, as compared with the low level of conflict over the central substantive agenda of market liberalization. Yet this explanation nonetheless shares several weaknesses with the following explanation, as discussed below.

Economic functionalism: The role of policy failure. The convergence of policy preferences in the major European states may also have resulted from the failure of purely national strategies of economic policy, which created or legitimated pressure for coordinated liberalization at the European level. According to the statements of European leaders, the plan for market liberalization by 1992 was in part a response to the declining industrial competitiveness of Europe. In the late 1970s and early 1980s, "Eurosclerosis"—the combination of persistent high unemployment, low growth rates relative to those of other countries in the Organization for Economic Cooperation and Development (OECD), and long-term decline in international com-

petitiveness vis-à-vis the United States and Japan in high-technology
industries such as electronics and telecommunications—was widely
interpreted as an indication of policy failure.

In the 1970s and early 1980s, the economic difficulties of
Britain, France, and Germany could ostensibly be attributed to problems common to all OECD countries, such as disruption from the two
oil shocks and the need for tight monetary policies to combat inflation. By 1982, however, French and German economic performance
lagged significantly behind that of the United States and Japan. This
relative failure in economic performance undermined the last excuse
for slow growth. After the British experience in the mid-1970s, the
German experience with internationally coordinated reflation in
1977, and the French experience with "Keynesianism in one country,"
reflation was no longer credible. The business-labor bargains on
which corporatism and incomes policy are based were disintegrating.

Poor economic performance may have been translated into
pressure for internal market liberalization through at least three distinct, though not mutually exclusive, mechanisms. The first mechanism is electoral. Although European integration itself is rarely an issue of electoral importance, leading politicians in advanced industrial
democracies face a structural imperative to provide steady economic
growth, on which electoral success often depends. Growth requires
constant investment, which in turn is stimulated by business confidence. Internal market reform can thus be seen as a way to generate
business confidence and stimulate investment by removing market
barriers.

The second mechanism is ideological. With other economic
policies discredited, European governments turned to new ideas, particularly the American and Japanese models of development. The
idea of creating an internal market the size of the United States was
one of the few untried policies. It seemed particularly attractive when
tied to firm-led high-technology cooperation programs patterned on
the Japanese model, such as ESPIRIT, the European Programme for
High Technology Research and Development (EUREKA), and Research in Advanced Communications for Europe (RACE). Moreover,
the idea of economic renewal through economies of scale and industrial flexibility underlies the 1992 initiative and reflects the new sup-
ply-side and privatization orthodoxy that was sweeping Europe during this period.

The third mechanism involves sectoral or firm-level business
pressure at the domestic level. In general, as trade and investment interdependence increase, these interests grow stronger. Specifically, the
more competitive a given firm or sector and hence the greater the

level of net exports or foreign investment, particularly within the EC, the greater is the likelihood that the firm or sector will support internal market liberalization. Moreover, as sectors become globalized and sensitive to competition from outside the EC, particularly from the United States and Japan, liberalization may appear necessary to create the economies of scale required to compete effectively. The greater the potential for common gains vis-à-vis non-EC countries, the greater is the incentive to bear the costs of adjustments to liberalization within Europe.

This sort of sectoral logic might also be used to explain the initial bargain upon which the EC was founded. In the early years of the EC, Germany agreed to finance a disproportionate share of the budget, much of which went to France in the form of subsidies to its relatively efficient agricultural sector, in exchange for market liberalization for industrial goods, in which Germany enjoyed a comparative advantage. Today, British support would be expected from the financial and business service sectors, while German support would draw on industrial and capital-goods exporters.

The economic functionalist explanation and the partisan support explanation are both more plausible than the first two explanations set forth above. Yet anomalies plague these accounts as well. Neither a functionalist nor a partisan sectoral approach seems to explain French support for internal market liberalization. France appears to lack a natural constituency analogous to German industry or British financial services. And if the 1992 initiative was a capitalist conspiracy, Mitterrand was a most unlikely instrument. The economic functionalist approach also faces difficulties in explaining the pressure in some member states for institutional change in areas other than internal market policy. Despite these anomalies, however, the activities of interest groups and political parties should serve as a springboard for further inquiry.

Domestic analysis is a precondition for systemic analysis, not a supplement to it. The existence of significant cross-national variance in state policy preferences and diplomatic strategies invites further research into the domestic roots of European integration. Yet most theories of international cooperation, including regime theory, have neglected the problem of domestic interest formation, often electing instead to specify interests by assumption. None of this is meant to exclude theories of state interests based on international processes, such as economic and social interdependence. But at the very least, domestic politics offers a mechanism—a "transmission belt"—by which international impulses are translated into policy. Testing domestic theories of integration invariably raises many questions traditionally treated by students of comparative politics: Which domestic actors take the lead in promoting and opposing economic liberalization? Are they state or societal actors? How do they perceive their interests? How do they influence one another? What is their relation to the world economy? Future research on these questions will necessarily connect the literatures on international cooperation and state-society relations in an interdependent world economy.

■ CONCLUSION: THE SEA IN PERSPECTIVE

Neofunctionalism remains the sole attempt to fashion a coherent and comprehensive theory of European integration. The standing of neofunctionalist theory among political scientists is a lagged function of the standing of the EC in the eyes of Europeans. When the EC stagnates, as in the 1970s, scholars speak of the obsolescence of regional integration theory; when it rebounds, as in 1985, they speak of the obsolescence of the nation state. Regional integration theory, we read today, has been "unjustly consigned to the dustbin."

This article challenges the notion, implicit in these statements, that progress in the EC necessarily supports all the claims of neofunctionalists. It does so by testing and rejecting a particular variant of neofunctionalism, supranational institutionalism, which rests on the argument that international institutions and transnational interest groups play a vital and increasing role as integration progresses. The approach proposed here, intergovernmental institutionalism, accords an important role to supranational institutions in cementing existing interstate bargains as the foundation for renewed integration. But it also affirms that the primary source of integration lies in the interests of the states themselves and the relative power each brings to Brussels. Perhaps most important, the intergovernmental approach demonstrates that even this explanation is incomplete, thus clearing the ground for further research into the international implications of European domestic politics.

22 Europe Before the Court: A Political Theory of Legal Integration

ANNE-MARIE BURLEY AND WALTER MATTLI

Wayne Sandholtz and John Zysman (Chapter 20) and Andrew Moravcsik (Chapter 21) staked out early in the 1990s the battle lines in the great debate of the decade. On one side were the supranationalists of various stripes who argued that the policymaking process in the European Union (EU) was undermining the central role of nation-states in European governance. National governments were just one set of (important) actors in a complex decisionmaking system. On the other side were intergovernmentalists—again of various persuasions, but most often rooted in a realist conception of international relations—who argued that European states still controlled the policies and processes at the heart of the EU. National governments were only using multinational cooperation and supranational institutions to achieve crucial objectives unattainable by more conventional means. The vast majority of scholars studying the EU sided explicitly or implicitly with the supranationalists, but it was the intergovernmentalists who seemed to drive the debate. No scholar attempting to make a theoretical contribution in the 1990s could ignore the approach no matter how misguided or misinformed he or she thought it was.

The next four chapters provide a strong dose of this anti-intergovernmentalism scholarship. The pieces offer strong criticism of a

Reprinted with permission from *International Organization* 47(1)(winter 1993):41–76. Copyright 1993 by the World Peace Foundation and the Massachusetts Institute of Technology. Notes omitted.

state-centered perspective, but they also make enormous positive contributions to our understanding of the European Union.

In their 1993 International Organization *article Anne-Marie Burley (now Anne-Marie Slaughter, Harvard Law School) and Walter Mattli (Columbia University) take on intergovernmentalism and other approaches to integration by turning back to neofunctionalism. They argue that neofunctionalism still provides a relevant description of integration within specific sectors, such as law where "the legal integration of the Community corresponds remarkably closely to the original neofunctionalist model developed by Ernst Haas." The drivers of the legal integration process, just as neofunctionalists predicted, are "supranational and subnational actors pursuing their own self-interests." These actors, following the logic of integration, have dramatically extended Community law and increased the power of the European Court of Justice. How has the EC legal system kept the member states from halting the process? Burley and Mattli argue that by operating within the constraints of legal reasoning, the Court has been able to hide political integration behind a legal mask, a role neofunctionalists originally forecast for economics.*

Burley and Mattli make a strong case for old-fashioned neofunctionalism, while placing new emphasis on Community law in the integration process, which had otherwise been ignored by (especially U.S.) political scientists.

European integration, a project deemed politically dead and academically moribund for much of the past two decades, has reemerged as one of the most important and interesting phenomena of the 1990s. The pundits are quick to observe that the widely touted "political and economic integration of Europe" is actually neither, that the "1992" program to achieve the Single Market is but the fulfillment of the basic goals laid down in the Treaty of Rome in 1958, and that the program agreed on for European monetary union at the Maastricht Intergovernmental Conference provides more ways to escape monetary union than to achieve it. Nevertheless, the "uniting of Europe" continues. Even the self-professed legion of skeptics about the European Community (EC) has had to recognize that if the Community remains something well short of a federal state, it also has become something far more than an international organization of independent sovereigns.

An unsung hero of this unexpected twist in the plot appears to be the European Court of Justice (ECJ). By their own account, now confirmed by both scholars and politicians, the thirteen judges quietly working in Luxembourg managed to transform the Treaty of

Rome (hereafter referred to as "the treaty") into a constitution. They thereby laid the legal foundation for an integrated European economy and polity. Until 1963 the enforcement of the Rome treaty, like that of any other international treaty, depended entirely on action by the national legislatures of the member states of the Community. By 1965, a citizen of a Community country could ask a national court to invalidate any provision of domestic law found to conflict with certain directly applicable provisions of the treaty. By 1975, a citizen of an EC country could seek the invalidation of a national law found to conflict with self-executing provisions of Community secondary legislation, the "directives" to national governments passed by the EC Council of Ministers. And by 1990, Community citizens could ask their national courts to interpret national legislation consistently with Community legislation in the face of undue delay in passing directives on the part of national legislatures.

The ECJ's accomplishments have long been the province only of lawyers, who either ignored or assumed their political impact. Beginning in the early 1980s, however, a small coterie of legal scholars began to explore the interaction between the Court and the political institutions and processes of the EC. However, these approaches do not explain the *dynamic* of legal integration. Further, they lack microfoundations. They attribute aggregate motives and interests to the institutions involved to illustrate why a particular outcome makes theoretical sense, but they fail to offer a credible account of why the actual actors involved at each step of the process might have an *incentive* to reach the result in question.

On the other side of the disciplinary divide, political scientists studying regional integration in the 1950s and 1960s paid, surprisingly, little attention to the role that supranational *legal* institutions may play in fostering integration. Even more puzzling is that much of the recent literature on the EC by American political scientists continues to ignore the role courts and Community law play in European integration.

We seek to remedy these deficiencies by developing a first-stage theory of the role of the Court in the Community that marries the insights of legal scholars in the area with a theoretical framework developed by political scientists. We argue that the legal integration of the Community corresponds remarkably closely to the original neofunctionalist model developed by Ernst Haas in the late 1950s. By legal integration, our dependent variable, we mean the gradual penetration of EC law into the domestic law of its member states. This process has two principal dimensions. First is the dimension of formal penetration, the expansion of (1) the types of supranational legal acts, from treaty law to secondary Community law, that take precedence over domestic law and (2) the range of cases in which individuals may invoke Community law directly in domestic courts. Second is the dimension of substantive penetration, the spilling over of Community legal regulation from the narrowly economic domain into areas dealing with issues such as occupational health and safety, social welfare, education, and even political participation rights. Cutting across both these categories is the adoption of principles of interpretation that further the uniformity and comprehensiveness of the Community legal system.

We find that the independent variables posited by neofunctionalist theory provide a convincing and parsimonious explanation of legal integration. We argue that just as neofunctionalism predicts, the drivers of this process are supranational and subnational actors pursuing their own self-interests within a politically insulated sphere. The distinctive features of this process include a widening of the ambit of successive legal decisions according to a functional logic, a gradual shift in the expectations of both government institutions and private actors participating in the legal system, and the strategic subordination of immediate individual interests of member states to postulated collective interests over the long term.

Law functions as a mask for politics, precisely the role neofunctionalists originally forecast for economics. The need for a "functional" domain to circumvent the direct clash of political interests is the central insight of neofunctionalist theory. This domain could never be completely separated from the political sphere but would at least provide a sufficient buffer to achieve results that could not be directly obtained in the political realm. Law, as Eric Stein recognized, is widely perceived by political decision makers as "mostly technical," and thus lawyers are given a more or less free hand to speak for the EC Commission, the EC Council of Ministers and the national governments. The result is that important political outcomes are debated and decided in the language and logic of law. Further, although we make the case here for the strength of neofunctionalism as a framework for explaining *legal* integration—an area in which the technicality of the Court's operation is reinforced by the apparent technicality of the issues it addresses—the principle of law as a medium that both masks and to a certain extent alters political conflicts portends a role for the Court in the wider processes of economic and even political integration.

This specification of the optimal preconditions for the operation of the neofunctionalist dynamic also permits a specification of the political *limits* of the theory, limits that the neofunctionalists themselves recognized. The strength of the functional domain as an incubator of integration depends on the relative resistance of that domain to politicization. Herein, however, lies a paradox that sheds a different light on the supposed naivete of "legalists." At a minimum, the margin of insulation necessary to promote integration requires that judges themselves appear to be practicing law rather than politics. Their political freedom of action thus depends on a minimal degree of fidelity to both substantive law and the methodological constraints imposed by legal reasoning. In a word, the staunch insistence on legal realities as distinct from political realities may in fact be a potent political tool.

The first part of this article surveys the political and legal literature on theories of the ECJ's contribution to the broad processes of European integration, offering a typology based on the extent to which these theories see the Court as having had a direct impact on economic and political integration. The second part focuses the inquiry on the more specific question of explaining legal integration and offers a brief review of the principal elements of neofunctionalist theory. The third part details the ways in which the process of legal integration as engineered by the Court fits the neofunctionalist model. The final part returns to the larger question of the relationship between the ECJ and the member states and reflects on some of the broader theoretical implications of our findings.

■ LEGAL AND POLITICAL THEORIES OF JURIDICAL CONTRIBUTION TO EUROPEAN INTEGRATION

In this section we review the main themes and conclusions of two sets of approaches inquiring about the role of the ECJ in European integration. Most of the European legal literature begins and ends with law, describing a legalist world that is hermetically closed to considerations of power and self-interest. A handful of "contextualists" do go further in an effort to place law in a broader political context. As an explanation of the actual process of legal integration, legalism fails for assuming that law can operate in a political vacuum. The contextual approaches are a considerable improvement in this regard and often yield a treasure trove of valuable information about the Court, but ultimately, they offer only hypotheses about underspecified relationships between law and politics.

The writings of American political scientists on European integration are equally unsatisfactory. Realism, the dominant paradigm in the field of international relations, assumes away the relevance of supranational institutions. Thus, the ECJ has received perfunctory attention at best—a most unsatisfactory state in light of the data that have accumulated over the past three decades. Nevertheless, even those writers most sympathetic to a neofunctionalist point of view have overlooked the Court's contribution to integration.

□ Legal Approaches

Legalism: pure law. Legalism is an approach to the study of the ECJ that denies the existence of ideological and sociopolitical influences on the Court's jurisdiction. Microfoundational explanations of the roles of individual actors give way to an all-purpose emphasis on the "rule of law." Martin Shapiro put the essence of legalism as follows: "The Community [is presented] as a juristic idea; the written constitution as a sacred text; the professional commentary as a legal truth; the case law as the inevitable working out of the correct implications of the constitutional text; and the constitutional court as the disembodied voice of right reason and constitutional teleology."

Legalism is embraced by the vast majority of European legal scholars specializing in EC law. Its appraisal of the Court's substantive contribution to European integration and of its juridical method of treaty interpretation is unanimously positive. Charges of judicial activism, that is, of undue judicial policy making, are either denied or viewed as a necessary stand against the complete disintegration of the Community. This argument, known as the "ruin"—or the "or else"—justification, runs as follows: The political actors in the Community, confronted with unexpected problems, often are unable or unwilling to stick to their treaty obligations. In such moments, the Court dutifully intervenes and temporarily assumes policy making leadership to prevent the rapid erosion of the Community, "a possibility that nobody really envisaged, not even the most intransigent custodian of national sovereignty."

Legalists thus uniformly view the ECJ as a great boon to European integration. The Court acts based upon its vast formal powers and according to its treaty-based duty to exploit those powers to their utmost. It thereby scrupulously observes the inherent limitations of the Community's judicial function.

Contextualism: law and politics. A few legal scholars recently have extended their analytic focus and proposed to substitute a law–politics duality for the "rule of law." They endeavor to analyze the reciprocal relationship between the legal and political spheres in European integration. These approaches suffer generally from two problems: first, the nature of the relationship is often fuzzy and claims of cause and effect are qualified so as to be rendered almost empty. Second, the incentives for action are not spelled out.

. . .

□ *Political Science Theories*

Realism. Realism is the antithesis of legalism. From a realist perspective, supranational organizations such as the ECJ are essentially ineffectual at forcing upon sovereign states a pace of integration that does not conform to the states' own interests and priorities. The ECJ's role is best described as fulfilling an essentially "technical servient" role. Faced with a dispute, legal technocrats simply apply treaty provisions and rules formulated by the policy making organs of the EC. Judicial interpretation, according to this model, is nothing more than a translation of these rules into operational language, devoid of political content and consequence.

Realists view the notion of supranational community law as an absurdity, on the ground that "if a national legislature decided to limit the effect of a Communities' regulation, or to nullify it, and if this intention was made plain to the national courts by the legislature . . . the national courts would not apply the Communities' law." In short, realism asserts the primacy of national politics over Community law and emphasizes the limits that the member states have imposed upon their involvement in Community affairs "which stops well short of any grant of sovereignty to the regional institutions."

. . .

Neorationalism. Geoffrey Garrett's and Barry Weingast's studies are two rare examples by political scientists that deal explicitly with the ECJ. They rely on a "rationalist" approach to the study of institutions, one that proceeds from the basic realist premises of sovereign and unitary actors but which accepts a role for institutions based on rational choice and game theoretic studies of cooperation.

Garrett begins with the proposition that the Court is in fact able to impose constraints on national political authorities within the Community. Its continued ability to play such a role, however, does not result from any autonomous power. Rather, the maintenance of the Community legal system is actually "consistent with the interests of member states." Member states' continuing collaboration within the EC indicates that they value the gains from effective participation in the internal market more highly than the potential benefits of defecting from Community rules. However, due to the complexity of the Community system, the incentives for unilateral defection may be considerable, especially if cheating is hard for other governments to spot or if the significance of defection is difficult to evaluate. Logically, if cheating is endemic, there are no gains from cooperation. It is thus in the member states' selfish interest to delegate some authority to the ECJ to enable it to *monitor* compliance with Community obligations, to facilitate "the logic of retaliation and reputation in iterated games," or, more broadly, to create a shared belief system about cooperation and defection in the context of differential and conflicting sets of individual beliefs that would otherwise inhibit the decentralized emergence of cooperation. The ECJ performs a further valuable role for the member states: it mitigates the *incomplete contracting problems* by applying the general rules of the Rome treaty to a myriad of unanticipated contingencies, thus obviating the costly need for the actors to make exhaustive agreements that anticipate every dispute that might arise among them."

These various benefits notwithstanding, however, the Court would still not be worth the costs it imposes on individual member states unless "it faithfully implement[s] the collective internal market preferences of [Community] members." Garrett concludes that the ECJ, and the domestic courts that follow its judgments, meets this criterion as well, on the ground that its rulings "are consistent with the preferences of France and Germany." This assertion is simply wrong. Garrett cites one case in support of his thesis, the Court's 1979 ruling in *Cassis de Dijon*, in which the Court reached a ruling consistent with Germany's export interests. Yet, in that case, as in five other landmark constitutional cases, the German government argued explicitly and strongly against the Court's ultimate position. Indeed, Germany's lawyers put forth views opposed to those of the Court more often than any other country. The French government did not make an appearance in any of these cases but battled the Court ferociously in other forums. Further, there is absolutely no evidence that the Court actually attempts, as Garrett and Weingast contend, to track the positions of the member states. Stein argues that the Court follows the lead of the *Commission*, using it as a political bellwether to ascertain how far member states can be *pushed* toward the Court and the Commission's vision of maximum integration.

With the luxury of hindsight and the ability to manipulate the analysis at a very high level of generality, it is easy to assert that a particular decision was "in the interests" of a particular state. Indeed, since the Garrett and Weingast approach assumes that states will only comply with judicial decisions if in fact those decisions are in their interests, they have an obvious incentive to deduce interest-compatibility from compliance. More generally, since the last five years have been a period in which all the principal EC member states have strongly supported continued integration, judicial decisions that retrospectively can be seen to have strengthened integration seem automatically congruent with the interests of those states. What we know is that at the time a particular case is brought, different governments strongly disagree as to its outcome. Over time, however, they tend to accept the Court's position and regard the path chosen as inevitable. *It is precisely this process that needs to be explained.* Here neorationalism is at a loss. Neofunctionalism is in its element.

Other approaches. Much of the remaining recent literature on the EC by political scientists has been characterized by (1) continuing disregard for the role of courts and EC law in the process of integration and (2) an increasingly eclectic methodology. Andrew Moravcsik's study [Chapter 21] on the negotiation of the SEA, for example, proposes an "intergovernmental institutionalist" approach that combines an emphasis on state power and national interests with the role of domestic factors in determining the goals that governments pursue. Wayne Sandholtz and John Zysman's study [Chapter 20] on Europe 1992 comes *in spirit* closest to a neofunctionalist analysis. Sandholtz and Zysman claim that the institutions of the Community, in alliance with a transnational industry coalition and aided by international structural changes as well as shifts in domestic politics, revived the Common Market project. Surprisingly, the Court remains unnamed. Finally, Sandholtz's article on monetary politics and Maastricht proposes an analytical framework that combines elements of intergovernmentalism, institutionalism, functionalism, and domestic politics. . . .

■ A RETURN TO NEOFUNCTIONALISM

An account of the impact of the Court in terms that political scientists will find as credible as lawyers must offer a political explanation of the role of the Court from the ground up. It should thus begin by developing a political theory of how the Court integrated its own domain, rather than beginning with legal integration as a fait accompli and asking about the interrelationship between legal and political integration. The process of legal integration did not come about through the "power of the law," as the legalists implicitly assume and often explicitly insist on. Individual actors—judges, lawyers, litigants—were involved, with specific identities, motives, and objectives. They interacted in a specific context and through specific processes. Only a genuine political account of how they achieved their objectives in the process of legal integration will provide the basis for a systematic account of the interaction of that process with the political processes of the EC.

Such an account has in fact already been provided, but it has never been applied to the Court as such. It is a neofunctionalist account.

□   *Neofunctionalism in Historical Perspective:*
    A Theory of Political Integration

The logic of political integration was first systematically analyzed and elaborated by Ernst Haas in his pioneering study *The Uniting of Europe* [Chapter 15]. This work and a collection of later contributions share a common theoretical framework called neofunctionalism. Neofunctionalism is concerned with explaining "how and why nation-states cease to be wholly sovereign, how and why they voluntarily mingle, merge, and mix with their neighbors so as to lose the factual attributes of sovereignty while acquiring new techniques for resolving conflicts between themselves." More precisely, neofunctionalism describes a process "whereby political actors in several distinct national settings are persuaded to shift their loyalties, expectations, and political activities towards a new and larger center, whose institutions possess or demand jurisdiction over the pre-existing national states."

As a theory of European integration, neofunctionalism was dependent on a set of highly contingent preconditions: a unique constellation of exogenous historical, international, and domestic variables. For present purposes, however, the principal contribution of neofunctionalist theory is its identification of the functional categories likely to be receptive to integration and its description of the actual mechanics of overcoming national barriers within a particular functional category *after the integration process has been launched.*

□   *Neofunctionalism as a Theory of the Integration*
    Process: Overcoming National Barriers

The actors: circumventing the state. The primary players in the integration process are above and below the state. Actors *below* the state include interest groups and political parties. Above the state are supranational regional institutions. These supranational institutions promote integration, foster the development of interest groups, cultivate close ties with them and with fellow-technocrats in the national civil services, and manipulate both if necessary.

The Commission of the European Communities, for example, has the "power of initiative." To have its proposals accepted by the Council of Ministers, the Commission forges behind-the-scene working alliances with pressure groups. As its policy making role grows, interest groups coalesce across national boundaries in their pursuit of Communitywide interests, thus adding to the integrative momentum. Note that these groups need not be convinced "integrationists." The very existence of the Community alters their situation and forces them to adjust.

What role is there for governments? According to neofunctionalism, government's role is "creatively responsive." As holders of the ultimate political power, governments may accept, sidestep, ignore, or sabotage the decisions of federal authorities. Yet, given their heterogeneity of interests in certain issue-areas, unilateral evasion or recalcitrance may prove unprofitable if it sets a precedent for other governments. Thus governments may either choose to or feel constrained to yield to the pressures of converging supra- and subnational interests.

The motives: instrumental self-interest. One of the important contributions of neofunctionalism is the introduction of an unambiguously utilitarian concept of interest politics that stands in sharp contrast to the notions of unselfishness or common goods that pervades functionalist writing. Assumptions of goodwill, harmony of interests, or dedication to the common good need not be postulated to account for integration. Ruthless egoism does the trick by itself. As Haas puts it, *"The 'good Europeans' are not the main creators of the . . . Community;* the process of community formation is dominated by nationally constituted groups with specific interests and aims, willing and able to adjust their aspirations by turning to supranational means *when this course appears profitable."* The supranational actors are likewise not immune to utilitarian thinking. They seek unremittingly to expand the mandate of their own institutions to have a more influential say in Community affairs.

The process: incremental expansion. Three related concepts lie at the very core of the dynamics of integration: functional spillover, political spillover, and upgrading of common interests.

Functional spillover is based on the assumption that the different sectors of a modern industrial economy are highly interdependent and that any integrative action in one sector creates a situation in which the original goal can be assured only by taking further actions in related sectors, which in turn create a further condition and a need for more action, and so forth. This process is described by Haas: "Sector integration . . . begets its own impetus toward extension to the entire economy even in the absence of specific group demands."

Political spillover describes the process of adaptive behavior, that is, the incremental shifting of expectations, the changing of values, and the coalescing at the supranational level of national interest groups and political parties in response to sectoral integration. It is crucial to note that neofunctionalism does not postulate an automatically cumulative integrative process. Again, in Haas's words, "The spillover process, though rooted in the structures and motives of the post-capitalist welfare state, is far from automatic," and "Functional contexts tend to be autonomous; lessons learned in one organization are not generally and automatically applied in others, or even by the same group in a later phase of its life." In other words, neofunctionalism identifies certain linkage mechanisms but makes no assumptions as to the inevitability of actor response to functional linkages.

Upgrading common interests is the third element in the neofunctionalist description of the dynamics of integration. It occurs when the member states experience significant difficulties in arriving at a common policy while acknowledging the necessity of reaching some common stand to safeguard other aspects of interdependence among them. One way of overcoming such deadlock is by swapping concessions in related fields. In practice, the upgrading of the parties' common interests relies on the services of an institutionalized autonomous mediator. This institutionalized swapping mechanism induces participants to refrain from vetoing proposals and invites them to seek compromises, which in turn bolster the power base of the central institutions.

The context: nominally apolitical. The context in which successful integration operates is economic, social, and technical. Here Haas seems to accept a key assumption of the predecessor to his theory, functionalism, which posits that functional cooperation must begin on the relatively low-key economic and social planes. In David Mitrany's words, "Any political scheme would start a disputation, any working arrangement would raise a hope and make for confidence and patience." However, economic and social problems are ultimately inseparable from political problems. Haas thus replaced the dichotomous relationship between economics and politics in functionalism by a continuous one: "The supranational style stresses the indirect penetration of the political by way of the economic because *the 'purely' economic decisions always acquire political significance in the minds of the participants."* "Technical" or "noncontroversial" areas of cooperation, however, might be so trivial as to remain outside the domain of human expectations and actions vital for integration. The area must therefore be economically important and endowed with a high degree of "functional specificity."

■ A NEOFUNCTIONALIST JURISPRUDENCE

The advent of the first major EC crisis in 1965, initiated by de Gaulle's adamant refusal to proceed with certain aspects of integration he deemed contrary to French interests, triggered a crescendo of criticism against neofunctionalism. The theory, it was claimed, had exaggerated both the expansive effect of increments within the economic sphere and the "gradual politicization" effect of spillover. Critics further castigated neofunctionalists for failing to appreciate the enduring importance of nationalism, the autonomy of the political sector, and the interaction between the international environment and the integrating region.

Neofunctionalists accepted most of the criticism and engaged in an agonizing reassessment of their theory. The coup de grace, however, was Haas's publication of *The Obsolescence of Regional Integration Theory*, in which he concluded that researchers should look beyond regional integration to focus on wider issues of international interdependence.

With the benefit of greater hindsight, however, we believe that neofunctionalism has much to recommend it as a theory of regional integration. Although it recognizes that external shocks may disrupt the integration process, it boasts enduring relevance as a description of the integrative process *within a sector*. The sector we apply it to here is the legal integration of the European Community.

The creation of an integrated and enforceable body of Community law conforms neatly to the neofunctionalist model. In this part of the article we describe the phenomenon of legal integration according to the neofunctionalist categories set forth above: actors, motives, process, and context. Within each category, we demonstrate that the distinctive characteristics of the ECJ and its jurisprudence correspond to neofunctionalist prediction. We further show how the core insight of neofunctionalism—that integration is most likely to occur within a domain shielded from the interplay of direct political interests—leads to the paradox that actors are best able to circumvent and overcome political obstacles by acting as nonpolitically as possible. Thus in the legal context, judges who would advance a pro-integration "political" agenda are likely to be maximally effective only to the extent that they remain within the apparent bounds of the law.

□   *Actors: A Specialized National and Supranational Community*

On the supranational level, the principal actors are the thirteen ECJ judges, the Commission legal staff, and the six advocates general, official members of the Court assigned the task of presenting an impartial opinion on the law in each case. Judges and advocates general are drawn from universities, national judiciaries, distinguished members of the Community bar, and national government officials. Judges take an oath to decide cases independently of national loyalties and are freed from accountability to their home governments by two important facets of the Court's decision-making process: secrecy of deliberation and the absence of dissenting opinions.

A quick perusal of the Treaty of Rome articles concerning the ECJ suggests that the founders intended the Court and its staff to interact primarily with other Community organs and the member states. Articles 169 and 170 provide for claims of noncompliance with Community obligations to be brought against member states by either the Commission or other member states. Article 173 gives the Court additional jurisdiction over a variety of actions brought against either the Commission or the Council by a member state, by the Commission, by the Council, or by specific individuals who have been subject to a Council or Commission decision directly addressed to them.

Almost as an afterthought, Article 177 authorizes the Court to issue "preliminary rulings" on any question involving the interpretation of Community law arising in the national courts. Lower national courts can refer such questions to the ECJ at their discretion; national courts of last resort are required to request the ECJ's assistance. In practice, the Article 177 procedure has provided a framework for links between the Court and subnational actors—private litigants, their lawyers, and lower national courts. From its earliest days, the ECJ waged a campaign to enhance the use of Article 177 as a vehicle enabling private individuals to challenge national legislation as incompatible with Community law. The number of Article 177 cases on the Court's docket grew steadily through the 1970s, from a low of 9 in 1968 to a high of 119 in 1978 and averaging over

90 per year from 1979 to 1982. This campaign has successfully transferred a large portion of the business of interpreting and applying Community law away from the immediate province of member states.

As an additional result of these efforts, the Community bar is now flourishing. Groups of private practitioners receive regular invitations to visit the Court and attend educational seminars. They get further encouragement and support from private associations such as the International Federation for European Law, which has branches in the member states that include both academics and private practitioners. Smaller practitioners' groups connected with national bar associations also abound. The proliferation of Community lawyers laid the foundation for the development of a specialized and highly interdependent Community above and below the level of member state governments. The best testimony on the nature of the ties binding that Community comes from a leading EC legal academic and editor of the *Common Market Law Review*, Henry Schermers. In a recent tribute to a former legal advisor to the Commission for his role in "building bridges between [the Commission], the Community Court and the practitioners," Schermers wrote,

> Much of the credit for the Community legal order rightly goes to the Court of Justice of the European Communities, but the Court will be the first to recognize that they do not deserve all the credit. Without the loyal support of the national judiciaries, preliminary questions would not have been asked nor preliminary rulings followed. And the national judiciaries themselves would not have entered into Community law had not national advocates pleaded it before them. For the establishment and growth of the Community legal order it was essential for the whole legal profession to become acquainted with the new system and its requirements. Company lawyers, solicitors and advocates had to be made aware of the opportunities offered to them by the Community legal system.

In this tribute, Schermers points to another important set of subnational actors: Community law professors. These academics divide their time between participation as private consultants on cases before the Court and extensive commentary on the Court's decisions. In addition to book-length treatises, they edit and contribute articles to a growing number of specialized journals devoted exclusively to EC law. As leading figures in their own national legal and political communities, they play a critical role in bolstering the legitimacy of the Court.

☐ *Motives: The Self-Interest of Judges,*
   Lawyers, and Professors

The glue that binds this community of supra- and subnational actors is self-interest. In the passage quoted above, Schermers speaks of making private practitioners aware of the "opportunities" offered to them by the Community legal system. The Court largely created those opportunities, providing personal incentives for individual litigants, their lawyers, and lower national courts to participate in the construction of the Community legal system. In the process, it enhanced its own power and the professional interests of all parties participating directly or indirectly in its business.

Giving individual litigants a personal stake in Community law. The history of the "constitutionalization" of the Treaty of Rome, and of the accompanying "legalization" of Community secondary legislation, is essentially the history of the direct effect doctrine. And, the history of the direct effect doctrine is the history of carving individually enforceable rights out of a body of rules apparently applicable only to states. In neofunctionalist terms, the Court created a pro-Community constituency of private individuals by giving them a direct stake in promulgation and implementation of Community law. Further, the Court was careful to create a one-way ratchet by permitting individual participation in the system only in a way that would advance Community goals.

The Court began by prohibiting individuals from seeking to annul legal acts issued by the Council of Ministers or the EC Commission for exceeding their powers under the Treaty of Rome. As noted above, Article 173 of the treaty appears to allow the Council, the Commission, the member states, and private parties to seek such an injunction. In 1962, however, the Court held that individuals could not bring such actions except in the narrowest of circumstances. A year later the Court handed down its landmark decision in *Van Gend & Loos*, allowing a private Dutch importer to invoke the common market provisions of the treaty directly against the Dutch government's attempt to impose customs duties on specified imports. *Van Gend* announced a new world. Over the explicit objections of three of the member states, the Court proclaimed:

> the Community constitutes a *new legal order* . . . for the benefit of which the states have limited their sovereign rights, albeit within limited fields, and *the subjects of which comprise not only Member States but also their nationals*. Independently of

the legislation of the Member States, Community law *therefore not only imposes obligations on individuals but it also intended to confer upon them rights which become part of their legal heritage.* These rights arise not only where they are expressly granted by the Treaty, but also by reason of obligations which the Treaty imposes in a clearly defined way upon individuals as well as upon the Member States and upon the institutions of the Community.

The Court effectively articulated a social contract for the EC, relying on the logic of mutuality to tell Community citizens that since Community law would impose new duties of citizenship flowing to an entity other than their national governments, which had now relinquished some portion of their sovereignty, they must be entitled to corresponding rights. Beneath the lofty rhetoric, however, was the creation of a far more practical set of incentives pushing toward integration. Henceforth importers around the Community who objected to paying customs duties on their imports could invoke the Treaty of Rome to force their governments to live up to their commitment to create a common market.

The subsequent evolution of the direct effect doctrine reflects the steady expansion of its scope. Eric Stein offers the best account, charting the extension of the doctrine from a "negative" treaty obligation to a "positive" obligation; from the "vertical" enforcement of a treaty obligation against a member state government to the "horizontal" enforcement of such an obligation against another individual; from the application only to treaty law to the much broader application to secondary Community legislation, such as Council directives and decisions. After vociferous protest from national courts, the Court did balk temporarily at granting horizontal effect to Community directives—allowing individuals to enforce obligations explicitly imposed by Council directives on member states against other individuals—but has subsequently permitted even these actions where member governments have failed to implement a directive correctly or in a timely fashion.

Without tracking the intricacies of direct effect jurisprudence any further, it suffices to note that at every turn the Court harped on the benefits of its judgments for individual citizens of the Community. In *Van Duyn*, for instance, the Court observed: "A decision to this effect (granting direct effect to Community directives) would undoubtedly strengthen the legal protection of individual citizens in the national courts." Conversely, of course, individuals are the best means of holding member states to their obligations. "Where Community authorities have, by directive, imposed on Member states the obligation to pursue a particular course of conduct, the useful effect of such an act would be weakened if individuals were prevented from relying on it before their national courts and if the latter were prevented from taking it into consideration as an element of Community law."

The net result of all these cases is that individuals (and their lawyers) who can point to a provision in the Community treaties or secondary legislation that supports a particular activity they wish to undertake—from equal pay for equal work to a lifting of customs levies—can invoke Community law and urge a national court to certify the question of whether and how Community law should be applied to the ECJ. When litigants did not appear to perceive the boon that had been granted them, moreover, the Court set about educating them in the use of the Article 177 procedure. The Court thus constructed a classically utilitarian mechanism and put it to work in the service of Community goals. Citizens who are net losers from integrative decisions by the Council or the Commission cannot sue to have those actions declared ultra vires. But citizens who stand to gain have a constant incentive to push their governments to live up to paper commitments. As Haas argued in 1964, a successful international organization can achieve "growth through planning . . . only on the basis of stimulating groups and governments in the environment to submit new demands calling for organizational action."

Courting the national courts. The entire process of increasing the use of the Article 177 procedure was an exercise in convincing national judges of the desirability of using the ECJ. Through seminars, dinners, regular invitations to Luxembourg, and visits around the Community, the ECJ judges put a human face on the institutional links they sought to build. Many of the Court's Article 177 opinions reenforced the same message. It was a message that included a number of components designed to appeal to the self-interest primarily of the lower national courts. It succeeded ultimately in transforming the European legal system into a split system, in which these lower courts began to recognize two separate and distinct authorities above them: their own national supreme courts, on questions of national law, and the ECJ, on questions of European law. Judge Mancini explains quite candidly that the ECJ needed the "cooperation and goodwill of the state courts."

Shapiro expresses surprise at the willingness of lower national courts to invoke Article 177 against the interests of their own national supreme courts, noting that lower court judges "must attend to their career prospects within hierarchically organized national judicial systems." Weiler offers several explanations, beginning with the legitimacy of ECJ decisions conferred by the national prestige of individual judges and the precise reasoning of the opinions themselves. He ultimately concludes, however, that the "legally driven constitutional revolution" in the EC is "a narrative of plain and simple judicial empowerment." And further, that "the E.C. system gave judges at the lowest level powers that had been reserved to the highest court in the land." For many, "to have de facto judicial review of legislation . . . would be heady stuff."

Perhaps the best evidence for this "narrative of empowerment" comes from the ECJ itself. Many of the opinions are carefully crafted appeals to judicial ego. In *Van Gend & Loos* itself the Belgian and Dutch governments had argued that the question of the application of the Treaty of Rome over Dutch or Belgian law was solely a question for the Belgian and Dutch national courts. The ECJ responded by announcing, in effect, that the entire case was a matter solely between the national courts and the ECJ, to be resolved without interference from the national governments. When the Belgian government objected that the question of European law referred by the national court could have no bearing on the outcome of the proceedings, the ECJ piously responded that it was not its business to review the "considerations which may have led a national court or tribunal to its choice of questions as well as the relevance which it attributes to such questions." In this and subsequent direct effect cases the ECJ continually suggested that the direct effect of Community law should depend on judicial interpretation rather than legislative action.

Finally, in holding that a national court's first loyalty must be to the ECJ on all questions of Community law, the Court was able simultaneously to appeal to national courts *in their role* as protectors of individual rights—a very effective dual strategy. Such argumentation simultaneously strengthens the force of the Court's message to national courts by portraying the construction of the European legal system as simply a continuation of the traditional role of European courts and, indeed, liberal courts everywhere: the protection of individual rights against the state. At the same time, as discussed above, the Court strengthens its own claim to perform that role, building a constituency beyond the Brussels bureaucracy.

Reciprocal empowerment. This utilitarian depiction of the integration process must include the ECJ itself. It is obvious that any measures that succeed in raising the visibility, effectiveness, and scope of EC law also enhance the prestige and power of the Court and its members, both judges and advocates general. In addition, however, by presenting itself as the champion of individual rights and the pro-

tector of the prerogatives of lower national courts, the ECJ also bur-
nishes its own image and gives its defenders weapons with which to
rebut charges of antidemocratic activism. Rasmussen points out that
the encouragement to use Article 177 procedure meant that the
Court visibly sided with "the little guy," the underdog against state
bureaucracies, "the 'people' against the 'power-elite.'" Strikingly
enough, this is a characterization with which Judge Koenrad
Lenaerts essentially concurs.

The empowerment of the ECJ with respect to the national
courts is more subtle. While offering lower national courts a "heady"
taste of power, the ECJ simultaneously strengthens its own legal legitimacy by making it appear that its own authority flows from the
national courts. It is the national courts, after all, who have sought
its guidance; and it is the national courts who will ultimately decide
the case, in the sense of issuing an actual ruling on the facts. The ECJ
only "interprets" the relevant provision of Community law, and
leaves it for the national court to apply it to the facts of the case. In
practice, of course, the ECJ frequently offers a virtual template for
the subsequent lower court decision. But, the all-important fiction is
preserved.

Finally, the empowerment of the ECJ simultaneously empowers
all those who make their living by analyzing and critiquing its decisions. Here Community law professors and their many assistants join
with members of the Community bar to form a Communitywide network of individuals with a strong stake in bolstering the Court's
prestige. On the most basic level, the growing importance of Community law translates into a growing demand for professors to teach
it and hence, funding for chaired professorships. The holders of these
chairs are likely, in turn, to aspire to become judges and advocates
general themselves, just as many current judges and advocates general are likely to return to the professorate when their terms expire.
This is a neofunctionalist interest group par excellence.

☐   *Process*

As discussed above, the neofunctionalist description of the actual
process of integration focused on three major features: functional
spillover, political spillover, and upgrading of common interests. All
three dynamics are clearly present in the building of the EC legal system.

Functional spillover: the logic of law. Functional spillover presupposes the existence of an agreed objective and simply posits that the

jurisdiction of the authorities charged with implementing that objective will expand as necessary to address whatever obstacles stand in the way. This expansion will continue as long as those authorities do not collide with equally powerful countervailing interests. Alternatively, of course, one objective might conflict with another objective. Such limits define the parameters within which this "functionalist" logic can work.

In the construction of a Community legal system, such limits were initially very few, and the functional logic was very strong. Judge Pierre Pescatore has attributed the ECJ's success in creating a coherent and authoritative body of Community law to the Court's ability—flowing from the structure and content of the Treaty of Rome—to use "constructive methods of interpretation." One of the more important of those methods is the "systematic method," drawing on "the various systematic elements on which Community law is based: general scheme of the legislation, structure of the institutions, arrangement of powers . . . , general concepts and guiding ideals of the Treaties. Here is a complete 'architecture,' coherent and well thought out, *the lines of which, once firmly drawn, require to be extended*." Interpretation according to the systematic method means filling in areas of the legal structure that logically follow from the parts of the structure already built.

A well-known set of examples confirms the power of this functional logic as applied by the ECJ. After *Van Gend & Loos*, the next major "constitutional" case handed down was *Costa v. Enel*, which established the supremacy of Community law over national law. In plain terms, *Costa* asserted that where a treaty term conflicted with a subsequent national statute, the treaty must prevail. Predictably, Judge Federico Mancini justifies this decision by reference to the ruin argument. He argues further, however, that the supremacy clause "was not only an indispensable development, it was also a logical development." Students of federalism have long recognized that the clash of interests between state and federal authorities can be mediated in several ways: either (1) by allowing state authorities to implement federal directives at the time and in the manner they desire, or (2) by allowing both state and federal authorities to legislate directly, which entails formulating guidelines to establish a hierarchy between the two. On this basis, Mancini (and Eric Stein before him) points out that because the Court had "enormously extended the Community power to deal directly with the public" in *Van Gend & Loos*, it now became logically necessary to insist that Community law must prevail over member state law in cases of conflict. In short, the "full impact of direct effect" can only be realized "in combination with" the supremacy clause.

The evolution of Community law also has manifested the substantive broadening typical of functional spillover. EC law is today no longer as dominantly economic in character as in the 1960s. It has spilled over into a variety of domains dealing with issues such as health and safety at work, entitlements to social welfare benefits, mutual recognition of educational and professional qualification, and, most recently, even political participation rights. Two notable examples are equal treatment with respect to social benefits of workers, a field developed almost entirely as a result of Court decisions, and the general system of Community trademark law—again formed entirely by the Court's case law. In both areas the Court gradually extended its reach by grounding each new decision on the necessity of securing the common market.

Political spillover: "transnational incrementalism." The neofunctionalists argued that integration was an adaptive process of gradually shifting expectations, changing loyalties, and evolving values. In trying to explain why member states responded positively to the Court's legal innovations, Joseph Weiler writes: "it is clear that a measure of transnational incrementalism developed. Once some of the highest courts of a few Member States endorsed the new Constitutional construct, their counterparts in other Member States heard more arguments that those courts should do the same, and it became more difficult for national courts to resist the trend with any modicum of credibility."

Beyond the Court's specific machinations, however, law operates as law by shifting expectations. The minute a rule is established as "law," individuals are entitled to rely upon the assumption that social, economic, or political behavior will be conducted in accordance with that rule. The creation and application of law is inherently a process of shifting expectations. A major function of a legal rule is to provide a clear and certain standard around which expectations can crystallize.

As long as those actors to which the Court's decisions are directed—member state governments, national courts, and individuals—accept one decision as a statement of the existing law and proceed to make arguments in the next case from that benchmark, they are shifting their expectations. This is precisely the process that court watchers, even potentially skeptical ones, have identified. Hjalte Rasmussen demonstrates that even governments overtly hostile to the Court's authority do not seek to ask the Court to overturn a previous ruling but rather accept that ruling as a statement of the law and use it as a point of departure for making arguments in subsequent cases. After reviewing an extensive sample of briefs submitted to the Court by member governments, Rasmussen was unable to find even one instance in which a member state suggested that a prior precedent be overruled.

This finding is particularly striking given that states do often strongly object to a proposed interpretation or application of a particular legislative term in its briefs and arguments *prior* to a particular decision. One of the most celebrated instances of member state defiance of the Court is the *Sheepmeat* case. This represented the culmination of a line of precedents in which the Court had held repeatedly that the treaty prohibited intra-EC agricultural trade restrictions created by national market organizations for specific products. The French government fought bitterly against this position at every turn but after losing in the first two cases, it chose to argue in the third for a delay in implementing its obligations—rather than to dispute the earlier decisions by the Court that had established those obligations in the first place.

Upgrading common interests. For the neofunctionalists, upgrading common interests referred to a "swapping mechanism" dependent on the services of an "institutionalized autonomous mediator." The Court is less a mediator than an arbiter and has no means per se of "swapping" concessions. What it does do, however, is continually to justify its decisions in light of the common interests of the members as enshrined in both specific and general objectives of the original Rome treaty. The modus operandi here is the "teleological method of interpretation," by which the court has been able to rationalize everything from direct effect to the preemption of member state negotiating power in external affairs in every case in which the treaty grants internal competence to Community authorities. All are reasoned not on the basis of specific provisions in the treaty or Community secondary legislation but on the accomplishment of the most elementary Community goals set forth in the Preamble to the treaty.

According to Judge Pescatore, the concepts employed in the teleological method include "concepts such as the customs union, equality of treatment and non-discrimination, freedom of movement, mutual assistance and solidarity, economic interpenetration and finally economic and legal unity as the supreme objective." He goes on to cite two examples from early cases concerning the free movement of goods and the customs union. He points out that "formulas" such as describing the customs union as one of the "foundations of the Community," the role of which is "essential for the implementation of the Community project . . . have been repeated and developed in very varied circumstances since this first judgment."

Rhetorically, these formulas constantly shift the analysis to a more general level on which it is possible to assert common interests—the same common interests that led member states into the community process in the first place. French sheepfarmers might fight to the death with British sheepfarmers, but the majority of the population in both nations have a common interest in "the free movement of goods." "Upgrading the common interest," in judicial parlance, is a process of reasserting long-term interest, at least as nominally perceived at the founding and enshrined in sonorous phrases, over short-term interest. In the process, of course, to the extent it succeeds in using this method to strengthen and enhance Community authority, the Court does certainly also succeed in upgrading its own powers.

□   *Context: The (Apparent) Separation of Law and Politics*

The effectiveness of law in the integration process—as Haas predicted for economics—depends on the perception that it is a domain distinct and apart from politics. Shapiro has argued, for instance, that the Court, aided and abetted by its commentators, has derived enormous advantage from denying the existence of policy discretion and instead hewing to the fiction, bolstered by the style and retroactivity of its judgments. An absolute division between law and politics, as between economics and politics, is ultimately impossible. Nevertheless, just as Haas stressed that overt political concerns are less directly engaged in economic integration, requiring some time for specific economic decisions to acquire political significance, so, too, can legal decision making function in a relative political vacuum. Although the political impact of judicial decisions will ultimately be felt, they will be more acceptable initially due to their independent nonpolitical justification.

The importance of undertaking integration in a nominally nonpolitical sphere is confirmed by the underlying issues and interests at stake in the nascent debate about judicial activism in the Community. As periodic struggles over the proper balance between judicial activism and judicial restraint in the United States have demonstrated, assertions about the preservation of the legitimacy and authority necessary to uphold the rule of law generally have a particular substantive vision of the law in mind. In the Community context, the response to Rasmussen's charge of judicial activism reveals that the substantive stakes concern the prospects for the Court's self-professed task, integration. In heeding widespread advice to maintain a careful balance between applying Community law and articulating and defending Community ideals, the Court is really preserving its ability to camouflage controversial political decisions in "technical" legal garb.

Maintaining the fiction. The European legal community appears to understand the importance of preserving the Court's image as a non-political institution all too well. The dominant theme in scholarship on the Court in the 1970s and 1980s was reassurance that the Court was carrying out its delicate balancing act with considerable success. Rasmussen describes a widespread refusal among Community lawyers and legal academics to criticize the Court on paper. The consensus seems to be that overt recognition of the Court's political agenda beyond the bounds of what "the law" might fairly be said to permit will damage the Court's effectiveness. Commenting on the same phenomenon, Shapiro has observed that the European legal community understands its collective writings on the Court as a political act designed to bolster the Court. By denying the existence of judicial activism and thus removing a major potential locus of opposition to the Court, they promote an institution whose pro-Community values accord with their own internalized values.

The Court itself has cooperated in burnishing this nonpolitical image. Pescatore set the tone in 1974, contending that the first reason for the "relative success of Community case law" is "the wide definition of the task of the Court as custodian of law." And certainly the Court has carefully crafted its opinions to present the results in terms of the inexorable logic of the law. To cite a classic example, in the *Van Gend & Loos* decision, in which the Court singlehandedly transformed the Treaty of Rome from an essentially nonenforceable international treaty to a domestic charter with direct and enforceable effects, it cast its analysis in the following framework: "To ascertain whether the provisions of an international treaty extend so far in their effects it is necessary to consider the spirit, the general scheme, and the wording of those provisions."

Judge Mancini recently has continued this tradition in his description of the Court's success in winning over national judges. Referring to the ECJ's "courteously didactic" method, Mancini ultimately attributes the rise of the Article 177 procedure to the "cleverness" of his colleagues not in devising political strategies but in fashioning the law in such a way that its autonomous power and ineluctable logic would be clear to the benighted national judges. He seems astonishingly candid, observing, with an insider's wink: "The national judge is thus led hand in hand as far as the door; crossing the threshold is his job, but now a job no harder than child's play." In fact, however, his "revelations" amount to a story about the power of law, thus continuing the Court's proud tradition of insisting on the legal-political divide.

Mancini also has joined with other judges, most notably Ulrich Everling, in public penance to reassure concerned onlookers that the Court was very aware of the need for prudence. By the early 1980s, responding to simmering criticism, Judge Everling published several articles announcing that much of the foundational work in establishing the Treaty of Rome as a Community constitution was done and that the Court could now afford to take a lower political profile. In 1989 Judge Mancini applauded the work of the Court to date but noted that the political relaunching of the Community embodied in the SEA and the progress of the 1992 initiative toward a genuine common market would now permit the Court essentially to confine its activities to the more purely legal sphere.

Transforming the political into the legal. Court watchers have long understood that the ECJ uses the EC Commission as a political bellwether. In any given case, the ECJ looks to the Commission's position as an indicator of political acceptability to the member states of a particular result or a line of reasoning. From the Court's own perspective, however, the chief advantage of following the Commission is the "advantage of objectivity," resulting from the Commission's supranational perspective. In neofunctionalist terms, the Court's reliance on what Pescatore characterizes as "well-founded information and balanced legal evaluations" as "source material for the Court's decisions" allows it to cast itself as nonpolitical by contrasting the neutrality and objectivity of its decision-making processes with the partisan political agendas of the parties before it.

Relatively less attention has been paid to the role of the Commission in depoliticizing potentially inflammatory disputes among the member states. Judge Pierre Pescatore credits the procedure set forth in Article 169 (whereby the *Commission* initiates an action against a member state for a declaration of default on a Community legal obligation) with defusing the potential fireworks of an Article 170 proceeding, in which one state would bring such a charge directly against another. By allowing default proceedings to be initiated by "an institution representative of the whole, and hence objective both by its status and by its task," this device "permits the Member States more easily to accept this process of control over their Community behavior and the censure which may arise for them from the judgments of the Court." Against this backdrop, it is of signal importance that the Court itself actively and successfully encouraged the increased use of the Article 169 procedure.

This perspective reveals yet another dimension of the Court's encouragement of the Article 177 procedure. The increased use of Article 177 shifted the vanguard of Community law enforcement (and creation) to cases involving primarily private parties. It thus further removed the Court from the overtly political sphere of direct conflicts between member states, or even between the Commission and member states. The political implications of private legal disputes, while potentially very important, often require a lawyer's eye to discern. Following Haas's description of economic integration, Article 177 cases offer a paradigm for the "indirect" penetration of the political by way of the legal.

Law as a mask. The above discussion of context reveals that the neofunctionalist domain is a domain theoretically governed by a distinct set of nonpolitical objectives, such as "the rule of law" or "economic growth and efficiency," and by a distinctive methodology and logic. These characteristics operate to define a purportedly "neutral" zone in which it is possible to reach outcomes that would be impossible to achieve in the political arena. Neofunctionalists also insisted, however, that this neutral zone would not be completely divorced from politics. On the contrary, "economic"—or, in our case, "legal"—decisions inevitably would acquire political significance. This gradual interpenetration was the mechanism by which economic integration might ultimately lead to political integration.

The key to understanding this process is that even an economic decision that has acquired political significance is not the same as a "purely" political decision and cannot be attacked as such. It retains an independent "nonpolitical" rationale, which must be met by a counterargument on its own terms. Within this domain, then, contending political interests must do battle by proxy. The chances of victory are affected by the strength of that proxy measured by independent nonpolitical criteria.

From this perspective, law functions both as mask and shield. It hides and protects the promotion of one particular set of political objectives against contending objectives in the purely political sphere. In specifying this dual relationship between law and politics, we also uncover a striking paradox. Law can only perform this dual political function to the extent it is accepted as law. A "legal" decision that is transparently "political," in the sense that it departs too far from the principles and methods of the law, will invite direct political attack. It will thus fail both as mask and shield. Conversely, a court seeking to advance its own political agenda must accept the independent constraints of legal reasoning, even when such constraints require it to reach a result that is far narrower than the one it might deem politically optimal.

In short, a court's political legitimacy, and hence its ability to advance its own political agenda, rests on its legal legitimacy. This premise is hardly news to domestic lawyers. It has informed an entire school of thought about the U.S. Supreme Court. It also accords with the perception of ECJ judges of how to enhance their own effectiveness, as witnessed not only by their insistence on their strict adherence to the goals of the Treaty of Rome but also by their vehement reaction to charges of activism. Mancini again: "If what makes a judge 'good' is his awareness of the constraints on judicial decision-making and the knowledge that rulings must be convincing in order to evoke obedience, the Luxembourg judges of the 1960s and 1970s were obviously very good."

What is new about the neofunctionalist approach is that it demonstrates the ways in which the preservation of judicial legitimacy shields an entire domain of integrationist processes, hence permitting the accretion of power and the pursuit of individual interests by specified actors within a dynamic of expansion. Moreover, the effectiveness of "law as a mask" extends well beyond the ECJ's efforts to construct a Community legal system. To the extent that judges of the European Court do in fact remain within the plausible boundaries of existing law, they achieve a similar level of effectiveness in the broader spheres of economic, social, and political integration.

■ IMPLICATIONS AND CONCLUSIONS

□ *The Maastricht Treaty*

The Maastricht Treaty on European Union reflects a determination on the part of the member states to limit the ECJ. The Court is entirely excluded from two of the three "pillars" of the treaty: foreign and security policy and cooperation in the spheres of justice and home affairs. In addition, a number of specific articles are very tightly drafted to prevent judicial manipulation. For instance, in the provisions on public health, education, vocational training, and culture, the treaty provides that the Council shall adopt necessary measures to achieve the common objectives set forth, "*excluding any harmonization of the laws and regulations of the Member States.*" This explicit prohibition of harmonization is an effort to ensure that the expedited decision-making procedures under Article 100 for the completion of the internal market cannot be interpreted to apply to those additional substantive areas. On the other hand, another amendment allows the Court for the first time, at the Commission's request, to impose a lump-sum or penalty payment on a member state that fails to comply with its judgment.

At first glance, the Maastricht provisions appear to confirm the Garrett-Weingast theory of the Court. The member states chose to strengthen the Court's power to monitor and punish defections from those areas of the treaty where it exercises jurisdiction; they chose to exclude it altogether in areas of lesser political consensus. Yet, Garrett and Weingast conclude that the single most important factor behind the maintenance of the Community legal system is not the Court's performance of monitoring and incomplete contracting functions but rather the alignment of its judgments with the interests of the member states holding the balance of power in the Community. If so, and if indeed the Court ensures the protection of its authority and legitimacy by assiduous fidelity to state interests rather than to the law, then why worry? Why should not the member states permit unrestricted jurisdiction, secure in the knowledge that the political constraints on the Court are safeguard enough? In areas of member state consensus, the Court will follow that consensus; in areas of continuing disagreement at least among the big states, the Court could be expected to decline jurisdiction or to decide on a technicality.

The answer can only be that the Court does have the power to pursue its own agenda, and that the personal incentives in the judicial and legal community, as well as the structural logic of law, favor integration. Further, the autonomy of the legal domain means that once started down a particular path, the Court's trajectory is difficult to monitor or control. It can be slowed by countermeasures carefully constructed on its own terms; the exclusion of harmonization, for instance, can be understood as a direct check on spillover crafted in legal language and according to legal rules. However, only exclusion provides certainty. Such exclusion will indeed stop the integration process in those areas; as fully admitted by neofunctionalists, neofunctionalism is a stochastic process, sensitive to political constraints. Absent such extreme measures, however, when not specifically cabined, the neofunctionalist dynamic does indeed produce incremental but steady change.

□ *The Sources of Judicial Autonomy*

Accepting our argument thus far, a larger question nevertheless remains to be addressed—one that exceeds the scope of this article but that intersects larger debates in international relations theory about the role of institutions. Why do nation-states permit law an autonomous realm, even on the condition that its practitioners will remain faithful to its language and logic? Why not politicize the courts? Another way to ask the same question is to ask why member states do not seek to control the Court on a much more micro level—not by cabining the scope of judicial interpretation or by jurisdiction-stripping provisions but by seeking to control the political orientation of individual judges or requiring the publication of the actual votes in individual cases.

The potential answers to these questions pit rationalism against reflectivism: the cool calculation of exogenously determined interests versus the culturally conditioned operation of shared belief systems. Reflectivists might argue that judicial independence is a bedrock norm of Western liberal democracies. It has arguably never even been questioned in civil law countries—the substantial majority of Community members—because the "law-making" functions of civil law courts are paltry in comparison with their common law brethren. Rationalists could counter with a demonstration of the utility of an independent judiciary for the "juridicization" of politics, the oppositional use of a third-party tribunal to check the power of the majority party. These are questions we can only pose, but their answers are important for theories about the power and strength of all institutions.

□   *A Return to Sophisticated Legalism*

Before concluding, it is worth returning for a moment to the various categories of existing theories about the role of the ECJ in European integration described in the first part of this article, particularly the contextualist theories. We argued that those theories lacked microfoundations and failed to specify causal mechanisms. A brief review of several of those theories here demonstrates that the neofunctionalist approach supplies the missing elements. . . .

In his most recent article, Weiler depicts much of the "systemic evolution of Europe" as the result of the self-created and internally sustained power of law. Shapiro made a similar point in the article in which he first threw down the gauntlet to Community legal scholars to take account of the larger political context in which the Court was acting. He concluded that the legalist analysis might ultimately be the more "politically sophisticated one" on the ground that "legal realities are realities too." Both Lenaerts and Rasmussen would agree, although Rasmussen fears that legal realities are likely to be overborne by political realities as a result of a loss of judicial legitimacy. This position might be described as the "sophisticated legalist" position—one that recognizes the existence of countervailing political forces but that nevertheless accords a role for the autonomous power of law.

The neofunctionalist approach integrates that insight with a carefully specified theory of the individual incentives and choices facing the servants of law and a description of the processes whereby they advance their own agenda within a sheltered domain. Thus, although we agree with Weiler's conclusion, we go far beyond his general claim that the power of law within the Community emanates from the "deep-seated legitimacy that derives from the mythical neutrality and religious-like authority with which we invest our supreme courts." The power flows from a network of strongly motivated individuals acting above and below the state. To enhance and preserve that power, they must preserve and earn anew the presumed legitimacy of law by remaining roughly faithful to its canons.

In conclusion, neofunctionalism offers a genuine political theory of an important dimension of European integration. It is a theory that should be equally comprehensible and plausible to lawyers and political scientists, even if European judges and legal scholars resist it for reasons the theory itself explains. Previously, those who would argue for the force of the law had to forsake "political" explanations, or at least explanations satisfactory to political scientists. Conversely, most of those seeking to construct a social scientific account of the role of the Court typically have eschewed "fuzzy" arguments based on the power of law. We advance a theory of the interaction of law and politics that draws on both disciplines, explaining the role of law in European integration as a product of rational motivation and choice. Lawyers seeking to offer causal explanations, as well as political scientists trying to explain legal phenomena, should be equally satisfied.

23 European Integration from the 1980s: State-Centric v. Multi-Level Governance

GARY MARKS, LIESBET HOOGHE, AND KERMIT BLANK

Gary Marks (University of North Carolina, Chapel Hill) and his colleagues, Liesbet Hooghe (University of Toronto) and Kermit Blank (University of North Carolina, Chapel Hill), provide a second challenge to intergovernmentalism (or what they refer to as the "state-centric model") by critiquing its description of the policymaking process in the European Union.

In this 1996 article, Marks, Hooghe, and Blank contest the intergovernmentalist notion that decisions in the EU are ultimately shaped by the member states. In their view, EU policy is produced by a complex web of interconnected institutions at the supranational, national, and subnational levels of government comprising a system of "multi-level governance." National governments play an important role in the system, but their sovereignty has eroded, almost imperceptibly, despite their best intentions. As the authors put it, "Instead of being explicitly challenged, states in the European Union are being melded gently into a multi-level polity by their leaders and the actions of numerous subnational and supranational actors." From their examination of EU policymaking in four stages—policy initiation, decisionmaking, implementation, and adjudication—Marks, Hooghe, and Blank argue that state "control of those living in their territories has significantly weakened."

The multi-level governance model does not discard the insights of intergovernmentalism but incorporates them into a much larger and more complex policymaking model. The model is highly descriptive and explains a great many policy outcomes, but it is not, nor does it claim to be, a theory of integration.

Developments in the European Union (EU) over the last decade have revived debate about the consequences of European integration for the autonomy and authority of the state in Europe. The scope and depth of policy-making at the EU-level have dramatically increased. The EU has almost completed the internal market and has absorbed the institutional reforms of the Single European Act (1986) which established qualified majority voting in the Council of Ministers and increased the power of the European Parliament. The Maastricht treaty (1993) further expanded EU competencies and the scope of qualified majority voting in the Council, and provided the European Parliament with a veto on certain types of legislation. The Maastricht treaty is a landmark in European integration quite apart from its ambitious plan for a common currency and European central bank by the end of this century.

Our aim in this article is to take stock of these developments. What do they mean for the political architecture of Europe? Do these developments consolidate nation-states or do they weaken them? If they weaken them, what kind of political order is emerging? These are large and complex questions, and we do not imagine that we can settle them once and for all. Our strategy is to pose two basic alternative conceptions—state-centric governance and multi-level governance—as distinctly as possible and then evaluate their validity by examining the European policy process.

The core presumption of state-centric governance is that European integration does not challenge the autonomy of nation-states. State-centrists contend that state sovereignty is preserved or even strengthened through EU membership. They argue that European integration is driven by bargains among member state governments. No government has to integrate more than it wishes because bargains rest on the lowest common denominator of the participating member states. In this model, supranational actors exist to aid member states, to facilitate agreements by providing information that would not otherwise be so readily available. Policy outcomes reflect the interests and relative power of member state executives. Supranational actors exercise little independent effect.

An alternative view is that European integration is a polity creating process in which authority and policy-making influence are shared across multiple levels of government—subnational, national, and supranational. While national governments are formidable participants in EU policy-making, control has slipped away from them to supranational institutions. States have lost some of their former authoritative control over individuals in their respective territories. In short, the locus of political control has changed. Individual state sovereignty is diluted in the EU by collective decision-making among national governments and by the autonomous role of the European Parliament, the European Commission, and the European Court of Justice.

We make this argument in this article along two tracks. First we analyze the variety of conditions under which central state executives will voluntarily or involuntarily lose their grip on power. Second, we examine policy-making in the EU across its different stages against the background of contending state-centric and multi-level approaches to European governance.

■ **TWO MODELS OF THE EUROPEAN UNION**

The models which we outline below are drawn from a large and diverse body of work on the European Union, though they are elaborated in different ways by different authors. Our aim here is not to replicate the ideas of any particular writer, but to set out the basic elements that underlie contending views of the EU so that we may evaluate their validity.

The core ideas of the *state-centric model* are put forward by several writers most of whom call themselves intergovernmentalists. This model poses states (or, more precisely, national governments) as ultimate decision-makers, devolving limited authority to supranational institutions to achieve specific policy goals. Decision-making in the EU is determined by bargaining among state executives. To the extent that supranational institutions arise, they serve the ultimate goals of state executives. The state-centric model does not maintain that policy-making is determined by state executives in every detail, only that the overall direction of policy-making is consistent with state control. States may be well served by creating a judiciary, for example, that allows them to enforce collective agreements, or bureaucracy that implements those agreements. But such institutions are not autonomous supranational agents. Rather, they have limited powers to achieve state-oriented collective goods.

EU decisions, according to the state-centric model, reflect the lowest common denominator among state executive positions. Although member state executives decide jointly, they are not compelled to swallow policies they find unacceptable because decision-making on important issues operates on the basis of unanimity. This allows states to maintain individual as well as collective control over outcomes. While some governments are not able to integrate as much as they would wish, none is forced into deeper collaboration than it really wants.

State decision-making in this model does not exist in a political vacuum. In this respect, the state-centric model takes issue with realist conceptions of international relations which focus on relations among unitary state actors. State executives are located in domestic political arenas, and their negotiating positions are influenced by domestic political interests. But—and this is an important assumption—those state arenas are discrete. That is to say, state decision-makers respond to political pressures that are *nested* within each state. So, the 15 state executives bargaining in the European arena are complemented by 15 separate state arenas that provide the sole channel for domestic political interests at the European level. The core claim of the state-centric model is that policy-making in the EU is determined primarily by state executives constrained by political interests nested within autonomous state arenas that connect subnational groups to European affairs.

One can envision several alternative models to this one. The one we present here, which we describe as *multi-level governance*, is drawn from several sources. Once again, our aim is not to reiterate any one scholar's perspective, but to elaborate essential elements of a model drawn from several strands of writing which makes the case that European integration has weakened the state.

The multi-level governance model does not reject the view that state executives and state arenas are important, or that these remain the *most* important pieces of the European puzzle. However, when one asserts that the state no longer monopolizes European level policy-making or the aggregation of domestic interests, a very different polity comes into focus. First, according to the multi-level governance model, decision-making competencies are shared by actors at different levels rather than monopolized by state executives. That is to say, supranational institutions—above all, the European Commission, the European Court, and the European Parliament—have independent influence in policy-making that cannot be derived from their role as agents of state executives. State executives may play an important role but, according to the multi-level governance model, one must also analyze the independent role of European level actors to explain European policy-making.

Second, collective decision-making among states involves a significant loss of control for individual state executives. Lowest common denominator outcomes are available only on a subset of EU decisions, mainly those concerning the scope of integration. Decisions concerning rules to be enforced across the EU (e.g., harmonizing regulation of product standards, labor conditions) have a zero-sum character, and necessarily involve gains or losses for individual states.

Third, political arenas are interconnected rather than nested. While national arenas remain important for the formation of state executive preferences, the multi-level model rejects the view that subnational actors are nested exclusively within them. Instead, subnational actors operate in both national and supranational arenas, creating transnational associations in the process. States do not monopolize links between domestic and European actors, but are one among a variety of actors contesting decisions that are made at a variety of levels. In this perspective, complex interrelationships in domestic politics do not stop at the nation-state, but extend to the European level. The separation between domestic and international politics, which lies at the heart of the state-centric model, is rejected by the multi-governance model. States are an integral and powerful part of the EU, but they no longer provide the sole interface between supranational and subnational arenas, and they share, rather than monopolize, control over many activities that take place in their respective territories.

. . .

■ POLICY-MAKING IN THE EUROPEAN UNION

The questions we are asking have to do with who decides what in European Union policy-making. If the state-centric model is valid, we would find a systematic pattern of state executive dominance. That entails three conditions. National governments, by virtue of the European Council and the Council of Ministers, should be able to impose their preferences collectively upon other European institutions, i.e., the European Commission, the European Parliament and the European Court of Justice. In other words, the latter three European institutions should be agents effectively controlled by state-dominated

European institutions. Second, national governments should be able to maintain individual sovereignty vis-à-vis other national governments. And thirdly, national governments should be able to control the mobilization of subnational interests, in the European arena. If, however, the multi-level governance model is valid, we should find, first, that the European Council and Council of Ministers share decisional authority with supranational institutions; second, that individual state executives cannot deliver the outcomes they wish through collective state executive decisions; and, finally, that subnational interests mobilize directly in the European arena or use the EU as a public space to pressure state executives into particular actions.

We divide the policy-making process into four sequential phases: policy initiation, decision making, implementation and adjudication. We focus on informal practices in addition to formal rules, for it is vital to understand how institutions actually shape the behavior of political actors in the European arena.

☐ *Policy Initiation: Commission as Agenda-Setter with a Price—Listen, Make Sense, and Time Aptly*

In political systems that involve many actors, complex procedures and multiple veto points, the power to set the agenda is extremely important. The European Commission alone has the formal power to initiate and draft legislation, which includes the right to amend or withdraw its proposal at any stage in the process, and it is the think-tank for new policies. From a multi-level governance perspective, the European Commission has significant autonomous influence over the agenda. According to the state-centric model, this formal power is largely decorative: in reality the European Commission draws up legislation primarily to meet the demands of state executives.

At first sight, the practice of policy initiation is consistent with state-centric interpretation. Analysis of 500 recent directives and regulations by the French Conseil d'Etat found that only a minority of EU proposals were spontaneous initiatives of the Commission. Regulatory initiative at the European level is demand driven rather than the product of autonomous supranational action, but the demands come not only from government leaders. A significant number of initiatives originate in the European Parliament, the Economic and Social Committee, regional governments, and various private and public-interest groups.

Such data should be evaluated carefully. For one thing, regulatory initiative at national and European levels is increasingly intermeshed. In its report, the Conseil d'Etat estimated that the European

Commission is consulted beforehand on 75–80 percent of French national legislation. Jacques Delors' prediction that by the year 2000 about 80 percent of national economic and social legislation would be of Community origin has a solid base in reality. Moreover, it is one thing to be the first to articulate an issue, and quite another to influence how that issue will be taken up, with whom, and under what set of rules. And in each of these respects the influence of the Commission extends beyond its formal role, partly because of its unique political and administrative resources, discussed below, and partly because the Council is stymied by intergovernmental competition.

An organization that may serve as a powerful principal with respect to the Commission is the European Council, the summit of the political leaders of the member states (plus the President of the Commission) held every six months. The European Council has immense prestige and legitimacy and a quasi-legal status as the body which defines "general political guidelines." However, its control of the European agenda is limited because it meets rarely and has only a skeleton permanent staff. The European Council provides the Commission with general policy mandates rather than specific policy proposals, and such mandates have proved to be a flexible basis for the Commission to build legislative programs.

More direct constraints on the Commission originate from the Council of Ministers and the European Parliament. Indeed, the power of initiative has increasingly become a shared competence, permanently subject to contestation, among the three institutions. The Council and, since the Maastricht treaty, the European Parliament can request the Commission to produce proposals, although they cannot draft proposals themselves. Council Presidencies began to exploit this window in the legal texts from the mid-1980s, when state executives began to attach higher priority to the Council Presidency. Several governments bring detailed proposals with them to Brussels when they take over the Council Presidency. Another way for the Council to circumvent the Commission's formal monopoly of legislative proposal is to make soft law, i.e., by ratifying common opinions, resolutions, agreements, and recommendations.

The effect of this on the Commission's agenda-setting role is double edged. On the one hand, the Commission finds it politically difficult to ignore detailed Council initiatives or soft law, even though their legal status is vague. On the other hand, state executives are intent on using the European arena to attain a variety of policy goals, and this gives the Commission allies for integrationist initiatives.

The European Parliament has made use of its newly gained competence in Article 138b. In return for the approval of the Santer

Commission in January 1995, it extracted from the Commission President a pledge to renegotiate the code of conduct (dating from 1990) between the two institutions in an effort to gain greater influence on the Commission's pen, its right of initiative.

The European Council, the Council, and the European Parliament have each succeeded in circumscribing the Commission's formal monopoly of initiative more narrowly, though none can claim that it has reduced the position of the Commission to that of an agent. Agenda-setting is now a shared and contested competence among the four European institutions, rather than monopolized by one actor.

But the diffusion of control over the EU's agenda does not stop here. Interest groups have mobilized intensively in the European arena and, while their power is difficult to pinpoint, it is clear that the Commission takes their input seriously. The passage of the Single European Act precipitated a rapid growth of European legislation and a corresponding increase in interest group representation in Europe. An outpouring of case study research suggests that the number and variety of groups involved is as great as, and is perhaps greater than, in any national capital. National and regional organizations of every kind have mobilized in Brussels, and these are flanked by a large and growing number of European peak organizations and individual companies from across Europe. According to a Commission report, some 3,000 interest groups and lobbies, or about 10,000 people, were based in Brussels in 1992. Among these there are 500 "Eurogroups" which aggregate interests at the European level. Most groups target their lobbying activity at the European Commission and the European Parliament, for these are perceived to be more accessible than the secretive Council.

Subnational authorities now mobilize intensively in Brussels. Apart from the Committee of the Regions, established by the Maastricht treaty, individual subnational authorities have set up almost 100 regional offices in Brussels and a wide variety of interregional associations.

Agenda-setting is therefore increasingly a shared and contested competence, with European institutions competing for control, and interest groups and subnational actors vying to influence the process. This is not much different from the situation in some national polities, particularly those organized federally.

As a consequence, it is often difficult to apportion responsibility for particular initiatives. This is true for the most intensively studied initiative of all—the internal market program—which was pressed forward by business interests, the Commission, and the European Parliament, as well as by state executives. Because the Commission plays a subtle initiating role, its influence is not captured by analysis of which institution formally announces a new policy. For example, the White Paper on *Growth, Competitiveness and Employment* was publicly mandated by the European Council in June 1993, but it did so in response to detailed guidelines for economic renewal tabled by the Commission President.

The Commission has considerable leverage, but it is conditional, not absolute. It depends on its capacity to nurture and use diverse contacts, its ability to anticipate and mediate demands, its decisional efficiency, and the unique expertise it derives from its role as think-tank of the European Union.

The Commission is always on the look-out for information and political support. It has developed an extensive informal machinery of advisory committees and working groups for consultation and pre-negotiation, some of which are made up of member state nominees, but others of interest group representatives and experts who give the Commission access to independent information and legitimacy. The Commission has virtually a free hand in creating new networks, and in this way it is able to reach out to new constituencies, including a variety of subnational groups.

· · ·

As a small and thinly staffed organization, the Commission has only a fraction of the resources available to central state executives, but its position as interlocutor with national governments, subnational authorities and a large variety of interest groups gives it unparalleled access to information. The Commission has superior in-house knowledge and expertise in agriculture, where one-quarter of its staff is concentrated. It has formidable expertise in external trade and competition, the two other areas where Commission competence is firmly established. In other areas, the Commission relies on member state submissions, its extensive advisory system of public and private actors, and paid consultants.

The European Commission is a critical actor in the policy initiation phase, whether one looks at formal rules or practice. If one surveys the evidence one cannot conclude that the Commission serves merely as an agent of state executives. The point is not that the Commission is the only decisive actor. We discern instead a system of multi-level governance involving competition and interdependence among the Commission, Council, and European Parliament, each of which commands impressive resources in the intricate game of policy initiation.

□   *Decision Making: State Sovereignty in Retreat*

According to the Treaties, the main legislative body in the EU is not the European Parliament, but the Council of Ministers, an assembly of member state executives. Until the Single European Act, the Council was the sole legislative authority. The thrust of the state-centric argument is to give great weight to the legislative powers of state executives in the decision making stage. At this stage, state executives may be said to be in complete control. They adjust policies to their collective preferences, define the limits of European collaboration, determine the role of the European Commission and the ECJ and, if need be, curtail their activities. If previous decisions have unintended consequences, these can be corrected by the Council.

There is some plausibility to this argument, but it is one-dimensional. In the first place, one must take into account the serious constraints under which individual governments have operated since the Single European Act. Second, one should recognize that even collectively, state executives exert conditional, not absolute, control. State executive dominance is eroded in the decision making process by the legislative power of the European Parliament, the role of the European Commission in overcoming transaction problems, and the efforts of interest groups to influence outcomes in the European arena.

The most transparent blow to state sovereignty has come from the successive extension of qualified majority voting under the Single European Act and the Maastricht treaty. Qualified majority voting is now the rule for most policy areas covered by the original Treaty of Rome, including agriculture, trade, competition policy, transport, and policy areas concerned with the realization of the internal market, though there are important exceptions which include the EU budget, taxation, capital flows, self-employed persons and professions, visa policy (qualified majority from 1 January 1996), free movement of persons, and rights of employed persons. The decision-making rules are complex, but the bottom line is clear: over broad areas of EU competence individual state executives may be outvoted.

The practice of qualified majority voting is complicated by the Luxembourg Compromise and by a "veto culture" which is said to have predominated in the Council of Ministers. Under the Luxembourg Compromise state executives can veto decisions subject to majority rule if they claim that their national vital interests are at stake. The Luxembourg Compromise features far more strongly in academic debates about the EU than in the practice of European politics. It was invoked less than a dozen times between 1966, and 1981, and it has been used even less frequently since that time.

The Luxembourg Compromise was accompanied by a "veto culture" which inhibited majority voting if a state executive expressed serious objections. During the 1970s, this led to the virtual paralysis of the Community as literally hundreds of Commission proposals were blocked. But the effectiveness of the veto culture was its undoing. It eroded during the 1980s as a result of growing intolerance with deadlock on the part of the European Parliament and most national leaders. The turning point was the inability of the British government in 1982 to veto a decision on agricultural prices to extract a larger British budgetary rebate. A qualified majority vote was taken at the meeting of Council of Ministers despite British objections.

Thereafter, state executives became more reluctant to invoke the compromise or tolerate its use by others. The last successful use of the Luxembourg veto was in June 1985, when the German government blocked a Council decision to reduce agricultural prices for cereals and colza. Since the Single European Act, which made majority voting the norm in a large number of areas, there has been just one attempt to invoke the compromise, and this failed. The Greek government vetoed a Council proposal concerning adjusted green exchange rates in 1988 in order to extract a more favorable exchange rate for the green drachma, but found itself isolated in the Council and was forced to retract the veto. In 1992–93, the French government threatened to veto the agricultural package of the GATT agreement, but eventually settled for a financial compensation package to cover what amounted to a "discreet climbdown." As Nugent has observed, the Luxembourg Compromise "is in the deepest of sleeps and is subject only to very occasional and partial awakenings."

In this context, second order rules about the adoption of alternative voting procedures are extremely important. Amendments to the Council's Rules of Procedure in July 1987 have made it much easier to initiate a qualified majority vote. While previously only the Council President could call a vote, it now suffices that one representative—and that could be the Commission—demands a ballot and is supported by a simple majority of the Council.

One of the most remarkable developments in the 1980s has been the transformation of the notion of "vital national interest." State executives wishing to exercise a Luxembourg veto have become dependent on the acquiescence of *other* state executives. They can no longer independently determine whether their vital national interest is at stake. As the British (1982), German (1985), Greek (1988) and French (1992–93) cases suggest, the conditions are restrictive. The Luxembourg Compromise has come to operate effectively only for decisions which involve some combination of the following characteristics: the perception of an unambiguous link to vital national interests; the prospect of serious domestic political damage to the government concerned; a national government which can credibly threaten to damage the general working of the European Union. While it originally legitimized unconditional defense of state sovereignty (de Gaulle vetoed the budgetary reform of 1965 on the grounds that it was too supranational), the notion of vital national interests has evolved to justify only defense of substantive interest, not defense of national sovereignty itself.

Even if a member state executive is able to invoke the Luxembourg Compromise, the veto remains a dull weapon. It cannot block alternative courses of action, as the German Federal government experienced in 1985 after it had stopped a Council regulation on lower prices for cereal and colza. The Commission simply invoked its emergency powers and achieved virtually the same reductions unilaterally. Moreover, a veto rarely settles an issue, unless the status quo is the preferred outcome for the vetoing government. But even in the two cases where the status quo was more desirable than the proposed change (the German and French cases), neither government was able to sustain the status quo. The German government was bypassed by the Commission; the French government was unable to block the GATT accord and, moreover, received only modest financial compensations in return for its acquiescence.

All in all, since the mid-1980s, the Luxembourg Compromise has been a weak instrument for the defense of state sovereignty. The British, German, Greek and French governments did not gain much by invoking or threatening to invoke it. Each came to accept that its options were severely constrained by European decision. The Luxembourg Compromise is now mainly symbolic for domestic consumption. In each of the four cases the ensuing crisis enabled embattled governments to shift responsibility in the face of intense domestic pressure. Although national governments were not able to realize their substantive aims, they could at least claim they fought hard to achieve them.

State executives have built a variety of specific safeguards into the Treaties. There are numerous derogations for particular states, especially on matters of taxation, state aids, monetary policy and energy policy. The Single European Act and the Maastricht treaty preserve unanimity for the most sensitive or contested policy areas.

These qualifications soften the blow to national sovereignty. But a sensible discussion of the overall situation turns on the *extent* to which national sovereignty has been compromised, rather than on whether this has happened. Even under the doubtful premise that the Council is the sole decision-maker, it is now the case that state sovereignty has been pooled among a group of states in most EU policy areas.

Collective state control exercised through the Council has diminished. That is first of all due to the growing role of the European Parliament in decision making. The SEA and the Maastricht treaty established cooperation and codecision procedures which have transformed the legislative process from a simple Council-dominated process into an complex balancing act between Council, Parliament and Commission. Since the Maastricht treaty, the two procedures apply to the bulk of EU legislation. The procedures are designed to encourage consensual decision making between the three institutions. It is impossible for the Council to take legislative decisions without the support of at least one of the two other institutions unless it is unanimous. Moreover, the procedures enhance the agenda-setting power of the European Parliament.

The cooperation procedure gives the Commission significant agenda-setting capacity. It may decide to take up or drop amendments from either the Council or Parliament, a power that makes it a broker—a consensus crafter—between the two institutions.

The intermeshing of institutions is particularly intricate under the codecision procedure, under which the Parliament obtains an absolute veto, although it loses some agenda-setting power to the Council. If the Parliament or Council rejects the other's positions, a conciliation committee tries to hammer out a compromise. The committee consists of representatives from both institutions, with the Commission sitting in as broker. A compromise needs the approval of an absolute majority in the Parliament and a qualified majority in the Council. If there is no agreement, the initiative returns to the Council, which can then make a take-it-or-leave-it offer, which the Parliament can reject by absolute majority. So the Parliament has the final word.

Even though the outcome of the codecision procedure is likely to be closer to the preferences of the Council than those of the Commission or Parliament, it does not simply reflect Council preferences. Under both procedures the Council is locked in a complex relationship of cooperation and contestation with the two other institutions. This is multi-level governance in action, and is distinctly different from what would be expected in a state-centric system.

The erosion of collective state control goes further than this. It is difficult for state executives to resolve transaction costs in the egalitarian setting of the Council, particularly now, given that there are 15 such actors. The Council usually lacks information, expertise, and the coordination to act quickly and effectively, and this induces it to rely on the European Commission for leadership.

The Commission, as a hierarchical organization, is usually able to present a more coherent position than the Council. Furthermore, Commission officials bring unusual skills to the negotiation table. As administrators, they have often been working on a particular policy issue for years; career mobility tends to be lower than for top echelons of most national administrations. In addition, they have access to information and expertise from a variety of sources in the European Union. They tend to be exceptionally skilled political negotiators acclimatized to the diverse political styles of national representatives and the need to seek consensual solutions. Formal decision rules in the Council help the Commission for focus discussion or broker compromise. While member state representatives preside at Council of Ministers' meetings and Council working groups, the Commission sits in to clarify, redraft, and finalize the proposal—in short, it holds the pen.

. . .

Cohesion policy offers an example of how the Commission may step beyond its role of umpire to become a negotiator. In establishing the framework for structural funds of 1994–99 in the summer of 1993, Commission officials negotiated bilaterally with officials from the relevant states. It was the Belgian presidency which acted as umpire. In such cases, the Commission becomes effectively a thirteenth (or, since 1995, a sixteenth) partner around the bargaining table. This can even be true for the most intergovernmental aspect of European Union politics: treaty bargaining, as an example from Maastricht illustrates. When the British government refused the watered down social provisions in the Maastricht treaty, Jacques Delors put on the table his original, more radical, social policy program of 1989 and proposed to attach it as a special protocol to the treaty, leaving Britain out. Faced with the prospect that the whole negotiation might break down, the other 11 state executives hastily signed up to a more substantial document than they had originally anticipated.

In sum, the Council is the senior actor in the decision-making stage, but the European Parliament and the Commission are indispensable partners. The Commission's power is predominantly soft in that it is exercised by subtle influence rather than sanction. Except for agriculture, external trade and competition policy, where it has substantial executive autonomy, it can gain little by confrontation. Its influence depends on its ability to craft consensus among institutions and among member state executives. However, extensive reliance on qualified majority voting has enabled the Commission to be bolder, as it does not have to court all state executives at once.

The European Parliament's position is based more on formal rules. Its track record under cooperation and codecision shows that it does not eschew confrontations with the Council. In return for its assent to enlargement and the GATT-agreement in 1994, it extracted from the Council a formal seat in the preparatory negotiations for the intergovernmental conference of 1996–97. In the meantime, it is intent on making the most of its power, even if it treads on the toes of its long-standing ally, the European Commission. During its hearings on the Santer Commission in January 1995, the European Parliament demanded that the Commission accept parliamentary amendments "as a matter of course," and withdraw proposals that it rejects. Commission officials have described these proposals as "outrageous" on the grounds that the Commission "would more or less lose it ability to operate."

As a whole, EU decision making can be characterized as one of multiple, intermeshing competencies, complementary policy functions, and variable lines of authority—features that are elements of multi-level governance.

☐ *Implementation: Opening the European*
  Arena—Breaking the State Mold

Multi-level governance is prominent in the implementation stage. Although the Commission has formal executive powers and national governments are in principle responsible for implementation, in practice these competencies are shared. On the one hand, national governments monitor the executive powers of the Commission closely, though they do so in conjunction with subnational governments and societal actors. On the other hand, the Commission has become involved in day-to-day implementation in a number of policy areas, and this brings it into close contact with subnational authorities and interest groups. As in the initiation and decision-making stage, mutual intrusion is contested.

The Commission's formal mandate gives it discretion to interpret legislation and issue administrative regulations bearing on specific cases. It issues 6–7,000 administrative regulations annually. However, only a tiny proportion of the Commission's decisions are unilateral. Since the 1980s, with the institutionalization of comitology, the Council and the individual national governments have become intimately involved. Many regulations have their own committee attached to them. Balancing Commission autonomy and state involvement is an open-ended and conflictual process in the European Union, and this is also apparent in comitology. Rules of operation vary across policy areas and are a source of contention between the Commission, usually supported by the Parliament, and the Council. Some committees are only advisory; others can prevent the Commission from carrying out a certain action by qualified majority vote; and a third category must approve Commission actions by qualified majority. In each case the Commission presides.

At first sight, comitology seems to give state executives control over the Commission's actions in genuine principal-agent fashion. But the relationship between state actors and European institutions is more complex. Comitology is weakest in precisely those areas where the Commission has extensive executive powers, e.g., in competition policy, state aids, agriculture, commercial policy and the internal market. Here, the Commission has significant space for autonomous action.

State-centrists may argue that state executives prefer to delegate these powers to achieve state-oriented collective goods, such as control over potential distortion of competition or a stronger bargaining position in international trade. But one result is that state executives have lost exclusive control in a range of policy areas. To mention just three examples among the many discussed in this chapter: they no longer control competition within their borders; they cannot aid national firms as they deem fit; they cannot autonomously conduct trade negotiations.

German regional policy had to be recast because it ran foul of the European Commission's competition authority. The Commission's insistence in the 1980s that regional aid to western Länder be curtailed has provoked several disputes among Länder and between Länder and the Federal government. By 1995, the traditional system of *Gemeinschaftsaufgabe* was on the brink of collapse.

Although comitology involves state actors in the European Commission's activities, this intermeshing is not necessarily limited to *central* state actors. Because the issues on the table are often technical in nature, member state governments tend to send those people who are directly responsible or who are best informed about the issued at home. These are regularly subnational officials, or representatives of interest groups or other nongovernmental bodies. Subnational participation in comitology is prevalent for member states organized along federal or semi-federal lines. But, in recent years, subnational actors have been drawn into the European arena from more centralized member states.

To the extent that EU regulations affect policy areas where authority is shared among central and subnational levels of government, effective implementation requires contacts between multiple levels of government. Environmental policy is an example of this, for in several European countries competencies in this area are shared across different territorial levels. To speed up implementation of environmental law, the Commission began in 1990 to arrange so-called "package" meetings to bring together central, regional and local government representatives of a member state. Such meetings are voluntary, but in the first year of its operation seven countries made use of them. The Spanish central government, for example, was keen to use the Commission's presence to pressure its autonomous provinces into compliance with EU environmental law, but to do so it conceded them access to the European arena.

The majority of participants in comitology are not national civil servants, but interest group representatives (particularly from farming, union, and employer organizations) alongside technical experts, scientists and academics. These people are mostly selected, or at least approved of, by their national government. One can plausibly assume that national governments find it more difficult to persuade technical experts, interest group representatives, and private actors than their own officials to defend the national interest. In practice therefore, comitology, which was originally a mechanism for central state oversight over Commission activities, has had the intended consequence of deepening the participation of subnational authorities and private actors in the European arena.

A second development which has received little attention in the literature is the direct involvement of Commission officials in day-to-day policy implementation. The Commission was never expected to perform ground-level implementation, except in unusual circumstances (such as competition policy, fraud, etc.). Yet, in some areas this has changed. The most prominent example is cohesion policy, which now absorbs about one-third of the EU budget. The bulk of the money goes to multi-annual regional development programs in the less developed regions of the EU. The 1989 reform prescribes the involvement of Commission, national, regional, local and social actors on a continuing basis in all stages of the policy process selection of priorities, choice of programs, allocation of funding, monitoring of operations, evaluation and adjustment of programs. To this end, each recipient region or country is required to set up an elaborate system of monitoring committees, with a general committee on top, and a cascade of subcommittees focused on particular programs.

Commission officials can and do participate at each level of this tree-like structure. Partnership is implemented unevenly across the EU, but just about everywhere it institutionalizes some form of direct contact between the Commission and non-central government actors including, particularly, regional and local authorities, local action groups and local businesses. Such links break open the mold of the state, so that multi-level governance encompasses actors within as well as beyond existing states.

□ *Adjudication: An Activist Court in a Supranational Legal Order*

State-centrists have argued that a European legal order and effective European Court of Justice (ECJ) are essential to state cooperation. Unilateral defection is difficult to detect, and thus it is in the interest of states to delegate authority to a European Court to monitor compliance. The ECJ also mitigates incomplete contracting problems by applying general interstate bargains to future contingencies. In this vein, the ECJ may be conceptualized as an agent of constituent member states. However, a number of scholars have argued convincingly that the ECJ has become more than an instrument of member states. The Court has been active in transforming the legal order in a supranational direction. But the Court could not have done this without a political ally at the European level: the European Commission. Nor could it have established the supremacy of European law without the collaboration of national courts, and this collaboration has altered the balance of power between national courts and national political authorities.

Through its activist stance, the ECJ has laid the legal foundation for an integrated European polity. By means of an impressive body of case law, the Court has established the Treaty of Rome as a document creating legal obligations directly binding on national governments and individual citizens alike. Moreover, these obligations have legal priority over laws made by the member states. Directly binding legal authority and supremacy are attributes of sovereignty, and their application by the ECJ indicates that the EU is becoming a constitutional regime.

·   ·   ·

ECJ decisions have become accepted as part of the legal order in the member States, shifting expectations about decision-making authority from a purely national-based system to one that is more multi-level. The doctrines of direct effect and supremacy were constructed over the strong objections of several member state executives. Yet, its influence lies not in its scope for unilateral action, but in the fact that its rulings and inclusive mode of operation create opportunities for other European institutions, particularly the Commission, for private interests, and national institutions (lower national courts), to influence the European agenda or enhance their power.

■ CONCLUSION

Multi-level governance does not confront the sovereignty of states directly. Instead of being explicitly challenged, states in the European Union are being melded gently into a multi-level polity by their leaders and the actions of numerous subnational and supranational actors. State-centric theorists are right when they argue that states are extremely powerful institutions that are capable of crushing direct threats to their existence. The institutional form of the state emerged because it proved a particularly effective means of systematically wielding violence, and it is difficult to imagine any generalized challenge along these lines. But this is not the only, or even the most important, issue facing the state. One does not have to argue that states are on the verge of political extinction to believe that their control of those living in their territories has significantly weakened.

It is not necessary to look far beyond the state itself to find reasons that might explain how such an outcome is possible. When we disaggregate the state into the actors that shape its diverse institutions, it is clear that key decision-makers, above all those directing the state executive, may have goals that do not coincide with that of projecting state sovereignty into the future. As well as being a goal in itself, the state may sensibly be regarded as a means to a variety of ends that are structured by party competition and interest group politics in a liberal democratic setting. A state executive may wish to shift decision making to the supranational level because the political benefits outweigh the cost of losing control. Or a state executive may have intrinsic grounds to shift control, for example to shed responsibility for unpopular decisions.

Even if state executives want to maintain sovereignty, they are often not able to do so. A state executive can easily be outvoted because most decisions in the Council are now taken under the decision rule of qualified majority, and moreover, even the national veto, the ultimate instrument of sovereignty, is constrained by the willingness of other state executives to tolerate its use. But the limits on state sovereignty are deeper. Even collectively, state executives do not determine the European agenda because they are unable to control the supranational institutions they have created at the European level. The growing diversity of issues on the Council's agenda, the sheer number of state executive principals and the mistrust that exists among them, and the increased specialization of policy-making have made the Council of Ministers reliant upon the Commission to set the agenda, forge compromises, and supervise compliance. The Commission and the Council are not on a par, but neither can their relationship be understood in principal-agent terms. Policy-making in the EU is characterized by mutual dependence, complementary functions and overlapping competencies.

The Council also shares decision-making competencies with the European Parliament, which has gained significant legislative power under the Single European Act and the Maastricht treaty. Indeed, the Parliament might be conceived of as a principal in its own right in the European arena. The Council, Commission and Parliament interact within a legal order which has been transformed into a supranational one through the innovative jurisprudence of the European Court of Justice. The complex interplay among these contending institutions in a polity where political control is diffuse often leads to outcomes that are second choice for all participants.

The character of the Euro-polity at any particular point in time is the outcome of a tension between supranational and intergovernmental pressures. We have argued that, since the 1980s, it has crystallized into a multi-level polity. States no longer serve as the exclusive nexus between domestic politics and international relations.

Direct connections are being forged among political actors in diverse political arenas. Traditional and formerly exclusive channels of communication and influence are being sidestepped. With its dispersed competencies, contending but interlocked institutions, shifting agendas, multi-level governance opens multiple points of access for interests, while it privileges those interests with technical expertise that match the dominant style of EU policy-making. In this turbulent process of mobilization and counter-mobilization it is patently clear that states no longer serve as the exclusive nexus between domestic politics and international relations. . . .

However, there is nothing inherent in the current system. Multi-level governance is unlikely to be a stable equilibrium. There is no widely legitimized constitutional framework. There is little consensus on the goals of integration. As a result, the allocation of competencies between national and supranational actors is ambiguous and contested. It is worth noting that the European polity has made two U-turns in its short history. Overt supranational features of the original structure were overshadowed by the imposition of intergovernmental institutions in the 1960s and 1970s. From the 1980s, a system of multi-level governance arose, in which national governmental control became diluted by the activities of supranational and subnational actors.

These developments have engendered strong negative reactions on the part of declining social groups represented in nationalist political movements. Ironically, much of the discontent with European integration has been directed towards state executives themselves and the pragmatic and elitist style in which they have bargained institutional change in the EU.

The EU-wide series of debates unleashed by the Treaty of Maastricht have forced the issue of sovereignty onto the agenda. Where governing parties themselves shy away from the issue, it is raised in stark terms by opposition parties, particularly those of the extreme right. Several member state governments are, themselves, deeply riven on the issues of integration and sovereignty. States and state sovereignty have become objects of popular contention—the outcome of which is as yet uncertain.

24 The Path to European Integration: A Historical Institutionalist Analysis

PAUL PIERSON

Paul Pierson, a colleague of Andrew Moravcsik's at Harvard University, also levels his intellectual guns at intergovernmentalism, but from a more sympathetic position than Anne-Marie Burley and Walter Mattli (Chapter 22) and Gary Marks, Liesbet Hooghe, and Kermit Blank (Chapter 23). Pierson aims with his historical institutionalist approach to develop a new theory of integration that draws on both neofunctionalism and intergovernmentalism. His central insight is that EU institutions and policies, which are created by the member states as a result of intergovernmental bargaining, evolve over time into something quite different than originally envisioned. Spillover occurs and gaps in member state control emerge, leading to an increase in responsibility for supranational institutions—just as neofunctionalists would predict. Once these gaps emerge, member states find it hard to claw back lost control because of the barriers Pierson identifies: the resistance of supranational actors, institutional barriers to reform, and high sunk costs. States must usually wait until the next interstate bargaining session (i.e., an intergovernmental conference) to try to re-exert control over certain policy areas or institutions, but this new agreement too may lead to further unintended consequences that inadvertently erode state power.

Intergovernmentalists believe that member states act on the basis of cold calculations of national interest: they make rational choices. Pierson's contribution to integration theory is an explanation for why states will sometimes irrationally (from an intergovernmentalist perspective) transfer control to supranational institutions. His answer, in a word, is that they don't mean to, but outcomes are unpredictable.

The evolution of the European Community (EC) has long fascinated political scientists. For four decades, some of the world's most enduring nation states have conducted an extraordinary political experiment. Progressing sporadically but in a consistent direction, the member states of the European Community have pooled increasing areas of policy authority, introducing prominent collective institutions. The creation of these institutions initiated a process that has transformed the nature of European politics.

How the evolution of these arrangements of collective governance can be explained and the nature of the current system understood remain matters of considerable controversy. Within American political science, students of international relations have maintained the most theoretically driven discussions of the EC. Despite significant internal disputes, the dominant paradigm in international relations scholarship regards European integration as the practice of ordinary diplomacy under conditions creating unusual opportunities for providing collective goods through highly institutionalized exchange. From this "intergovernmentalist" perspective, the EC is essentially a forum for interstate bargaining. Member states remain the only important actors at the European level. Societal actors exert influence only through the domestic political structures of member states. Policy making is made through negotiation among member states or through carefully circumscribed delegations of authority. Whether relying on negotiation or delegation, Chiefs of Government (COGs) are at the heart of the EC, and each member state seeks to maximize its own advantage. Debate within this perspective has concerned such questions as why member states desired certain observed outcomes, which member states have the most influence on collective decision making, and which alignment of member-state interests can best explain policy or institutional development in the EC.

This perspective has not been without its challengers. European scholars have generally depicted the EC as a more complex and pluralistic political structure, less firmly under member-state control. Much of this scholarship is not particularly concerned with advancing broad theories of integration, concentrating instead on the detailed investigation of day-to-day policy development in areas where the EC's role is prominent. From this perspective, the Community looks more like a single (if highly fragmented) polity than the site of diplomatic maneuvering among autonomous member states. Within Europe, analyses that treat the EC as a quasi-federal system—"an obvious reference point for the European Community," in the words of one prominent analyst—are now quite common.

This is equally true within the ranks of comparativists, who have turned their attention recently to the EC [see Chapter 25]. The principal reason for this new interest is revealing: Students of a wide range of government activities, including industrial, regional, social, and environmental policies, have found that they can no longer understand the domestic processes and outcomes that interest them without addressing the role of the EC. These investigations also portray a complex and pluralistic political process, not firmly under member-state control and not explicable in terms of simple diplomatic bargaining. Coming from the detailed investigation of particular domestic policy arenas to address a strikingly new phenomenon, however, comparativists possessed few theoretical tools that appeared directly applicable. Like European analysts, they have tended to depict the Community as a quasi-federal, *multilevel* or *multitiered* political system. Yet these terms are used more to describe the current state of affairs than to explain it. Thus, if a growing body of detailed research reveals considerable unease about the dominant international relations models of EC politics, critics have so far had little to offer as an alternative to intergovernmentalist accounts.

In practice, the critics of intergovernmentalism have tried to move forward in two ways. Some have continued to investigate particular policy areas, content to reveal the density and pluralism of actual policy making while simply observing that the focus of international relations theory on grand diplomacy among sovereign member states does not square with what is actually occurring "on the ground." However, it is almost always possible, *ex post*, to posit some set of member-state preferences that reconciles observed outcomes with the image of near total member-state control. Where policy outcomes do not conform to the expected preferences of member states, they may be explained as part of a "nested game" or as an instance of side payments. Drawing on rational choice theory, intergovernmentalism possesses flexible conceptual tools that can explain why member states would favor the observed outcomes. Thus, absent a theoretically based explanation for the constraints on member states, these detailed investigations will not persuade proponents of intergovernmentalism.

More theoretically oriented critics have drawn on aspects of the *neofunctionalist* tradition in international relations, showing how spillover processes and the autonomous actions of supranational actors (including the Commission and European Court of Justice) contribute to European policy making. Recent efforts to update neofunctionalism have successfully highlighted important limitations in intergovernmentalist accounts, and I will rely in part on these arguments in developing my own analysis. Yet neofunctionalism has serious problems of its own. Given the strong institutional position of member states in the EC, neofunctionalists seem to attribute greater autonomy to supranational actors than can plausibly be sustained. Although neofunctionalist arguments about the independent action of the Commission and Court of Justice have some merit, there is little doubt that the member states, acting together in the Council, remain the most powerful decision makers. In most cases, it seems equally probable that these decision makers act to secure their own interests, whatever those are deemed to be. Crucially, these principals retain the legal authority to rein in their agents if they find it in their interests to do so. Thus, *at any given point in time*, the key propositions of intergovernmentalist theory are likely to hold.

This article seeks to lay the foundation for a more persuasive account of member-state constraint. My focus is on why gaps emerge in member-state control over the evolution of European institutions and public policies, why these gaps are difficult to close, and how these openings create room for actors other than member states to influence the process of European integration while constraining the room for maneuver of all political actors. The basis for this challenge to intergovernmentalism lies in insights from what I will term *historical institutionalism*. The label covers a diverse range of scholarship, much of it with little theoretical focus. Indeed, a principal goal of this article is to strengthen the theoretical foundations of historical institutionalism. There are, however, two unifying themes within this broad research orientation. This scholarship is *historical* because it recognizes that political development must be understood as a process that unfolds over time. It is *institutionalist* because it stresses that many of the contemporary implications of these temporal processes are embedded in institutions—whether these be formal rules, policy structures, or norms.

The crucial claim I derive from historical institutionalism is that actors may be in a strong initial position, seek to maximize their interests, and nevertheless carry out institutional and policy reforms that fundamentally transform their own positions (or those of their successors) in ways that are unanticipated and/or undesired. Attempts to cut into ongoing social processes at a single point in time produce a "snapshot" view that is distorted in crucial respects. Central parts of my analysis emphasize temporal aspects of politics: the lags between decisions and long-term consequences, as well as the constraints that emerge from societal adaptations and shifts in policy preferences that occur during the interim. When European integration is examined over time, the gaps in member-state control appear far more prominent than they do in intergovernmentalist accounts.

In contrast to the functional account of institutions that underpins intergovernmentalism, historical institutionalism stresses the difficulties of subjecting institutional evolution to tight control. Two brief historical examples can illustrate the broad point explored in this article. The first concerns the changing institutional position of state governments in the United States. Because approval of the U.S. Constitution required state ratification, the interests of states received considerable attention in the process of institutional design. The framers intended the Senate to serve as a strong support of state interests. In an arrangement that partly echoes the EC's emphasis on member-state participation in collective deliberations, state legislatures were to appoint senators, who were expected to serve as delegates representing states in the formation of policy. Over time, however, senators seeking greater autonomy were able to gradually free themselves from state oversight. By the early 1900s, the enactment of the 17th Amendment requiring popular election of senators only ratified the result of a lengthy erosion of state legislative control.

The development of Canadian federalism provides another example. The designers of the Canadian federation sought a highly centralized form of federalism—in part as a reaction to the ways in which decentralization contributed to the horrors of the American Civil War. Yet the Canadian federation is now far less centralized than the American one. Among the reasons: the Canadian federation left to the provinces sole responsibility for many activities that were then considered trivial. With the growing role of government in social policy and economic management, however, these responsibilities turned out to be of tremendous importance.

In both cases, the current functioning of institutions cannot be derived from the aspirations of the original designers. Processes evolving over time led to quite unexpected outcomes. Similarly, I will argue that what one makes of the EC depends on whether one examines a photograph or a moving picture. Just as a film often reveals meanings that cannot be discerned from a single photograph, a view of Europe's development over time gives us a richer sense of the nature of the emerging European polity. At any given time, the diplo-

matic maneuvering among member states looms large, and an intergovernmentalist perspective makes considerable sense. Seen as a historical process, however, the scope of member-state authority appears far more circumscribed, and both the interventions of other
actors and the cumulative constraints of rule-based governance more
considerable.

My argument is developed in . . . [two] stages. In the first, I review the main features of intergovernmentalist analyses of the EC. In
the second, I develop a historical institutionalist critique. . . .

■ INTERGOVERNMENTALIST THEORIES AND
MEMBER-STATE AUTONOMY

The accelerated activity of the EC in the past decade coincided with a
growing focus among international relations scholars on international regimes, which were conceptualized as institutionalized forms
of collective action among nation states. Although some analysts of
European integration have continued to echo the earlier international
relations literature on neofunctionalism, the dominant intergovern-

mentalist perspective has treated the EC as a standard (albeit unusu-
ally well-developed and multifaceted) international regime. It would
be unrealistic to attempt a thorough review of this diverse and sophisticated literature here. Instead, I focus on three core features of
intergovernmentalism: the emphasis on member-state preoccupation
with sovereignty; the depiction of institutions as instruments; and the
focus on "grand bargains" among member states.

□   The Centrality of Sovereignty

Intergovernmentalism itself generally takes member-state preferences
as given, focusing instead on how member states seek to pursue those
preferences. Yet despite this apparent openness, intergovernmentalist
accounts tend to stress member-state preoccupation with preserving
sovereignty. As Keohane maintains, "governments put a high value
on the maintenance of their own autonomy, [so] it is usually impossible to establish international institutions that exercise authority over
states."

Of course, much of the writing on international regimes arose
as a reaction to realist perspectives that were seen as putting *too
much* weight on sovereignty concerns—suggesting that collective action among states would almost never be possible. Regime theorists

have argued that in contexts where security concerns have diminished, nation states may care about absolute gains as well as relative ones. Nonetheless, the realist focus on sovereignty carries over into intergovernmentalist treatments of the EC. Most intergovernmentalist analyses suggest that member-state preferences are heavily weighted toward preserving sovereignty, leading COGs to be vigilant guardians of national autonomy in evaluating proposals for international cooperation. The issue is often posed in principal-agent terms. The principals (member states) may delegate certain responsibilities to agents (international institutions), but only with the strictest oversight. The core calculation for member states is whether the benefits of collective action outweigh any possible risk to autonomy. According to Moravcsik, "in the intergovernmentalist view, the unique institutional structure of the EC is acceptable to national governments *only* [italics added] insofar as it strengthens, rather than weakens, their control over domestic affairs."

□ The Instrumentality of Institutions

Work on international regimes has drawn heavily on the insights of Transaction Cost Economics (TCE), which analyzes institutions in functional terms. As Moravcsik summarizes, "Modern regime theory views international institutions as deliberate instruments to improve the efficiency of bargaining between states." Drawing on sophisticated work in game theory and economic theories of organizations, intergovernmentalists note that collective action among autonomous nation states is often desired yet enormously difficult. A critical issue concerns problems of information. Uncertainty about the preferences, intentions, and reliability of other actors makes agreements difficult to execute and enforce. Institutions can help surmount these problems, reducing information asymmetries, monitoring compliance, and creating linkages across issues that diminish the likelihood of defection. According to Keohane,

> Far from being threats to governments (in which case it would be hard to understand why they exist at all), they permit governments to attain objectives that would otherwise be unattainable. They do so in part by facilitating intergovernmental agreements. Regimes facilitate agreements by raising the anticipated costs of violating others' property rights, by altering transaction costs through the clustering of issues, and by providing reliable information to members. Regimes are relatively efficient institutions, compared with the alternative of having a myriad of unrelated

agreements, since their principles, rules, and institutions create linkages among issues that give actors incentives to reach mutually beneficial agreements.

In intergovernmentalist accounts, self-conscious, maximizing actors (member states) create institutions because these institutions help them surmount collective action problems and achieve gains from exchange. The best way to understand the development of international institutions is to identify the functions they fulfill, especially the lowering of bargaining costs and the reduction of uncertainty through the provision of "a forum and vocabulary for the signaling of preferences and intentions."

□   *The Centrality of Intergovernmental Bargains*

Students of the EC frequently distinguish between the intermittent grand bargains (e.g., the Treaty of Rome, the Single European Act, Maastricht) that establish basic features of institutional design and the day-to-day policy making in the Community that occurs between these agreements. For intergovernmentalists, the grand bargains are where the action is. Because, as Moravcsik puts it, "functional regime theory view[s] . . . international institutions as passive, transaction-cost reducing sets of rules," it is the design of those rules that is central. The EC, he adds, "has developed through a series of celebrated intergovernmental bargains, each of which sets the agenda for an intervening period of *consolidation* [italics added]. The most fundamental task facing a theoretical account of European integration is to explain these bargains." The intergovernmentalist research agenda clearly reflects this line of thinking, focusing overwhelmingly on explaining aspects of two grand bargains: the Single European Act and the Maastricht treaty. Political developments during the periods between these bargains, or that concern matters not hotly contested during those bargains, have received almost no attention.

These three aspects of intergovernmentalist accounts are closely connected. The depiction of member states as profoundly concerned about sovereignty contributes to a functional view of regimes. Given the preoccupation with sovereignty, the institutional underpinnings for cooperation will only be created or extended after a careful weighing of long-term costs and benefits. The benefits are the transaction-cost reducing functions that regimes perform; the costs often relate to any risk of lost autonomy. Similarly, the emphasis on member-state bargains follows logically from the functional analysis of institutions. If the EC is an international regime in which member states have carefully designed passive instruments to allow them to carry out collective goals, periods of consolidation are of little interest. It is the bargains themselves that create or change the rules of the game, therefore demanding attention. The post-bargain period simply plays out the implications intended in the grand bargains. Together, these three positions have contributed to a powerful argument about the process of European integration. As I suggest in the next section of this article, however, all three are open to serious challenge.

■ A HISTORICAL INSTITUTIONALIST CRITIQUE

Historical institutionalism is a loose term covering a range of scholarship that has tried to combine social science concerns and methods with a recognition that social processes must be understood as historical phenomena. In my own usage, historical institutionalism cuts across the usual sharp dichotomy between rational choice and nonrational choice work, drawing instead on research within both traditions that emphasizes the significance of historical processes. Thus it includes rational choice analyses that consider issues of institutional evolution and path dependence crucial. It excludes much research in political science that uses history only as a technique for widening the universe of available cases.

The core arguments of historical institutionalism contrast with a more common view in the social sciences, which, as March and Olson observe, assumes (often implicitly) that "institutions and behavior . . . evolve through some form of efficient historical process. An efficient historical process . . . is one that moves rapidly to a unique solution, conditional on current environmental conditions, and is independent of the historical path." Given this orientation, Skocpol notes, "Analysts typically look only for synchronic determinants of policies—for example, in current social interests or in existing political alliances. In addition, however, we must examine patterns unfolding over time."

Recent research focusing on institutional evolution and path dependence has challenged the expectation that institutions embody the long-term interests of those responsible for original institutional design. Where the legal authority of the institutional designers is as unquestionable as that of the member states in the EC, I will argue that such a challenge must be based on two sets of claims. First, there must be an account of why gaps—by which I mean significant divergences between the institutional and policy preferences of member states and the actual functioning of institutions and policies—would emerge. Second, critics must explain why, once such gaps emerge, they cannot reliably be closed. One can find scattered elements of such accounts in recent theoretical treatments of institutional change. When brought together, they provide a compelling response to the claim that institutional development in the European Union can be understood in functional terms.

I focus first on the factors that are likely to create considerable gaps in member-state control. Four are of fundamental importance: the autonomous actions of European institutional actors, the restricted time horizons of decision makers, the large potential for unintended consequences, and the likelihood of changes in COG preferences over time. Each of these factors requires more detailed discussion.

□   *The Partial Autonomy of EC Institutions*

The main contribution of recent neofunctionalist analysis has been to emphasize the autonomous role of supranational actors, especially the Commission and the Court. I begin by summarizing these arguments and suggesting that, by themselves, they constitute an inadequate response to intergovernmentalism.

The central objections raised by neofunctionalists can be cast in terms of the same principal-agent framework used in many intergovernmentalist accounts. Member states created the EC, and they did so to serve their own purposes. In order to carry out collective tasks, however, the member states felt compelled to create new institutions. As Moe has argued, the results are predictable.

> A new public agency is literally a new actor on the political scene. It has its own interests, which may diverge from those of its creators, and it typically has resources—expertise, delegated authority—to strike out on its own should the opportunities arise. The political game is different now: there are more players and more interests to be accommodated.

In the European context, the member states' problem has been especially difficult. They have needed to create arrangements that would allow reasonably efficient decision making and effective enforcement despite the involvement of a large number of governments with differing interests, and despite the need for decision making, implementation, and oversight on a wide range of complex and tightly coupled policy areas. These considerations generated pressure to grant those who run these institutions considerable authority. Thus, the political organs of the EC are not without resources; as a result, they are not simply passive tools of the member states.

Over time, EC organizations will seek to use grants of authority for their own purposes, especially to increase their autonomy. They will try to expand the gaps in member-state control, and they will use any accumulated political resources to resist efforts to curtail their authority. The result is an intricate, ongoing struggle that is well-known to students of the European Union but would also be familiar to American observers of, say, relations between congressional committees and administrative agencies. Member states generally (but not always) seek to rein in EC institutions. They recognize, however, that these crucial collective organizations cannot function without significant power and that the authority required will grow as the tasks addressed at the European level expand and become more complex.

For their part, European institutions such as the Commission, the European Court of Justice, and the European Parliament are always looking for opportunities to enhance their powers. Neofunctionalist analyses have emphasized the significant successes of these supranational actors. The Council, to be sure, continues to stand watch over proposed legislation and actively protects member-state interests. Yet the Commission, Parliament, and Court possess considerable ability to advance their own interests. For the Commission, two assets are particularly important. The first concerns the setting of agendas, a source of influence it frequently shares with the European Parliament. Choosing which proposals to consider is a tremendously important (if frequently unappreciated) aspect of politics, and here European institutional actors often have primacy. Obviously, this power is far from unlimited; the Commission cannot expect to pass proposals that ignore the preferences of member states. Usually, however, it will have some room for maneuver. Entrepreneurial European actors, such as the Delors Commission, may be able to frame issues, design packages, and structure the sequence of proposals in ways that maximize their room for independent initiative. The expansion of qualified majority voting has widened the range of possible winning coalitions, further increasing the agenda-setting powers of the Commission and Parliament. Neofunctionalists have argued persuasively that the Commission's effective use of agenda-setting powers has advanced European integration and increased its own role in policy reform.

The Commission's second major asset is its role as what Eichener calls a *process manager*. Policy making at the EC level, as many have noted, is heavily tilted toward regulation—a type of policy making with its own distinctive qualities. The development of complex social regulations requires the assembly and coordination of complex networks of experts. This task falls to the Commission, and with it comes additional room for influence. Especially in the labyrinths of regulatory policy making, this role may give the Commission significant power. The political resources of the European Court are at least as significant. If the United States in the 19th century had a "state of courts and parties," the EC looks at times like a "state of courts and technocrats." In the process of European integration, the European Court has taken an active, even forcing stance, gradually building a remarkable base of authority and effectively "constitutionalizing" the emerging European polity. The Court has more extensive powers of judicial review than most of its national counterparts and fewer impediments to action than other EC decision-making bodies. If the Council is prone to gridlock, the necessity of deciding cases inclines the Court to action. This inclination is strengthened by rules allowing simple majority decisions and by a secrecy (neither actual votes nor dissenting views are made public) that shelters judges from member-state and popular pressures. European Court judges also share a common professional background, legal culture (at least on the continent), and sense of mission that seems to effectively limit the influence of the member states in judicial decision making.

Neofunctionalist accounts of these supranational institutions have certainly demonstrated their prominent role in the EC, as even some intergovernmentalists have acknowledged. Yet the true influence of the Courts, Commission, and Parliament on policy making and future institutional development remains uncertain. Do these organizations create genuine gaps in member-state control, or do they simply act as agents, fulfilling monitoring, information-gathering, and implementation roles under tight member-state scrutiny? As Martin, among others, has suggested, autonomy may be more apparent than real:

> Politicians and academic observers often infer from such a pattern [of activity] autonomy of the Commission and/or of government leaders. However, consideration of institutional constraints leads us to examine delegation of authority . . . because of the costs of exercising tight control over agents, an optimal structure of delegation may be one with little active oversight or overt interference in the negotiating process from principals. Agents rationally anticipate the responses of those they represent. The law of anticipated reactions suggests that we cannot

infer a lack of political influence from a lack of observed oversight activity.

Thus what appears to be autonomy may simply reflect the principals'
deft use of oversight. Relying on the disciplining power of anticipated reactions and the use of "fire alarms"—signals derived from
reporting requirements or interest-group monitoring activity—to
identify significant problems, member states can stay in the background while remaining firmly in charge.

Again, given the ease of assembling plausible ex post accounts
of why given outcomes served member-state interests, these arguments about delegation are difficult to refute, although they are
equally difficult to demonstrate. To foreshadow a point pursued at
length below, the intergovernmentalist claim that supranational actors are agents rather than autonomous actors is strengthened if we
believe that member states can react powerfully to observed losses of
control. If the Commission, Court, and Parliament anticipate that
their efforts to produce or exploit gaps will be detected, punished,
and reversed, they are indeed unlikely to strike out on their own.
Thus a crucial problem with neofunctionalism is that it lacks a coherent account of why the threat of such a member-state reaction is not
always credible. I address this problem below.

Before proceeding to that issue, however, the case for constraints on member-state control can be greatly strengthened if other
sources of gaps can be identified. Here, the historical institutionalist
focus on the temporal dimension of politics is invaluable. It highlights three additional sources of gaps: the short time horizons of decision makers, the prevalence of unanticipated consequences, and the
prospect of shifting member-state policy preferences.

□   *The Restricted Time Horizons of Political Decision Makers*

A statement attributed to David Stockman, former President Rea-
gan's budget director, is unusual among political decision makers
only for its candor. Asked by an adviser to consider pension reforms
to combat Social Security's severe long-term financing problems,
Stockman dismissed the idea out of hand, exclaiming that he had no
interest in wasting "a lot of political capital on some other guys'
problem in [the year] 2010."

Many of the implications of political decisions—especially
complex policy interventions or major institutional reforms—only
play out in the long run. Yet political decision makers are frequently

most interested in the short-term consequences of their actions; long-term effects are often heavily discounted. The principal reason is that of the logic of electoral politics. Keynes once noted that in the long run, we are all dead; for politicians in democratic polities, electoral death can come much faster. Because the decisions of voters, which determine political success, are taken in the short run, politicians are likely to employ a high discount rate. They have a strong incentive to pay attention to long-term consequences only if these become politically salient, or when they have little reason to fear short-term electoral retribution.

The gap between short-term interests and long-term consequences is often ignored in arguments about institutional design and reform. As a number of critics have noted, choice-theoretic treatments of institutions often make an intentionalist or functionalist fallacy, arguing that the long-term effects of institutions explain why decision makers introduce them. Instead, long-term institutional consequences are often the by-products of actions taken for short-term political reasons. The evolution of the congressional committee system in the United States—a central institutional feature of contemporary American governance—is a good example. As Shepsle notes, Henry Clay and his supporters introduced the system to further their immediate political goals without regard to long-term consequences: "The lasting effects of this institutional innovation could hardly have been anticipated, much less desired, by Clay. They were by-products (and proved to be the more enduring and important products) of self-interested leadership behavior." In this case, the system's long-term functioning was not the goal of the actors who created it. By the same token, the reasons for the institution's invention cannot be derived from an analysis of its long-term effects.

Recognizing the importance of policy makers' high discount rates raises a challenge for intergovernmentalist theories of the EC. As noted above, most international relations approaches to European integration stress the tenacity with which nation states cling to all aspects of national sovereignty. The design of collective institutions is assumed to reflect this preoccupation. Yet, in democratic politics, sustained power requires electoral vindication. Under many circumstances, the first concern of national governments is not with sovereignty per se but with creating the conditions for continued domestic political success. By extension, where the time horizons of decision makers are restricted, *functional* arguments that are central to transaction-cost views of international regimes also come into question. Rather than being treated as the goals of policy makers under such circumstances, long-term institutional effects should often be seen as the by-products of their purposive behavior.

□   *Unanticipated Consequences*

Gaps in member-state control occur not only because long-term consequences tend to be heavily discounted. Even if policy makers do focus on long-term effects, unintended consequences are likely to be widespread. Complex social processes involving a large number of factors always generate elaborate feedback loops and significant interaction effects that decision makers cannot hope to fully comprehend. Although social scientists possess limited tools for dealing with such outcomes, many models—such as core neoclassical arguments about the dynamics of market systems—are based on them.

Unanticipated consequences are likely to be of particular significance in the European Union because of the presence of high *issue density*. In sharp contrast to any existing international organization, the range of decisions made at the European level runs almost the full gamut of traditionally domestic issues, from the setting of agricultural prices to the regulation of auto emissions and fuel content to the enforcement of trade restrictions. In the past decade, there has been a massive expansion of EC decision making, primarily because of the single market project. The sheer scope of this decision making limits the ability of member states to firmly control the development of policy.

.   .   .

Growing issue density has two distinct consequences. First, it generates problems of overload. As European-level decision making becomes both more prevalent and more complex, it places growing demands on the gatekeepers of member-state sovereignty. In this context, time constraints, scarcities of information, and the need to delegate decisions to experts may promote unanticipated consequences and lead to considerable gaps in member-state control. Member-state scrutiny will usually be extensive in the formation of the grand interstate bargains that are the favorite subject for intergovernmentalists, such as the Treaty of Rome, the Single European Act, and the Maastricht treaty. In the intervals between these agreements, however, flesh must be added to the skeletal frameworks. In this context, where much policy actually evolves, the ability of member states to control the process is likely to be weaker. As Marks has put it, "Beyond and beneath the highly visible politics of member-state bargaining lies a dimly lit process of institutional formation." Marks, for instance, has demonstrated how the Commission exploited its more detailed knowledge of the policy process and its manager role in policy formation to generate influence over the structural funds that the British government failed to anticipate.

As previously discussed, problems of overload are especially consequential when member states must contend with supranational organizations eager to extend their authority. In the development of complex regulatory judgments and the legal determination of what previous decisions actually require, essential policy-making authority is often in the hands of bodies of experts, where the Commission plays a crucial role, or in the hands of the Court. This is, of course, one of the central insights of principal-agent theory. Agents can use their greater information about their own activities and the requirements connected to their work to achieve autonomy from principals. *Asymmetrical access to information*, which is ubiquitous in complex decision-making processes, provides a foundation for influence.

The second consequence of issue density is the oft-cited process of spillover: the tendency of tasks adopted to have important consequences for realms outside those originally intended, or to empower actors who generate new demands for extended intervention. One of the key arguments in much writing on contemporary political economics stresses precisely the embeddedness of economic action within networks of tightly coupled social and political institutions. Efforts to integrate some aspects of complex modern societies, without changing other components, may prove problematic because the sectors to be integrated cannot be effectively isolated. The more "tightly coupled" government policies are, the more likely it is that actions in one realm will have unanticipated effects in others. McNamara, for example, has demonstrated the significance of such interaction effects in the cases of monetary and agricultural policies. Similar connections between the single-market initiative and social policy development have also been documented. As the density of EC policy making increases, such interaction effects become more prevalent, unintended consequences multiply, and the prospect of gaps in member-state control will grow.

□   *Shifts in COG Policy Preferences*

Intergovernmentalist theories tend to treat the institutional and policy preferences of the member states as essentially fixed. This is one of a number of crucial respects in which intergovernmentalism involves a too-easy translation from the world of economic organizations to the world of politics. It may make some sense to assume stable policy preferences when studying firms, or even when one discusses the enduring issues of grand diplomacy. However, as one moves from traditional foreign policy issues such as national security toward the traditionally domestic concerns where the EC has become quite significant, this becomes a more dubious premise.

The policy preferences of member states may shift for a number of reasons. Altered circumstances or new information may lead governments to question previous arrangements. Equally important, changes in government occur frequently, and governments of different partisan complexions often have quite distinct views on policy matters dealt with at the EC level. Governments come and go. Each inherits a set of arrangements from the past; each tries to place its own imprint on this heritage. The result, over time, is that evolving arrangements will diverge from the intentions of original designers, while any newly arriving COG is likely to find institutional and policy arrangements considerably out of synch with its own preferences.

Thus, there are a number of reasons that gaps in member-state control are likely to emerge. Two general points about these sources of gaps deserve emphasis. First, most of these processes have a temporal quality, which makes them invisible to a synchronic analysis of institutional and policy choice. The role of restricted time horizons, unintended consequences, and shifting member-state preferences will only be evident if we examine political processes over time. Second, most of the processes highlighted are much more likely to be prevalent in the EC than in the more purely international settings that were the subject of original efforts to develop and refine regime theory. Because many of the more domestic issues that the EC considers have significant electoral implications, the time horizons of decision makers are likely to be shorter. Unanticipated consequences are also more prevalent, because unlike a typical international regime, the EC deals with many tightly coupled issues. Electoral turnover is more likely to cause shifts in COG preferences on the more domestic issues that the EC considers than on the traditional diplomatic agenda of most international regimes. In short, the EC's focus on core concerns of traditional domestic politics makes it more prone to all the sources of gaps in member-state control that historical institutionalism identifies.

At this point, however, the claim of member-state constraint is incomplete. Transaction-cost approaches are compatible with the possibility of at least some sorts of gaps, although these are rarely addressed in practice. After all, although it has not emphasized unanticipated consequences, TCE is based in large part on how uncertainty about future events provokes particular organizational responses. It is not enough to demonstrate that gaps emerge; one must also show that once such losses of control take place, they often cannot be corrected.

For intergovernmentalists, even where the possibility of gaps is acknowledged, these losses of control are considered theoretically unproblematic. Should outcomes occur that principals do not desire, TCE describes two routes to restored efficiency: competition and learning. Competitive pressures in a market society mean that new organizations with more efficient structures will develop, eventually replacing suboptimal organizations. Learning processes among principals can also lead to correction. According to Williamson, one can rely on

> the "far-sighted propensity" or "rational spirit" that economics ascribes to economic actors. . . . Once the unanticipated consequences are understood, these effects will thereafter be anticipated and the ramifications can be folded back into the organizational design. Unwanted costs will then be mitigated and unanticipated benefits will be enhanced. Better economic performance will ordinarily result.

Both these corrective mechanisms, however, are of limited applicability when one shifts from Williamson's focus on firms in private markets to the world of political institutions. This is clearest for the mechanism of competition. Political institutions rarely confront a dense environment of competing institutions that will instantly capitalize on inefficient performance, swooping in to carry off an institution's "customers" and drive it into bankruptcy. Political environments are typically more permissive. Within Europe, there is nothing like a market place for competition among international regimes in which new market entrants can demonstrate that their efficiency (however that might be defined and measured) is greater than the EC's.

Whereas arguments based on competition are weak, learning arguments would appear to be more applicable to political environments. Indeed, Marks, who has pointed to the significance of unanticipated consequences in limiting member-state control, concedes that the use of such arguments "is tricky in the context of ongoing political relationships where learning takes place." The process through which actors learn about gaps in control and how to address them has received little attention. However, at least on the biggest issues, intergovernmentalists can reasonably assert that member states will gradually become aware of undesired or unanticipated outcomes and will become more adept at developing effective responses over time. Learning thus seems to offer an effective mechanism for closing gaps and returning institutional and policy designs to an efficient (from the point of view of the member states) path.

Yet the efficacy of the learning argument depends crucially on the capacity of member states to fold new understandings back into the organizational design. Put differently, once gaps appear and are identified, how easy is it for principals to regain control? Here the distinction between economic and political institutions becomes crucial. In economic organizations, owners (or principals) may face few barriers to such efforts. In the political world, however (and in the EC, in particular), incorporating new understandings into institutions and policies is no simple task. The next stage of the argument, then, is to consider why gaps, even when identified, might be hard to close. There are three broad reasons: the resistance of EC institutional actors, the institutional obstacles to reform within the EC, and the sunk costs associated with previous actions. If these barriers are sufficiently high, learning will not provide a sufficient basis for correction, and member-state control will be constrained.

□   *The Resistance of Supranational Actors*

To the extent that neofunctionalism has had an implicit argument about the difficulty of closing gaps, it has centered on supranational actors. The Court, Commission, and Parliament have accumulated significant political resources. They can be expected to use these resources to resist member-state efforts to exercise greater control over their activities. Yet neofunctionalism has failed to address the question of why, in an open confrontation between member states and supranational actors, the latter could ever be expected to prevail. Member states, after all, have substantial oversight powers, along with control over budgets and appointments. More fundamentally, they possess the legal authority to determine (and alter) the basic rules of the game, including those affecting the very existence of the EC's supranational organizations. The resources of the Court, Commission, and Parliament, such as the capacity to play off one member state against another in the agenda-setting process and perhaps exploit information asymmetries, are not trivial, but they are clearly modest by comparison. A persuasive account of member-state constraint must draw on more than the political resources of supranational actors.

□ *Institutional Barriers to Reform*

The efforts of principals to reassert control will be facilitated if they can easily redesign policies and institutions. In the economic realm, principals are generally in a strong position to remake their organizations as they choose. Lines of authority are clear, and the relevant decision makers are likely to share the same broad goal of maximizing profits. In politics, however, the temporal dimension raises distinct problems. Political decision makers know that continuous institutional control is unlikely. This lack of continuous control has implications both for how institutions are designed and for the prospects of changing institutions once they are created. In particular, those designing institutions must consider the likelihood that future governments will be eager to overturn their designs, or to turn the institutions they create to other purposes. As Moe notes, the designers of institutions

> do not want "their" agencies to fall under the control of opponents. And given the way public authority is allocated and exercised in a democracy, they often can only shut out their opponents by shutting themselves out too. In many cases, then, they purposely create structures that even they cannot control.

Thus, political institutions are often "sticky"—specifically designed to hinder the process of institutional and policy reform. This is, of course, far more true of some national polities than others. Yet the barriers in most national political systems pale in comparison to the obstacles present in the EC. In principle, the member states decide: They have the authority, if they so choose, to reform or even abolish the Court, Commission, or Parliament. But in fact, the rules of the game within the Community were designed to inhibit even modest changes of course. The same requirements that make initial decision making difficult also make previously enacted reforms hard to undo, even if those reforms turn out to be unexpectedly costly or to infringe on member-state sovereignty.

Efforts to employ the most radical vehicle of institutional redesign, a treaty revision, face extremely high barriers: unanimous member-state agreement, plus ratification by national parliaments and (in some cases) electorates. Given the chances for disagreements among COGs, let alone the problems connected to ratification, the chances of achieving such a high degree of consensus are generally quite low. Use of this process is now widely recognized to be extraordinarily difficult and unpredictable. As Pollack notes, "The threat of treaty revision is essentially the 'nuclear option'—exceedingly effective, but difficult to use—and is therefore a relatively ineffective and non-credible means of member state control."

Efforts to produce more modest changes in course confront more modest hurdles, but these remain far tougher than the obstacles facing, for example, a congressional committee trying to rein in a rogue federal agency. Member states will often be divided on significant issues, but in many policy areas, change requires a unanimous vote of the member states. In other cases, Qualified Majority Voting (QMV) is the rule. This makes reform easier, but the standard—roughly five sevenths of the weighted votes of member states—still presents a threshold that is considerably tougher to cross than that required in most democratic institutions.

The extent to which these barriers constrain member states has recently been questioned. Where it was once understood that participation in the EC was an all-or-nothing proposition, Maastricht has enhanced the prospects for a Europe à la carte, or a Europe of "variable geometries." Britain and Denmark received opt-outs on monetary union; the 11 other member states circumvented the British veto by opting "up and out" with the Social Protocol. As Anderson summarizes the new situation, Maastricht "and attached protocols established an important precedent, opening the door to a multitrack Europe in which the treaties and resulting secondary legislation do not apply uniformly to each member." This new flexibility, however, refers only to *additional* treaty obligations. Member-state governments may be able to obtain opt-outs from future treaty provisions. Unless they succeed in navigating the difficult EC decision rules for reversing course, however, they are not free to review and discard the commitments of previous governments, even if those earlier governments were preoccupied by short-term goals, had quite different policy preferences, or acted in ways that produced many unanticipated consequences. And as new policies are enacted, the scope of this restrictive *acquis communautaire* continues to grow.

The rules governing institutional and policy reform in the EC create what Scharpf calls a "joint-decision trap," making member-state efforts to close gaps in control highly problematic. The extent of the institutional obstacles will vary from issue to issue. Obviously, if the benefits of acting are high enough, member states will be able to act. But often the benefits must be quite high. In shutting out their potential successors, COGs have indeed shut themselves out as well.

☐   *Sunk Costs and the Rising Price of Exit*

The evolution of EC policy over time may constrain member states not only because institutional arrangements make a reversal of course difficult when member states discover unanticipated consequences or their policy preferences change. Individual and organizational adaptations to previous decisions may also generate massive sunk costs that make policy reversal *unattractive*. When actors adapt to the new rules of the game by making extensive commitments based on the expectation that these rules will continue, previous decisions may lock in member states to policy options that they would not now choose to initiate. Put another way, social adaptation to EC institutions and policies drastically increases the cost of exit from existing arrangements for member states. Rather than reflecting the benefits of institutionalized exchange, continuing integration could easily reflect the rising costs of "non-Europe."

Recent work on path dependence has emphasized the ways in which initial institutional or policy decisions—even suboptimal ones—can become self-reinforcing over time. These initial choices encourage the emergence of elaborate social and economic networks, greatly increasing the cost of adopting once-possible alternatives and therefore inhibiting exit from a current policy path. Major initiatives have major social consequences. Individuals make important commitments in response to government actions. These commitments, in turn, may vastly increase the disruption caused by policy shifts or institutional reforms, effectively locking in previous decisions.

Work on technological change has revealed some of the circumstances conducive to path dependence. The crucial idea is the prevalence of increasing returns, which encourage a focus on a single alternative and continued movement down a specific path once initial steps are taken. Large set-up or fixed costs are likely to create increasing returns to further investment in a given technology, providing individuals with a strong incentive to identify and stick with a single option. Substantial learning effects connected to the operation of complex systems provide an additional source of increasing returns. Coordination effects occur when the individual receives increased benefits from a particular activity if others also adopt the same option. Finally, adaptive expectations occur when individuals feel a need to "pick the right horse" because options that fail to win broad acceptance will have drawbacks later on. Under these conditions, individual expectations about usage patterns may become self-fulfilling.

As North has argued, all of these arguments can be extended from studies of technological change to other social processes, making path dependence a common feature of institutional evolution. Path dependence may occur in policy development, as well, because policies can also constitute crucial systems of rules, incentives, and constraints. In contexts of complex social interdependence, new institutions and policies will often generate high fixed costs, learning effects, coordination effects, and adaptive expectations. For example, housing and transportation policies in the United States after World War II encouraged massive investments in particular spatial patterns of work, consumption, and residence. Once in place, these patterns sharply constrained the alternatives available to policy makers on issues ranging from energy policy to school desegregation. Many of the commitments that locked in suburbanization were literally cast in concrete, but this need not be the case. Social Security in the United States became gradually locked in through its financing system, which created a kind of rolling intergenerational contract. Institutions and policies may encourage individuals and organizations to develop particular skills, make certain investments, purchase particular goods, or devote time and money to certain organizations. All these decisions generate sunk costs. That is to say, they create commitments. In many cases, initial actions push individual behavior onto paths that are hard to reverse.

Lock-in arguments have received relatively little attention within political science, in part because these processes have a tendency to depoliticize issues. By accelerating the momentum behind one path, they render previously viable alternatives implausible. The result is often not the kind of conflict over the foregone alternative that political scientists would quickly identify, but the absence of conflict. Lock-in leads to what Bachrach and Baratz called *non-decisions*. This aspect of politics can probably be identified only through careful, theoretically grounded, historical investigation of how social adaptations to institutional and policy constraints alter the context for future decision making.

Over time, as social actors make commitments based on existing institutions and policies, the cost of exit from existing arrangements rises. Within the EC, dense networks of social, political, and economic activity have grown up around past institutional and policy decisions. In speculating about a hypothetical effort to stem the power of Court and Commission, member states must ask themselves if this can be done without, for instance, jeopardizing the single-market project. Thus, sunk costs may dramatically reduce a member-state government's room for maneuver. In the EC, one can see this development in the growing implausibility of member-state exit threats. Although "sovereign" member states remain free to tear up treaties and walk away at any time, the constantly increasing costs of exit in a densely integrated polity have rendered this option virtually unthinkable for EC member states.

Williamson's confident assertion that learning allows firms to adjust to unanticipated consequences applies far less well to an analysis of politics. Member-state learning from past events may lead, as it did at Maastricht, to greater restrictions on supranational actors in new initiatives. Recapturing ground in previously institutionalized fields of activity, however, will often be quite difficult. Member states do not inherit a blank slate that they can remake at will when their policy preferences shift or unintended consequences become visible. Decision rules hamper reform, and extensive adaptations to existing arrangements increase the associated costs. Thus a central fact of life for member states is the *acquis communautaire*, the corpus of existing legislation and practice. As Shackleton notes,

> However much member states might deplore certain aspects of Community policy, there is no question that all find themselves locked into a system which narrows down the areas for possible change and obliges them to think of incremental revision of existing arrangements.

As has always been true in domestic politics, new governments in member states now find that the dead weight of previous institutional and policy decisions at the European level seriously limits their room for maneuver.

The need to examine political processes over time is the crucial feature linking all the arguments presented in this section. None of these processes are likely to be captured by a snapshot view. Historical institutionalism provides a clear account of why gaps emerge in member-state authority. Member states are often preoccupied with short-term outcomes. Their decisions are certain to produce all sorts of unanticipated consequences. The preferences of member states may also shift, leaving them with formal institutions and highly developed policies that do not fit their current needs. At least as important, historical institutionalism provides a coherent account of why learning processes and fire alarms may not be sufficient to prompt the reassertion of member-state control. If member states decide that their agents have captured too much authority, they may well seek to rein them in. Gaps, however, open possibilities for autonomous action by supranational actors, which may in turn produce political resources that make them more significant players in the next round of decision making. Decision rules and the proliferation of sunk costs may make the price of reasserting control too high.

In short, historical institutionalist analysis can incorporate key aspects of neofunctionalism while offering a stronger and expanded analytical foundation for an account of member-state constraint. There are important points of compatibility between the two approaches. Both suggest that unintended consequences, including spillover, are likely to be significant for institutional development. Both point to the significance of supranational actors. A crucial difference is that neofunctionalism sees political control as a zero-sum phenomenon, with authority gradually transferred from member states to supranational actors, whereas historical institutionalism emphasizes how the evolution of rules and policies along with social adaptations creates an increasingly structured polity that restricts the options available to all political actors. What has been missing from neofunctionalism—and what historical institutionalist arguments can supply—is a more convincing analysis of member-state constraint. Intergovernmentalists challenge neofunctionalism with two key questions: Why would member states lose control, and even if they did, why would they not subsequently reassert it? Historical institutionalism gives clear and plausible answers to both.

.   .   .

■ CONCLUSION

The arguments advanced in this article present major challenges to an intergovernmentalist account of European integration. By providing explicit microfoundations for an analysis that places much more emphasis on member-state constraint, historical institutionalism increases the pressure on intergovernmentalists to offer convincing evidence that the causal processes they posit are actually at work. Rather than simply inferring policy and institutional preferences post hoc from an examination of outcomes, intergovernmentalists will need to show that the desire to achieve these functional outcomes actually motivated key decision makers.

In principle, important aspects of a historical institutionalist analysis could be integrated with intergovernmentalism. Indeed, this article accepts the starting point of intergovernmentalism: member states are the central institution builders of the EC, and they do so to serve their own purposes. Although it has rarely been done in prac tice, many intergovernmentalist arguments could incorporate a temporal dimension. Keohane, for instance, has recognized the possibility that COGs might anticipate the potential for preference shifts in successor governments. Other challenges, however, will not be so easy to reconcile, such as the possibility that COGs employ a high discount rate in making decisions about institutional design, unintended consequences are ubiquitous, and gaps that emerge are difficult to close. It is hard to see how these factors could be systematically incorporated into intergovernmentalism without undermining the three pillars of that approach: the emphasis on member-state sovereignty concerns, the treatment of institutions as instruments, and the nearly exclusive focus on grand bargains.

The challenge for those wishing to advance a historical institutionalist account is also daunting. The temporal processes outlined here would have to be carefully specified to generate clear hypotheses concerning such matters as when we should expect policy makers to employ short time horizons, when to expect that unintended consequences will be widespread, or how particular decision rules influence the prospects for closing gaps in control. As Pollack has persuasively argued, such analyses should focus on the factors that can explain variation in outcomes across issues and among institutional arenas, as well as over time. To develop the historical institutionalist line of argument will require difficult efforts to trace the motivations of political actors in order to separate the intended from the unintended. Determining the impact of sunk costs on current decision making also represents a considerable challenge. Studying political arenas in detail over long periods of time is arduous. The evidentiary requirements encourage a focus on detailed analyses of particular cases, rendering investigations vulnerable to the critique that the cases examined are unrepresentative. However, if one accepts the conclusion that intergovernmentalists must now show that the processes they hypothesize are actually at work, rather than simply inferring those processes from observed outcomes, it is not clear that their research tasks are any less formidable.

The purpose of the current investigation is not to pursue these difficult questions but to set an agenda by identifying plausible causal processes that can lead to growing constraints on COGs over time. Although it is only the first step, such an effort can be a prelude to empirically grounded research. . . . Indeed, this first step is a significant one. Historical institutionalist arguments can provide a compelling account for a remarkable development that is widely accepted by European scholars and most Americans working in the field of comparative politics: The EC is no longer simply a multilateral instrument, limited in scope and firmly under the control of individual member states. Instead, the EC possesses characteristics of a supranational entity, including extensive bureaucratic competencies, unified judicial control, and significant capacities to develop or modify policies. Within Europe, a wide range of policies classically seen as domestic can no longer be understood without acknowledging the EC's role within a highly fragmented but increasingly integrated polity. Historical institutionalism provides the analytical tools for thinking of the EC, not as an international organization, but as the central level—albeit still a weak one—of an emergent multitiered system of governance. The power of the member states in this polity is not merely pooled but increasingly constrained.

It would be folly to suggest that the member states do not play a central part in policy development within the European Union. Rather, my point is that they do so in a context that they do not (even collectively) fully control. Arguments about intergovernmental bargaining exaggerate the extent of member state power. In their focus on grand intergovernmental bargains, they fail to capture the gradually unfolding implications of a complex and ambitious agenda of shared decision making. Although the member states remain extremely powerful, tracing the process of integration over time suggests that their influence is increasingly circumscribed. The path to European integration has embedded member states in a dense institutional environment that cannot be understood in the language of interstate bargaining.

25

The Study of the European Community: The Challenge to Comparative Politics

SIMON HIX

Integration theory tries to explain how several states come together to form one—or something like one—state. The theory is about international relations until the moment the several become "one" and international relations become domestic politics. The tricky part is deciding when the "one" has emerged.

Simon Hix (London School of Economics and Political Science) does not think the European Union (he uses "Community") constitutes a single state, but he does believe it has developed to the point where comparative politics approaches have become more appropriate for studying its "politics." In this 1994 article, Hix discusses each of the important international relations theories used to explain integration (not reprinted here), then compares them with approaches aimed at understanding politics in single states. He concludes that international relations approaches are still appropriate for explaining behavior in areas where "member states remain sovereign," but that comparative politics approaches will yield greater insights in most issue areas.

The article is a bold call to treat the European Union as though it were a domestic polity that could be compared to other national political systems. Whether you agree with Hix or not will depend on your perception of the EU. Is it an international organization composed of

Reprinted with permission from *West European Politics*, 17(1)(1994):1–30. Published by Frank Cass & Co., Ltd., 900 Eastern Avenue, Ilford, Essex IG2 7HH, England. Copyright 1994 by Frank Cass. Notes omitted.

sovereign states; a federal state with a domestic polity; or is it sui
generis*? Each answer requires a different set of explanatory theories.*

Although the political system of the European Community (EC) may
only be "part formed" and largely *sui generis*, politics in the EC is
not inherently different to the practice of government in any democratic system. As in all modern polities, EC "politics" is dominated by
questions of representation and participation, the distribution and allocation of resources, and political and administrative efficiency. To
study the connection between political "inputs" and "outputs" on
these issues, one would naturally use the discourse of "comparative
politics"—the subfield of political science concerned with the study
of the "internal" politics of "political systems."

Since its birth in the 1950s, however, the EC has mainly been
studied as an example of the supranational integration of, or intergovernmental cooperation between, (previously) sovereign nation-
states. It was thus appropriate that the traditional analysis of the EC
used the discourse of International Relations (IR). However, now
that the EC is more than an "international organization," theories of
international politics are of limited use for studying the "internal"
politics of the Community. For example, from an IR perspective political conflict in the EC is primarily along a single dimension; where
actors (be they nation-states in the Realist approach, or interest
groups in the Pluralist approach) either support or oppose further
supranational integration. As the "political" nature of the EC develops, however, there is also conflict over questions of allocation and
distribution of resources. On these socioeconomic issues, political
competition is along a fundamentally different dimension, which in
comparative political terms is classically referred to as the
"Left-Right." However, this limitation of the IR approach is not by
itself sufficient to claim the superiority of a "comparative" approach
to the EC. A more rigorous investigation needs to be undertaken.

· · ·

■ **COMPARATIVE POLITICS PARADIGMS
AND EC POLITICS**

The field of comparative politics has only recently woken up to the
possibility of applying its theories and principles to political behavior
and action in the Community. . . . However, direct applications of
comparative politics to the EC remain few and far between. Hence,

although this section will involve an analysis of these recent approaches, it will also include a discussion of possible further applications within the comparative politics paradigms for the study of EC politics.

☐ *Pluralist Approaches*

Like pluralist theories in international relations, pluralism in comparative politics is an agent-biased paradigm, which assumes that political outcomes in a democratic system are shaped by competing economic and social interests. Evolving from the "group theories" of the 1950s, the interest group process is a main component of pluralist approaches in both fields. Politics for most citizens is believed to be a "remote, alien and unrewarding activity." Hence, issues must be of great personal importance when individuals group together in an attempt to influence the political process. Moreover, the pluralist "ideal type" is when interest groups are multiple, voluntary, competitive, non-hierarchically ordered, self-determined, not recognized or subsidized by the state, not monopolistic, and internally democratic. Although there are few explicit pluralist approaches to the EC in the field of comparative politics, several authors claim that interest aggregation and articulation in the Community is close to this ideal type.

Comparative pluralist interpretations of the EC argue that the decision-making process in the Community is more like the United States in the 1960s than the (neocorporatist) European tradition. The understaffing of most Commission Directorates and the multiple channels of access to EC decision making—because the same draft directive is dealt with in several divisions in the Commission, in several committees of the European Parliament (EP), as well as in COREPER and the Council of Ministers—give organized interests at the European level more opportunity to be heard than in the more corporatist national systems where decision making is traditionally controlled by the governing parties and the "coopted" peak organizations of business and labor. Moreover, business groups, who are primarily interested in the regulation of their products or services in the market place, have been motivated to organize at the European level by the Single Market program which passed such market regulation from the national governments to the EC. Consequently, since the mid-1980s there has been a rapid growth of "lobbying" in the Community, and the number of officially recognized interest groups [European Interest Groups (EIGs)] has risen from approximately 500 in 1985 to over 1,500 by 1990.

However, this vision of the EC as a pluralist dream is slightly misleading. As with the criticism of the pluralist analysis of US politics, there is little "countervailing power" in the Community. The decision-making process is fragmented into specific interest areas, and each area is controlled by "special interest coalitions." The access of all interest groups to EC policy channels is far from equal, despite the Commission policy of subsidizing non-economic interests. Moreover, because of the high organizational costs of establishing a pan-European group, the larger economic interests (such as in the agriculture and petrochemicals sectors) are able to lobby the Commission far more effectively than the "counter" interests (such as consumer or environment groups). Hence, although there is multiple and open access for organized interests in the Community, the EC is perhaps closer to American "Post-pluralism," where decision makers are no longer neutral arbiters but proactively take account of countervailing interests; or even "neocorporatism," where there is a combination of pluralist articulation and special representation for the "two sides of industry" (as in the special status of UNICE [Union of Industrial and Employers' Confederation of Europe] and the ETUC [European Trade Union Confederation] in the development of legislation under the Social Charter).

However, although the comparative politics pluralist approaches to the EC may be at a primitive stage they have begun to make an important contribution to the analysis of the political process in the Community. Moreover, from the same ontological and methodological assumptions as the international relations pluralist theories, the comparative politics approaches shed light on the nature of decision making at the European level, rather than on the importance of organized interests for the development of national positions towards integration. If the Community is treated as a system of government decision making, the substantial comparative literature on interest organization and representation can be applied to politics in the EC. In contrast, in analyzing the power of interest groups in the EC, the international relations pluralist approaches, such as neofunctionalism, are constrained by their discourse which does not use such theoretical tools as "countervailing power," "interest group stasis," "the theory of plural elites," or "corporatist tripartitism."

□   *Rational Choice Approaches*

As with the realist theories in international relations, rational choice approaches treat actors as fundamentally self-interested. Rational choice also assumes, however, a logical connection between rationally ordered preferences (ends) and rationally-evaluated behavior (means). By assuming rationality, the observer can use techniques, such as decision-theory or game theory, to understand individual behavior when faced with uncertainty. This can either be "natural" uncertainty, arising from environmental factors, or "strategic" uncertainty, when facing other actors. The rational choice modeler does not claim that when making a decision an actor actually goes through the same methodological (and often mathematical) processes as the observer, but simply that the actor behaves "as if" she is following the same procedures. Unlike the realist approaches in international relations, however, there have been relatively few rational choice applications to the EC.

Consciously attempting to "move beyond the approaches prevalent in the international relations literature on cooperation," Garrett employs a game-theoretical framework for understanding the EC decision to adopt the internal market program. Apart from arguing that his approach is more rigorous, Garrett also criticizes the realist approaches to the EC for wrongly assuming "that the institutions associated with international cooperation have little impact on the political structure of the international system and represent little or no challenge to the sovereignty of the nation-states." Using techniques from spatial theories of competition, Garrett's two main conclusions are that: first, rather than the internal market being a simple question of transactions costs economics, a specific set of political and economic principles were chosen from many possible "Pareto-nearing outcomes" because of "institutional and ideological constraints"; and, second, despite the final agreement being by unanimity, the outcome accorded closely to the wishes of the more powerful member states.

Other rational choice approaches appear to confirm this second conclusion. Utilizing the Shapley-Shubik and Banzhaf indices of voting power, Herne and Nurmi find that the larger member states are clearly dominant in the Council of Ministers, regardless of whether simple majority, qualified majority or unanimity voting procedures are used; and in negotiations with the European Parliament, Tsebelis also finds that the outcome is closer to the preferences of the larger member states. However, although these findings appear to confirm the qualitative findings of the realist approaches in international relations, rational choice approaches to the EC have suggested some interesting developments that have not been highlighted by the IR theories. For example, rational choice approaches have also illustrated the importance of ideology in the internal market negotiations, that the EP is a "conditional agenda setter," and that there is an integral link between party competition in the national and EC arenas.

Hence, from the same basic assumptions as the realist approaches in international relations, the few rational choice approaches to the EC have already begun to discover some important features of EC decision making. As with all the comparative politics approaches, the rational choice theorists accept the EC system as a "given" and ask questions about the nature of political behavior "within," and between, the EC's institutional settings. However, even the rational choice approaches have their limitations. First, like the realists, the rational choice applications tend to regard the member states as unitary actors, with "hierarchically-ordered" and "single-peaked" preferences. Second, and also like the realist approaches, they tend to view political conflict in the EC as single-dimensional, with the actors (be they the member states, the EC institutions themselves, or the parties in the European Parliament) positioned on a single continuum between "more" and "less" integration. Even though Garrett highlights the importance of economic ideology, he bases his spatial analysis of the internal market negotiations on the single "integration" continuum. . . .

Hence, although rational choice approaches to the EC have produced fruitful observations . . . they fail to formally integrate internal national competition or institutional and ideological considerations into their models. As the number of rational choice approaches to the EC increases, however, more complex models of decision making in the EC are likely to evolve. We may thus see a rational choice analysis of EC politics which is multi-dimensional, structurally constrained, and ideological oriented. At present, however, and without the technical ability of the public choice theorists, these issues may also be incorporated into non-rational choice comparative approaches to the EC—within the sociological and institutional paradigms.

□   *Sociological Approaches*

As with the structural approaches in international relations, there are few (if any!) direct sociological approaches to the EC. By treating the EC as a "political system," however, one is implicitly making reference to the sociologically-derived "systems theories" of politics. Developing his approach from Parsons' and Easton's theories, Almond states, "the sociological approach . . . suggests how the application of certain sociological and anthropological concepts may facilitate systematic comparison among the major types of political systems."

This sociological approach thus laid the foundations for the study of the different elements and the development of political systems, much of which can be used in the analysis of the EC. For example, an approach derived from Parsons and Almond, which can be applied to the dimensions of political conflict in the EC, is the Lipset and Rokkan theory of nation-building. First, however, there is one theory which explicitly applies a sociological approach to EC politics.

Starting from the assumption that the EC has "developed beyond the role of a traditional international organization," Shackleton asks: "What kind of institution or set of institutions is the European Community?" Using "cultural theory," from political sociology, there are two dimensions of the relationship between the individual and the political system: "group," the extent to which an individual is incorporated into bounded units; and "grid," the degree to which an individual's life is circumscribed by externally imposed restrictions. Hence, in the EC, "group" refers to the degree of supranational integration, whereas "grid" refers to the degree of central regulation. The interaction of these two dimensions thus produces four possible "ways of life": hierarchical, fatalistic, egalitarian, and individualistic. Shackleton hence concludes that the present sociological and institutional structure of the EC means that it is closest to the "egalitarian" (low regulation and high integration) way of life; but there is also an inherent tension between two other ways of life—the "hierarchical" and "individualistic." More relevant to this research, however, cultural theory also suggests that there are inherently two types of political conflict in the EC: "group conflict," between supranational centralization and national independence (a pro- and anti-integration dimension); and "grid conflict," between economic and social regulation and deregulation (an ideological dimension).

The existence of these two fundamental dimensions of conflict in the EC is also implied by the application of the sociological theories of nation-building to the development of the EC. From the sociological assumptions of Talcott Parsons' "theory of action," Lipset and Rokkan proposed a model of nation-building to explain the matrix of social and political "cleavages" in contemporary political systems. The cleavages arise from dichotomous conflicts created by "critical junctures" in the historical development of each system. For example, the National Revolution produced Church versus State and center versus periphery conflicts, and the Industrial Revolution produced landed versus urban and middle-class versus working-class conflicts. However, whereas center-periphery and church-state conflicts do not exist in every system because of different national revolution experiences, socioeconomic conflicts are prevalent in all West-

ern nations because of the common experience of industrialization
and the prevalence of the capitalist system of economic exchange.

Applying cultural theory and the Lipset-Rokkan thesis to the
EC system, therefore, there are two fundamental lines of conflict produced by two separate critical junctures. Moreover, because cultural
theory and Lipset and Rokkan both derive their models from the Par-
sonian theory of socialization, it is not a coincidence that Lipset and
Rokkan's "territorial-cultural" and "functional" cleavage dimensions correspond closely to cultural theory's "group" and "grid"
conflicts, respectively. Hence, first, as with the process of national integration, supranational integration produces a center versus periphery cleavage, between national-interest and European-interest. This
cleavage is thus manifest in the conflict between pressures for further
supranational integration and the desire to preserve national sovereignty. Second, the industrial revolution produces a socioeconomic or
Left-Right cleavage. The movement from an agrarian to an industrial
economy introduces conflicts between more or less state intervention
in the market and more or less redistribution. Hence, this Left-Right
cleavage is manifest at the European level with the "politicization" of
the EC, as decisions on questions of market regulation (such as in the
Single Market program) and redistribution (social and regional policies) begin to be taken at the supranational level.

·   ·   ·

□   *"Old" and "New" Institutional Approaches*

The study of political institutions has always been a central pillar of
comparative politics. Although the traditional legal-formal institutional approaches were abandoned for more sophisticated sociological and behavioral methods in the 1950s, 60s and 70s, there has recently been a re-emphasis of the importance of institutions for
structuring individual behavior. In the comparative analysis of the
EC one also finds these "old" and "new" institutional approaches.

Although contemporary, most analyses of the EC within comparative constitutional law and comparative public law are "old" institutional approaches because of their emphasis on formality and
objectivity. Illustrating "the difference between the political (traditional IR perspective) and legal assessment of the Community," juridical approaches make a distinction between the conventional international treaty elements of EC law and the novel and
unprecedented "supranational" elements of the Community System.
Moreover, scholars of EC law point out that the European Court of
Justice (ECJ) has contributed significantly to the integration process,

and illustrate how the Community has begun to develop a "constitution." Thus, the main elements of the EC's constitution are "the undisputed supremacy clause," which places EC law above national law in a similar fashion to a federal constitution; the direct effect of EC regulations and the immediate enforceability of certain directives; the growing case law rights of EC "citizens"; and the EC's powers of judicial review of all other organs of the Community. As a result, the political system of the EC already rests on a fairly firm legal base which contains elements of administrative and judicial review and a division of competences similar to those in a federal constitution.

However, there are also "new" institutional approaches to the EC, which use contemporary decision-making theories, and compare the EC's institutional rules and environment to classic models of government. Like the legal approaches, one group of these neoinstitutionalists argues that the EC can be analyzed using the concept of federalism. However, in this approach, "federalism" does not have to imply that the EC is an explicit federation of states. Furthermore, the Community does not fit comfortably into the traditional Anglo-American typologies of federal systems where the clarity of the division of authority between the central government and the constituent units is regarded as a crucial indicator of the degree of federalism. The complexity of the EC system of "mixed" and "shared" competences implies that tasks do not simply have to be *either* in the hands of the central organs *or* in the hands of the constituent governments in perpetuity. Thus, the new institutionalists prefer to use the concepts of "subsidiarity" and "cooperative federalism," where the majority of competences are "concurrent," to describe decision making in the EC. For example, in the EC, as in Germany and Switzerland, the majority of (concurrent) decisions display elements of both intergovernmentalism and supranationalism; hence, "a mixed national/community system . . . in which the emphasis is placed on the 'pooling of sovereignties.'"

A second new institutionalist approach to the EC suggests that the Community is a "consociational" democracy. The concept of consociational democracy was first proposed to illustrate how, in contradiction of Almond's sociological typology of comparative systems, deeply divided (segmented) societies can remain stable as a result of behavior and rules that produce "elite accommodation." Consequently, there are features of a consociational democracy: a pillarized society, elite predominance, a "cartel of elites," segmental autonomy, proportionality, minority veto, and oversized coalitions—all of which exist in the EC. First, the EC is a "territorially" pillarized system because individual interaction and loyalty is primarily focused within the EC nation-states. Second, elites predominate within their "pillars" because the national governments control the allocation of resources and maintain a monopoly over the forces of coercion within the national territory. Third, there is a "cartel of elites" at the European level because of the elite/governmental nature of EC decision making and because of the rules to ensure elite accommodation. Fourth, in the EC the desire of governments to protect their national sovereignty is the equivalent of segmental autonomy within territorially pillarized federal states. Fifth, proportionality is ensured in the EC in the systems of representation in the Council of Ministers and the European Parliament, in the allocation of jobs in the institutions' administrations, and in the allocation of EC resources. Sixth, mutual veto is guaranteed in the EC by the Luxembourg Compromise, which allows a member state to exercise a veto if there is a threat to a "vital national interest." Finally, oversized coalitions exist because of the qualified majority voting in the Council of Ministers and the majority requirements in the EP, which facilitates a *de jure* Socialist-Christian Democrat coalition.

As a result, the institutional approaches to the EC have illustrated how comparative politics types can be beneficially used to analyze the institutional features of the Community system. In contrast to the international relations institutional approaches, the comparative approaches thus seek less to *prescribe* an institutional structure than to *describe* the decision-making environment as it stands at the present time. Moreover, the observation that the EC displays elements of "cooperative federalism" and "consociational democracy" has important implications for the analysis of political conflict in the Community. It is these institutional features that organize the behavior of the actors, and structure the conflict. Describing the EC in these terms thus allows further comparisons to be drawn from politics in other federally organized and territorially pillarized systems.

In contrast to IR approaches to EC politics, a comparative analysis thus suggests that there are two fundamental dimensions of politics in the Community. First, there is the national-supranational dimension highlighted by the pluralist and realist approaches in international relations, and which is used in rational choice approaches to the EC. However, sociological approaches to the Community illustrate that there is also a socioeconomic conflict, which is present ("latent") in all European systems because of the common problems involved in governing a capitalist economy. The Lipset-Rokkan model also suggests, however, that the Left-Right dimension emerges (is "manifest") in the EC only when basic socioeconomic issues are tackled at the European level. This thus reinforces the intuitive argument that "party-political divisions" will only exist at the EC level as a result of the "politicization" of the Community.

However, the interaction between these two dimensions is also dependent upon the institutional environment in the EC—the constraints inherent in "cooperative federalism" and "consociationalism." In consociational systems where the "pillars" are not based on class divisions, the Left-Right conflict is often subsidiary (or only equal) to the conflict between the pillars, which may be a territorial, linguistic or religious cleavage. Furthermore, the institution of elite accommodation works to "control" the development of conflicts that cut across (and thus undermine) the internal cohesion of the pillars. In a similar way, the institution of federalism limits the salience of ideological conflicts, and restricts the evolution of party structures. Nevertheless, in the "European" tradition of federalism, the ideological tradition of the *Parteienstaat* is often stronger than the institution of the *Bundestaat*. Despite these constraints, therefore, on Left-Right issues (such as the Social Charter) party-political positions may be better indicators of EC policy-outcomes than the "national interests" of the governments.

■ CONCLUSION—A CALL FOR COMPARATIVIST RESEARCH

Consequently, comparing the comparative politics and international relations approaches derived from the same ontological and methodological assumptions suggests that the comparative politics paradigms often produce more profitable insights for the study of EC "politics." Whereas IR pluralist theories concentrate on the attitudes of actors towards "integration," "comparative" pluralist approaches describe the nature of interest representation and intermediation in the Community. Furthermore, whereas realist and rational choice approaches both regard actors as aligned on a single "independence-integration" continuum, rational choice models also determine the relative strength of each actor and illustrate the importance of the institutional mechanisms. Moreover, whereas structuralist theories simply regard EC politics as the interaction of the West European states' attempts to come to terms with global changes, sociological theories provide a framework for understanding the EC as a "political system." Finally, whereas IR institutional approaches prescribe a "politics-free" supranational system, the comparative institutional approaches use traditional concepts to describe the shape of the EC's institutional structures and environment.

The international relations approaches may be appropriate for the study of European *integration*. However, comparative politics approaches are more appropriate for the analysis of European Community *politics*. As sub-fields of the same discipline (political science), international relations and comparative politics have a certain amount of literature in common. However, because they have focused on diametrically opposed areas of the discipline—the politics "among" against the politics "within" nations—the academic discourse of IR scholars and comparativists has grown apart as the fields have matured. Consequently, in their application to the EC, it is natural that international relations and comparative politics theories are applicable for different aspects of the EC system. Hence in areas where the EC member states remain sovereign, international relations theories of "cooperation" may still produce accurate and parsimonious explanations. However, where decisions are taken which involve crosscutting party-political and national interests, decision and coalition theories from comparative politics are likely to have a higher explanatory value. Moreover, because of the focus of the comparative literature, this will probably be true for most areas of EC politics: from general questions such as the connection between political inputs and outputs, or the relationship between the EC institutions, to specific matters such as the representation of territorial and functional interests, or the choice of voting procedures.

Only recently, however, has a textbook on EC politics appeared which attempts to claim the study of the "internal" politics of the Community for the field of comparative politics. In the introduction to this groundbreaking collection of essays, Sbragia argues that "thinking about the Community comparatively will prove to be more fruitful analytically than simply describing the Community as 'unique' and consequently analyzing it exclusively on its own terms. Theories, concepts, and knowledge drawn from the study of other polities can in fact be illuminating when applied to the study of the Community." The above discussion appears to support this argument. As more academics and students become interested in the significance and functioning of the European Community the time is right for "comparativists" to take up their pens and challenge the dominance of the international approaches.

26

Economic and Monetary Union: The Primacy of High Politics

LOUKAS TSOUKALIS

*After Bela Balassa (Chapter 18), grand theories of economic and po-
litical integration were left largely to political scientists. Economists
continued to work on specific technical aspects of economic integration, such as fixed exchange rate systems, trade diversion, benefits of
the single market, and the pros and cons of economic and monetary
union, but few cared to venture into areas where politics and economics intersect. Loukas Tsoukalis (University of Athens and the College of Europe, Bruges, Belgium) is the exception.*

*Tsoukalis, in this 1996 article on economic and monetary union
(EMU), makes it clear that economists are skeptical about the benefits
of a single currency for the EU. Europe is not an "optimum currency
area" where labor and capital mobility can easily substitute for currency revaluations. The EU therefore runs the risk of creating pockets
of economic depression that governments will have few tools to fix.
So why is the EU embarking on such a risky policy? In a word, politics. Tsoukalis argues that European political leaders see EMU "as an
economic means to a political end, rather than an end in itself." A
united and economically dominant Germany had to be tied closely
to the West; completing economic integration would force political*

Reprinted with permission of Oxford University Press from *Policy-Making
in the European Union*, ed. Helen Wallace and William Wallace (3rd ed.,
1996). Copyright 1996 by Loukas Tsoukalis and Oxford University Press.
Notes omitted.

*integration that would guarantee European security. Economics be-
comes high politics.*

*Tsoukalis, perhaps reflecting the attitude of his own profession,
is skeptical about the need for EMU, but he is worried about more
than economics. His greatest concern is that Europe is establishing a
economic policy process that lacks legitimacy and democratic accountability. The only answer seems to be a European federation.*

And so we come full circle—back to Spinelli.

Economic and monetary union (EMU) has occupied a prominent place on the European agenda for many years. It has had a che-
quered history, and it remains a subject of considerable controversy
among policy-makers and academic economists. There is a rapidly
growing literature on the pros and cons of EMU, the necessary preconditions to be fulfilled before the adoption of a single currency,
and the requirements for its successful operation. Much of it has
built on the early literature dealing with the advantages and disad-
vantages of fixed exchange rates. Perhaps inevitably, most writings
on the subject are of a highly technical nature. Thus the initiated are
separated by high fences from the ordinary folk and political debate
is rendered difficult—difficult, though of course not futile, given the
political significance and the symbolism which money carries in relation to national sovereignty, not to mention its wider economic rami-
fications.

EMU is an important subject in itself but not only for economic
reasons. Money has also been frequently seen as an instrument for
the achievement of wider political objectives. It may, therefore, be
rather unfortunate that markets and economic fundamentals do not
always oblige by adjusting themselves to the exigencies of high politics. The history of European monetary integration can be seen, using
a slightly old-fashioned terminology, as a dialectical process between
wider political objectives and market realities.

EMU constitutes the most important and also concrete part of
the Maastricht revision of the treaty as the Treaty on European
Union (TEU). Following the old political maxim that difficult decisions are best left for later, it adopts a back-loaded approach: a relatively long transitional period, with minor changes envisaged for the
early stages, while the crucial transfer of power from the national to
the European level has been put off until the end of the century.

· · ·

■ **ECONOMISTS ARE SCEPTICAL . . .**

Although EMU has been on the table of European Councils for many years, it has not generated much enthusiasm among academic economists, who have been, arguably in their majority, sceptical about the whole project. True, several economists, among the most reputable and also among the most prolific on the subject, have argued in its favour, but the arguments put forward were often political rather than economic. European institutions, and the Commission in particular, have invested much money and mental energy in order to influence informed opinion; and the effect has not been insignificant.

To put it in simple terms, the opposition to EMU among professional economists is based on the following reasoning: western Europe is not yet an optimum currency area where the gains from a common currency can outweigh the losses resulting from the abandonment of the exchange rate as a policy instrument for the correction of external imbalances. Economic integration in Europe has not yet reached the level where capital and especially labour mobility can act as near substitutes for changes in the exchange rate; or that wages and price movements in different countries correspond to changes in productivity rates so as to make exchange-rate realignments redundant; or even that the European economy is sufficiently homogeneous so that different countries and regions are not frequently subject to asymmetric external shocks. But is this true of the United States or even Italy? It is largely a question of degree.

Inter-regional budgetary transfers play a major role in reducing economic disparities within all existing federations. Despite the remarkable growth of structural funds since 1989, there is hardly any prospect of a similar development occurring inside the EU. Can we expect a much greater flexibility of European labour markets as a means of absorbing asymmetrical shocks in the future, or would still higher rates of unemployment (and wider income disparities) become the necessary price to pay for EMU?

In the discussion on EMU, some differentiation is needed with respect to individual countries. The effectiveness of the exchange rate as a policy instrument is closely related to the openness of an economy to international trade, while the relative importance of intraregional trade is also an important factor to be taken into consideration before entering a monetary union. The UK is not the same as Luxembourg, or even Belgium. Countries with small and open economies can use the exchange rate only sparingly as an instrument of adjustment; a devaluation, for example, has a strong effect on domestic inflation, which in turn helps to undo very quickly the initial positive effects on the external competitiveness of the economy. It is not, therefore, surprising that the Benelux countries, Denmark, and also Ireland have shown in practice greater attachment to the system of fixed exchange rates than other countries which have also tried their luck with the same system.

The scepticism with respect to EMU shown by many academic economists (and central bankers, until they began to discover with considerable delight that participation in the EMS usually went hand in hand with greater independence for themselves vis-à-vis national governments) does not necessarily mean that they are in favour of floating. The experience of the 1970s helped to dissipate any enthusiasm that might have existed. Exchange markets, and all financial markets, have shown repeatedly their inherent instability. Economic fundamentals play little role in the short term, and the herd instinct leads to the so-called overshooting. The real question then becomes: what is the price of market instability and how much confidence should we have in the ability of governments to manage?

Many economists would be in favour of a system of fixed but adjustable exchange rates for a group of countries with a high degree of economic interdependence, such as the members of the EU. But they would also be wary of the apparent tendency of governments to forget progressively the adjustable part of the arrangement. The experience of the EMS is very indicative. The combination of fixed exchange rates and free capital movements means that governments can no longer use monetary policy for the achievement of domestic objectives; and this has proved a very unpleasant political conclusion which governments often refuse to draw.

■   . . . BUT MONEY IS HIGHLY POLITICAL

With the notable exception of the British, especially during the Thatcher years when the magic of the market-place was almost unchallenged, the large majority of European policy-makers have shown strong attachment to exchange-rate stability. The common market, now elevated to the higher stage of the internal market, is generally considered to be incompatible with widely fluctuating exchange rates. Indeed, the direct cost of foreign exchange transactions, to which the cost of exchange-rate uncertainty should be added, has been treated as yet another barrier to be eliminated in the construction of the internal market. Thus EMU has been presented as the logical consequence of the 1992 program.

The caution of economists has usually been overcompensated by the enthusiasm shown by some political leaders. EMU has been seen as an economic means to a political end, rather than an end in itself. This was true of the 1960s, when plans for European monetary integration were used mainly as a means of rallying the other Europeans behind the French challenge of the dollar standard. It was even more true of the ill-fated attempt to establish an EMU in the 1970s. Together with European Political Cooperation (EPC), it was then chosen as the main weapon to fight against a possible dilution of the Community after the entry of the British "Trojan horse." It was also to serve as the basis for Franco-German cooperation and as *"la voie royale vers l'union politique."*

The same story was repeated once again with the establishment of the EMS in 1979: it was the peak of Franco-German cooperation and the apotheosis of high politics, with money being used as the instrument of high politics *par excellence* and with political leaders imposing their will on recalcitrant and "narrow-minded" technocrats. With the benefit of hindsight, it can be argued that the setting up of the EMS was indeed a major turning point in the process of European integration, after a long period of crisis which threatened to undo the very foundations of the European edifice. Giscard d'Estaing and Schmidt proved capable of longer vision than several of their colleagues, not to mention those in charge of monetary policy and the exchange rate.

The 1991 Intergovernmental Conference (IGC) followed the same pattern. EMU was seen as the main instrument for the strengthening of the EC, which was in turn linked directly to German unification and the creation of a new political and economic order in the East. Monetary union was the preferred way of integrating the German giant more tightly into the Community system. Money was thus part and parcel of the European balance of power, as it, perhaps, ought to be.

Earlier initiatives in the field of European monetary integration had been largely motivated by external preoccupations; the instability of the dollar and US policies of "unbenign neglect" had served as powerful federalizing factors in Europe. This was not true of the various initiatives which finally led to the new treaty provisions adopted at Maastricht for the establishment of EMU—or, at least, not to the same extent as in the past. True, the reform of the international monetary system was not in the cards and the lack of unity among European countries remained an important factor behind the continuing asymmetry in the international system. But this asymmetry was now less evident, the US administration did not adopt the aggressive stance of its predecessors, and intra-ERM [Exchange Rate Mechanism] exchange rates appeared at the time less vulnerable to the gyrations of the dollar. Perhaps less preoccupation with external factors was also a sign of the new collective confidence of the Europeans.

The driving force for the latest relaunching of monetary union came from Brussels and Paris, with EMU representing the flagship of the European strategy of both the Commission (Jacques Delors in particular) and the French government. There was also strong support from Belgium, Italy, and, with some qualification, Spain. Initially, Germany showed little enthusiasm: the government and the central bank were happy with the *status quo* and any move towards monetary union was perceived, quite rightly, as leading to an erosion of Germany's independence in the monetary field. In purely economic terms, there was in fact precious little for the Germans in a monetary union. What later tipped the balance was the perceived need to reaffirm the country's commitment to European integration in the wake of German unification. This is how the matter was presented in Brussels and Paris. Thus the German decision (Helmut Kohl's to be precise) to proceed with EMU was highly political, as it was indeed in most other member countries.

Once a Franco-German agreement had been reached on the subject of EMU, the process appeared almost unstoppable, thus becoming a repetition of earlier patterns of European decision making. The Dutch shared much of the economic scepticism of the Germans, but their margin of maneuver was extremely limited. The main concern of the small and less developed economies was to link EMU to more substantial budgetary transfers and also to avoid an institutionalization of two or more tiers in the Community. As for Britain, it remained the only country to question in public the desirability and feasibility of EMU, on both economic and political grounds. The situation had apparently changed little since 1979. Realizing its isolation, the Conservative government made a conscious effort to remain in the negotiating game. In the end, it reconciled itself with an "opt-out" provision in the TEU for the final stage of EMU.

In terms of decision-making, the negotiation on EMU during the Maastricht IGC bears considerable resemblance to earlier European initiatives and especially the one which had led previously to the adoption of the internal-market program. The gradual build-up of momentum, the steady expansion of the political support base through coalition-building, and the isolation of opponents were combined with an effective marketing campaign orchestrated by the Commission and addressed primarily towards opinion leaders and the business community. Central bankers were closely involved early on, notably through their participation in the Delors Committee which produced the report on EMU. Later, they played an active role in the drafting of the relevant articles of the treaty. Functional spillover was also successfully mixed with high politics and the appeal to "Eurosentiment"—a recipe which had proved quite powerful in the past.

■ **SOME FUNDAMENTALS: THE PROBLEMS OF TURNING AMBITION INTO REALITY**

Money and macroeconomic policy in general remained in the exclusive domain of national governments for a long time; the external constraints imposed on their freedom of action were much more the result of international economic interdependence than European integration. The Community started to be considered as a possible focus of attention in response to instability in international markets and the desire to assert Europe's role. External factors progressively lost in importance as money became more and more directly linked with the internal construction of Europe. Geopolitical considerations, European ideology, and symbolism have characterized much of the debate on EMU conducted at the highest political level.

Initiatives came from the very top, and the role of personalities was absolutely crucial. The role of European institutions was essentially supportive, except for the period of the Delors presidency, when the Commission often succeeded in entering the top league. One can hardly detect an important role played by pressure groups. As for public opinion, it provided at best some kind of permissive consensus. Monetary union has been a subject for the select few: difficult to penetrate because of its technical nature and also rather distant as a goal. Plans for EMU have always included long transitional periods, with the real transfer of power being postponed for the final stage.

Things have, however, started to change as the D-day approaches. The German public shows little enthusiasm at the prospect of the DM being replaced by a "softer" European currency, while the champions of national sovereignty seem to touch a sensitive nerve of the British public. Furthermore, EMU is becoming increasingly identified in the public eye with austerity policies: stabilization measures are frequently justified by governments with reference to Maastricht and the need to prepare for entry into the final phase of EMU. Austerity measures are never popular, even less so in times of recession and high unemployment. Thus public opinion could become a much more important factor in relation to EMU, and not necessarily a positive one.

While the main parameters of the European debate on EMU have been set at the highest political level, the negotiations of specific arrangements and the everyday running of monetary "regimes" have been entrusted to small numbers of technocrats and most notably central bankers, who often had more in common with each other than with their national political masters, to the extent that this term can be used in relation to more or less independent central banks. Informal transnational alliances have developed in this area.

Collective management of European monetary "regimes" has not been so far accompanied by the development of common institutions. The setting up of the European Monetary Institute (EMI) is the first step leading to the creation of the European Central Bank (ECB), but which will happen only in the final stage. This will be the moment when power over the conduct of monetary policy is transferred from the national to the European level.

Economic globalization, especially as it is manifested in capital markets, has substantially narrowed the autonomy of national governments in terms of economic policy. Time and time again, member governments have experienced major set-backs on the road to monetary union, when the particular combination of national policies was deemed by markets to be incompatible with fixed exchange rates. Political agreements reached in European Councils are not by themselves sufficient to secure the stability of exchange rates, and even less so to guarantee a workable monetary union.

The part of the TEU devoted to EMU is a typical Community compromise. The French secured a clear commitment enshrined in the treaty, as well as a specific date. The Germans made sure that the date would be distant, with little happening in between, and that the new European model would be as close as possible to their own. The British secured an "opt-out" for themselves, followed later by the Danes, while the poor countries obtained a more or less explicit link with redistribution. Unfortunately, political compromises do not always stand the test of time and markets.

The conditions for admission to the final stage of EMU, otherwise known as convergence criteria, are quite explicit and they concentrate exclusively on monetary variables. The first refers to a sustainable price performance, defined as a rate of inflation which should not exceed that of the three best performing member countries by more than 1.5 percentage points. The second relates to national budgets: actual or planned deficit should not be above 3 percent of GDP, while the accumulated public debt should not be above 60 percent of GDP. With respect to this criterion, however, the treaty leaves some room for interpretation.

Exchange-rate stability is the third criterion: the national currency must have remained within the "normal" fluctuation margins of the ERM for at least two years; after August 1993 "normal" seems to be defined as 15 percent, which makes this criterion easy to meet. The fourth criterion is meant to ensure that the exchange-rate stability is not based on excessively high interest rates; thus the average nominal interest rate on long-term government bonds should not exceed that of the three best-performing member states by more than two percentage points.

The convergence criteria can be criticized on many grounds: they are mechanistic; some of them are arbitrary and, perhaps, also superfluous. They do, however, reflect the strong influence of Germany as well as prevalent economic orthodoxy; and the two are closely interrelated. The same applies to the whole approach towards macroeconomic policy in the context of EMU. Monetary policy will be run by independent technocrats in the ECB, the Community budget will remain very small, and the coordination of fiscal policies will be almost exclusively addressed towards profligate members. But who will set macroeconomic priorities for the EU as a whole? And will the system prove flexible enough to accommodate a possible change of the economic paradigm in the future?

The TEU said that before the end of 1996 the Council would decide, by qualified majority and on the basis of reports from the Commission and the EMI, whether the majority of member countries met the four convergence criteria and would thus give the green light for the beginning of the third and final stage of EMU. A qualified majority decision would be reached about whether there is a majority fit to enjoy the fruits of paradise (and EMU): this would be a rather uncommon case in international and even domestic politics. Under French pressure the authors of the treaty went further. It was stipulated that the third stage would start on 1 January 1999 at the latest, irrespective of how many members are found then to fulfil the necessary conditions, again the Council deciding on each case and on the basis of qualified majority.

. . .

Although EMU has been used consistently as a means of accelerating the process of political integration in Europe, it has been so far the most concrete manifestation of asymmetrical relations inside the

Community. Because of the need to fulfil the convergence criteria, the establishment of a complete EMU may be expected to strengthen further the division of member countries into different tiers. . . .

The most fundamental question, however, relates to the feasibility of monetary union without political union, and indirectly to the question of legitimacy. Can we have a central bank with absolute authority in terms of monetary policy at the European level, whose decisions will have a direct impact on unemployment in Andalusia or Attica, without a corresponding political authority and the political system that it implies? The last Intergovernmental Conference failed to deliver the political system which would match EMU. It remains to be seen whether the next one will be more successful.

Index

Philadelphia Convention, 90
Philip, André, 179
Pierson, Paul, 295–296
Pinder, John, 189–190
Pluralism, 58, 121–122, 325–326
Pluralistic community. *See* Security-community, pluralistic
Policymaking, 310–311; multi-level, 277–278; state-centric, 277–278
Policymaking process: adjudication, 290–291; decisionmaking, 282–287; implementation, 287–290; policy initiation, 278–281
Political capabilities: conditions for integration, 129
Political elites, 196–198, 201, 205
Political integration, 77, 147–148; conditions for, 150; defined, 139–140, 149–150; process of, 148–149, 150; variable factors, 150–151
Political reforms: disintegration and, 134
Pompidou, Georges, 193
Post-pluralism, 326. *See also* Pluralism
Potential welfare, 181–182
Power, 57, 62, 88, 89–90, 92; balance of, 4, 121, 339; condition for integration, 125; dispersion of, 52; division of, 74–75; economic, 196–197, 203; legal, 256; loss of, 87–88; redistribution of, 190–191. *See also* Authority; Autonomy; Control; Sovereignty
Power politics, 111
Privatization, 200
Productivity: European approach to, 206
Protectionism, 53–54
Prussia, 122, 124, 125

QMV. *See* Qualified Majority Voting
Quai d'Orsay, 234
Qualified Majority Voting (QMV), 274, 315

RACE. *See* Research in Advanced Communications for Europe
Rasmussen, Hjalte, 262–263, 270
Rational choice theory, 297–298, 326–328, 333
Real-income (component of potential welfare), 181–182
Realism, 245–246, 247, 333

Reconstruction, 102–103
Regime theory, 146, 300–302
Regional development funds, 201
Regional integration, 160–161, 253. *See also* Neofunctionalism
Relaunching, 45, 218, 227
Research and development, 209–210, 227
Research in Advanced Communications for Europe (RACE), 210
Resource allocation, 182–184
Responsiveness: condition for integration, 125
Reykjavik (Iceland), 197
Rocard, Michel, 226–227, 235
Roosevelt, Franklin D., 60, 100–101
Röpke, 179
Rossi, Ada, 3
Rossi, Ernesto, 3
Roundtable of European Industrialists, 212–213, 221, 230
Rule of law, 246, 264
Russia, 73

Sandholtz, Wayne, 195, 217, 222, 241, 249
Santer Commission, 279–281
Scandinavia, 77–78
Schäuble, Wolfgang, 71
Schengen Agreement, 76
Schermer, Henry, 255
Schmidt, Helmut, 193, 339
Schuman, Robert, 13–14, 19, 22, 192, 193
Schuman Declaration, 15
Science/technology, 209–210; national policy and, 200
Scotland. *See* Britain
SEA. *See* Single European Act
Sectoral integration, 146, 183–185
Security, 74, 202; community and, 106–107; EU and, 79; functional organizations and, 110; Germany and, 201–202; member states, 35; 1992 project and, 197
Security-community, 118, 120, 127; amalgamated, 120–122; defined, 117–118, 147–148; pluralistic, 118, 121–122, 134. *See also* Union
Self-determination, 160, 161
Shapiro, Martin, 246, 265, 270

Telematics, 209–210
Tennessee Valley Authority (TVA), 101, 111
Thatcher, Margaret, 208, 209, 233, 234, 237; Delors's response to, 55; European Community budget policy, 228; speech at Bruges, 49–54
Thatcher government, 227–229
Thorn-Davignon Commission, 221
Totalitarianism, 104
Trade, 174–175, 176, 179, 192, 203; agreements/barriers, 178, 183; liberalization, 179; outside of EC, 53–54; restrictions, 176
Transactionalism, 115–117
Transaction Cost Economics (TCE), 301, 311–312
Transnational business groups, 220–221, 229–230
Transnational coalitions, 200
Transnational incrementalism. See Spillover
Treaties, 96–97. See also Constitution; and specific treaties
Treaty of Paris, 15, 16. See also European Coal and Steel Community; Treaty of Rome
Treaty of Rome, 22, 60–61, 193, 195; adjudication and, 290; Article 177, 254–260, 265, 267; competences and, 191; constitutional function, 242–243; ECJ and, 248, 254; France and, 38–40; grand bargains, 302, 309; jurisprudence and, 256–257; lowest-common-denominator bargaining and, 233; national goals and, 154; national separatism and, 146; policy areas of, 282; preamble, 15–17; SEA and, 58, 211, 212; Thatcher on, 50, 53. See also European Economic Community; Single European Act
Treaty on European Union. See Maastricht Treaty
Trilateral powers, 233, 236–237; EC reform and, 219, 225–229, 230; economic difficulties of, 238. See also Britain; France; Germany
Tsoukalis, Loukas, 335–336
"Two-track" Europe, 219

Unemployment, EMU and, 337
UNICE. See Union des Confederations de l'Industrie et des Employeurs d'Europe
Unification, 40–41, 85–86; attitudes towards, 91; Britain's opposition to, 7; controversy over, 140; de Gaulle on, 34; democratization and, 87; economic, 112; failure factors, 159–160; force and, 87; France's demands, 40–41; Franco-German relations, 35–36; Germany and, 339; global, 5–6, 93–113; historical view of, 3; industrial groups, 141–142; motives for, 5–6, 15, 21, 25, 46–47, 160; necessity of, 62; obstacles to, 36–37; political sphere, 42; public opinion and, 87; role in world peace, 13–14. See also Integration
Union des Confederations de l'Industrie et des Employeurs d'Europe (UNICE), 221, 230, 326
United Kingdom. See Britain
United Nations, 9, 11, 160, 162
United States: Articles of Confederation, 136; challenge to Union, 192; Common Market and, 21; Constitution, 90, 299; economic decline of, 195; economic performance, 238; formation of, 178; functionalism and, 136; institutional evolution, 308; institutions of, 305; model for unification, 52; 1992 project and, 196–197; role in integration, 78–79; security policy role, 79; state governments and, 299; trade and, 24
United States, colonial: example of amalgamation, 125
United States-European partnership, 24–25
United States of Europe (USE), 7–8, 10–11, 13, 85–86, 189

Van Duyn (ECJ case), 257
Van Gand & Loos (ECJ case), 256, 259, 261, 265
Ventotene Manifesto, 85; text, 4–6
Veto. See Luxembourg Compromise
Veto culture, 282–284

About the Book

This popular reader on EU politics and integration theory is now even better! The first section presents the various visions of a united Europe expressed by some of the primary shapers of the union. The expanded second section introduces the seminal work of early scholars as they struggled to understand postwar European integration; the ideas of federalism, functionalism, neofunctionalism, intergovernmentalism, and other classic integration "isms" are developed here. Finally, the completely updated third section features pathbreaking contemporary scholarship on the integration process.

This volume offers students a chance to be party to a long-running, sometimes heated, and always engaging conversation among political leaders and scholars devoted to creating, maintaining, or simply understanding the European Union.

Brent F. Nelsen is associate professor of political science at Furman University. He is author of *The State Offshore: Petroleum, Politics, and State Intervention on the British and Norwegian Continental Shelves* and editor of *Norway and the European Community: The Political Economy of Integration.* His current work is on religion and European integration. **Alexander C-G. Stubb** received degrees from Furman University, Université de la Sorbonne, and the College of Europe (Bruges, Belgium) before working as an adviser on Intergovernmental Conference affairs at the European Union Secretariat of the Ministry of Foreign Affairs in Finland. He is currently working on his Ph.D. at the London School of Economics and Political Science.